JUST IN CASE

A Passenger's Guide to
Airplane Safety and Survival

JUST IN CASE

A Passenger's Guide to
Airplane Safety and Survival

DANIEL A. JOHNSON

PLENUM PRESS • NEW YORK AND LONDON

Library of Congress Cataloging in Publication Data

Johnson, Daniel A., 1937–
   Just in case.

   Includes bibliographical references and index.
   1. Survival (after airplane accidents, shipwrecks, etc.) I. Title.
TL553.7.J57   1984   613.6′9   83-26892
ISBN 0-306-41576-3

© 1984 Daniel A. Johnson
Plenum Press is a Division of
Plenum Publishing Corporation
233 Spring Street, New York, N.Y. 10013

Printed in the United States of America

Dedicated to

IRV STREIMER

whose enthusiasm for the teaching
and applying of human factors
has changed the course of many lives

PREFACE

The purpose of this book is to provide you, the airline passenger, with a greater confidence in your ability to survive aircraft accidents. It gives specific steps that can improve your chances of surviving an accident, whether that accident occurs in flight, on the ground, or in the water. It is not a book that indicts the aviation community for not improving airline safety. There have been numerous books, as well as magazine articles and television documentaries, which have attempted this. They have decried, sometimes hysterically, apparent inadequacies in how airplanes are manufactured, how they are maintained by the airlines, how they are flown by the pilots, and how they are controlled by the air traffic controllers.

When an accident occurs and passengers are injured and killed, there is much concern about who is to blame and what changes must be made. The causes of accidents must be determined, and any inadequacies in the design, maintenance, and control of the plane must be eliminated. However, the entire responsibility for accidental deaths or injuries cannot be shifted to others. We, as passengers, must assume some responsibility for our own well-being. There has been no media coverage of passengers who disregard their own safety, and in so doing jeopardize the safety of others. Yet many in the airline industry have heard people say, almost proudly, that they never pay attention to the flight attendant or read the safety pamphlet. If there is such a passenger between you and the only exit aboard a burning plane, his self-imposed ignorance about how to operate that exit affects *your* survival.

I won't quote numerous statistics that prove how safe flying on commercial airplanes is as compared to driving on the highways. Most people know that flying is safer, and realize that it is not only more convenient, but frequently it is more economical than other forms of transportation.

One thing I will try to do is to give you a realistic assessment of aircraft accidents. The chance that you, as a passenger, would be killed or injured in an accident aboard an American scheduled airline is very low: between 1972 and 1981 an average of 161 people were killed each year—the accident rate was less than one fatal accident for every one million takeoffs. Even then, in many fatal accidents most passengers survived. If you were aboard a commuter or air-taxi airline, the chance of being in a fatal accident, though higher than on scheduled airlines, was still relatively low.[1] Nevertheless the chance of being in a fatal plane accident on *some* airlines in various parts of the world appears to be much higher than in the United States. In fact two of these airlines, one in North Africa and one in an Eastern bloc country, had such high accident rates during the 1960–1975 period that if a certain major U.S. airline had had the same accident rate, it would have experienced one major crash every eleven days.[2] On the other hand there are many carriers throughout the world whose safety records are comparable to those set by U.S. airlines.

Even though airline travel on American and many foreign airlines is very safe, there is still the possibility of being in an accident. In this case there is certain information which could be invaluable to you. Some of this information is routinely given by flight attendants aboard the plane, or sometimes shown on a passenger briefing movie. Another important source is the passenger safety information card. Crucial information may also be found on the emergency equipment itself. And additional information is provided in the following chapters.

The book is laid out in this manner. The first two chapters delve into the different types of accidents, and how people behave during them. The third chapter investigates decompressions and some common misconceptions passengers have about the emergency oxygen system, and why some passengers have difficulty using it. Chapter Four describes other emergencies, such as turbulence, which can occur in flight. Chapter Five looks at the relative safety of various seat locations on the plane. Chapter Six describes how to prepare for an unexpected crash on landing or takeoff—the most common phases of flight for severe but survivable accidents. Fire aboard airplanes is discussed in Chapter Seven, and Chapter Eight illustrates the different ways of escaping from accidents on the ground. Chapter

Nine examines some of the problems passengers have experienced when using life jackets and rafts, as well as problems encountered when escaping from a ditched aircraft. The book concludes with a chapter on postaccident psychological and physiological reactions and some methods of dealing with them.

Much of the background for this book was gained after I started working as a human factors specialist in the passenger safety program for a large aircraft manufacturer in the late 1960s. Human factors is a discipline which deals with problems experienced by people attempting to operate machines. Many specialists in human factors (which is also known as human engineering, engineering psychology, and ergonomics, a term found mostly in Europe) have had formal training in research psychology, medicine, or physiology. They conduct research on the problems that occur when men and machines interact. The products of their research are guidelines for equipment designers which describe, in part, what information the person using the equipment must have, how that information is to be displayed, the size and shape of the controls to be operated, and the effects of adverse environments, such as cold water or high altitude, on performance.

McDonnell-Douglas Aircraft, the Boeing Company, and Lockheed Aircraft, the three major manufacturers of commercial aircraft in the United States, have conducted considerable research to reduce the probability of pilots' making errors and causing accidents, and to increase the safety of passengers once an accident has occurred. It is apparent that following an accident, the safety of everyone on board is greatly dependent on three factors: (1) how well the emergency equipment (emergency exits, life jackets) was designed for performing the task it was meant to perform; (2) how easily the piece of equipment can be operated by the person meant to use it; and (3) whether the user, either a passenger or a crewmember, has received adequate training to use the equipment.

But problems in these three areas have not been addressed evenly. Much effort has been expended by the airplane manufacturers in designing highly reliable equipment, equipment which is very effective in performing the task it was meant to perform. And human factor specialists have worked with the aircraft designers to make sure that the equipment can be used easily by the crewmembers. The airlines which operate the airplanes spend considerable effort training the pilots and flight attendants how to use the equipment. But it has become apparent to me that there has been no concerted effort to try to ensure that the passenger is able, or knows how to operate the safety equipment. It is obvious that one area in which significant improvement in passenger safety could still be achieved involves the education of the passenger about safety procedures and equipment.

In the past it has been mistakenly assumed that if the aircraft manufacturers did all they could to ensure the passengers' surviving an accident (eliminating hard surfaces and sharp edges around the passenger seat, providing safety belts, putting in emergency lighting, making the aisle big enough for passengers to move quickly out of the plane, and so on), and if the pilots and the flight attendants were well trained, then when an emergency occurred the passengers would simply know what to do, and would do it. Sometimes passengers might panic, but it was thought that nothing could be done about it. However, over the past ten or fifteen years there has been a growing realization that the problem is more complicated: passengers don't always behave as they are expected to, and crewmembers are not always there to help.

It has become apparent to many in the airline industry that passengers must know beforehand what to do in different types of emergencies if they are to act quickly, without making mistakes. Because of the growing realization of the importance of passenger education, many airlines have improved their passenger briefing techniques by redesigning their safety information cards. Some have also started showing briefing movies prior to takeoff. But these efforts, alone, are not enough. It is also the responsibility of the passenger to pay attention to this information. You, as the passenger, need to know what emergency equipment is aboard the plane, and you should also have some idea of how to use it.

It is toward this end that this book was written. There is more information in this book than could possibly be provided in a flight attendant's briefing or given on a safety information card, though both of these sources of information are very important. You will know that if you ever are in an aircraft accident, you should listen to, and follow, the commands issued by the captain or the flight attendant. But you will also realize that in a very severe accident, these crewmembers may not be there to issue commands. In this case you will have to rely on what *you* know and what *you* can do. As one man, who had survived a severe aircraft accident in which many had died, told me, "You can't depend on anyone but yourself, not other passengers or stewardesses. . . . You've got to get out on your own."

REFERENCES

1. *Safety Information Bulletin,* SB 82–4, National Transportation Safety Board, Washington, D.C., Jan. 28, 1982.
2. Arnold Barnett, Michael Abraham, and Victor Schimmel, "Airline Safety: Some Empirical Findings," *Management Science* 25, no. 11 (Nov. 1979).

ACKNOWLEDGMENTS

I want to thank Toni Steadman, Linda Goff, Peter Bonneau, and Randy Hunting for their effort in producing and compiling the art used in this book, and Jeanne Elliott, Dave Zamarin, Rosalind Hanaway, and especially Linda Regan for critical and helpful comments.

CONTENTS

Chapter One

THE SURVIVABLE ACCIDENT

You are a passenger aboard a jetliner which has flown you thousands of miles in just a few hours high above the clouds. The flight attendants have taken good care of you, serving you food and drink along the way. You haven't had to worry about the many details of flying the plane. Then, just as you're landing, the impossible happens. For some reason the plane is unable to stop on the runway. It could be an unsuspected layer of ice or gusts of wind or brake failure, but the plane continues off the end of the runway. It seems to take an interminable period before it comes to a stop, but while it's still in motion, you see fire and smoke erupting from the wings and engines. You are now experiencing something that few people have experienced—an airplane accident. You've read about how dangerous they are, and you believe—incorrectly, as many do—that there's very little chance of getting out of one of these accidents alive.

Up until now you have not had to concern yourself with any of the details involved in flying from one place to another. It has made little difference to you how much fuel your plane has had to carry, or even at what altitude you were flying, although the pilot did mention it. But now as the plane comes to a stop you will have to make a number of decisions of extreme importance which can be correctly made only if you have learned some important facts. First, should you remain in your seat and wait for help or should you get up and head for an exit? Should you bring your briefcase with you or leave it on board? Which direction should you move to get to the closest exit? If there is debris blocking the aisle, would you know the best method of getting around it? You finally get to the exit, but it hasn't yet been opened. Before you attempt to open it there are certain things you should do and certain things you should not do—will you know what they are? You finally open the exit and there is an inflatable escape slide hanging down from the door sill—will you know how to inflate it? Once the slide is inflated, will you know the best way to get into it?

Many people survive airplane accidents. Most of them do so because they are lucky and because the cabin crew is alert, well trained, and uninjured. Others survive because they have learned some important facts about the plane on which they are flying. In the following chapters the different types of emergencies that can occur will be discussed and a number of descriptions of actual accidents will be given. You will learn how to prepare for each type of emergency and what to do once the emergency has occurred. In so doing, you will become more aware of the types of accidents that can occur. Most passengers seem not to be vigilant or alert to their surroundings aboard the plane, at least as far as emergency situations are concerned. Therefore some graphic descriptions of what has occurred in a number of accidents by people who were there will let you experience "secondhand" what it was like. These accounts are given not only because they make some important points; they are also given in the hope that you will become a more vigilant passenger. In addition, you should feel more confident because what you will have learned will make you better able to survive the survivable accident.

TYPES OF SURVIVABLE ACCIDENTS

If you are aboard an aircraft that is about to crash, it will bring you little solace to know that there is probably a combination of reasons why your accident is about to happen. One reason may be directly attributable to the aircraft manufacturer, another to the airline which trains and supervises the crews which fly and maintain the aircraft, a third to the pilots of your aircraft, or even the pilot of another aircraft. Yet another reason may lie with the air traffic controller or even with the airport designer. There are many potential causes for an accident. Even though the rate of aircraft accidents has been reduced significantly over the past thirty years, and airline travel is the safest way that you can travel, it is not possible at this time to eliminate aircraft accidents altogether.

For you, the passenger on a stricken aircraft, the reason for the accident is beside the point. After all, what can you do to prevent an accident? Even if you saw an aircraft speeding down the runway toward your plane (as happened when two B-747s collided on the island of Tenerife in 1977), or you felt that your aircraft was descending for a landing too quickly, or you heard your plane's engines quit during flight, there would be little you could do to prevent the impending accident.

But there are some actions you can take to increase your chances of surviving the accident, actions that are not particularly difficult, and which take very little time and effort.

Much information on how to react in an emergency is readily available to passengers, but many, oblivious to its importance, pay scant attention to it. Here I will give you information about equipment and procedures aboard commercial airplanes which can affect your safety during and after a survivable accident.

A "survivable" accident is one in which some or all of the passengers may survive the impact of a crash or a collision. People who live through such an accident may still, however, succumb to the subsequent hazards of fire, smoke, or water. But knowing what to do before and after one of these accidents can increase your chances of survival. There is considerable evidence to support this assertion, evidence based on actual accident reports as well as on experimental studies. For example, in a survivable accident of a B-707 at Pago Pago in 1974, all but 5 of the 101 occupants were killed. These 5 passengers, all of whom stated they had read the passenger safety information cards and listened to the pretakeoff briefing, used the overwing exits for escape. Other passengers in their vicinity went to the forward or aft cabin doors where they perished—along with the flight attendants. The National Transportation Safety Board (NTSB) speculated that the flight attendants may not have been able to open the doors since the crowding passengers prevented them from moving the doors inward to open them. (The doors open in an inward direction to keep them from being opened at high altitudes by accident or otherwise.) It was concluded that more passengers could have survived had they known the location of the emergency overwing exits and used them.[1]

This brings up the question of safe evacuation of an airplane directly after an accident. The NTSB conducted a study on this question in the early 1970s and evaluated the effects of: (1) the weather conditions outside the aircraft (if the wind were blowing at too great a speed, and at a critical angle, an inflatable escape slide might not be usable); (2) the terrain around the airplane (not surprisingly, more passengers can be hurt escaping from an aircraft onto pavement than onto grass); (3) the attitude or position of the airplane after it has come to rest (an aircraft tilted to its side could render the escape slides in an almost vertical position; the steepness of the slide could cause the escapees to exit at too great a speed); (4) the presence of fire and smoke either inside or outside the aircraft (these obviously make safe escape not only more difficult, but more urgent).[2]

The report also examined problems associated with evacuation slides. They frequently fail to inflate, and sometimes they deflate too soon— before all of the passengers are out. Emergency lighting was also reported to have its limitations, one of which was its installation close to or on the ceiling. If smoke should fill the cabin, it will usually be thickest near the ceiling, which would thereby cut down the amount of available light. In addition to other problems, the NTSB also evaluated how well prepared the passengers were for an emergency. The report noted that during one B-747 emergency evacuation, 55 percent of those who had not read the safety information card were injured compared with only 16 percent of those who had read the card. The report did not, however, delve further into how knowledge of safety procedures could have served to reduce injuries.

Other research, on the other hand, has demonstrated that people who learn what to do and what not to do before an emergency are less likely to make mistakes during an actual emergency. Photographs and well-designed illustrations can effectively instruct people on how to use life jackets and oxygen masks,[3] and increase their ability to use the emergency equipment quickly and effectively.

There is also evidence that prior knowledge of how to act in an emergency can help overcome an unfortunate, yet common, reaction which people exhibit in an emergency. It is commonly thought that following an accident—such as after a landing accident when an aircraft may begin to burn, or when a plane begins to sink—the occupants will panic and scramble madly to get out of every available exit. In a number of cases this has not occurred. In fact panic seldom occurs, and then only under a set of rather unusual circumstances.

What is more common than panic, and probably more deadly, is a reaction called "behavioral inaction." In those accidents where panic flight occurs, at least some of the passengers may get out. But the passenger who remains behaviorally inactive will have little chance of surviving.

One woman told me that as she sat in a burning aircraft, uninjured, and near several exits, she could only think that she was going to die. Luckily, her husband was able to jar her out of the inactive state. She later estimated that another hundred people could have survived had they simply gotten out of their seats and gone to the exits.[4] There have been numerous instances of behavioral inaction in similar conditions, and it appears to have been produced in the laboratory with both humans and other animals,[5] as will be covered in Chapter Two.

Based on this research with humans, it seems that those people who know what to do before an emergency arises are most likely to react quickly and do whatever is necessary to save their lives. As mentioned before, some of this critical information is already available on the safety information card in the seat pouch usually located directly in front of each passenger, from the flight attendant's instructions, or printed on the emergency equipment itself. Other important information is provided in this book.

INJURIES, ACCIDENTS, AND INCIDENTS

According to United States Federal Aviation Regulations, to be qualified as serious an injury must meet one of the following criteria: (1) the injured person is admitted to a hospital within the first week following the accident, needing hospitalization for more than forty-eight hours; (2) the person has fractured any bone, with the exception of simple fractures of the fingers, toes, or nose; (3) the person has suffered a severe hemorrhage or other major injury; (4) the injury has occurred to an internal organ; or (5) the injured person has received second- or third-degree burns over 5 percent or more of the surface of the body. An "accident-caused" death must occur within thirty days of the accident; otherwise it would be considered a serious injury.[6]

An "aircraft accident" has occurred whenever serious injury, death, or major damage to an aircraft has taken place when people are aboard the plane for the purpose of flying. This therefore rules out injury or damage resulting from maintenance or other causes not related to flying.

An accident is also said to have occurred if damage renders the aircraft nonairworthy, or if there is major damage to the airframe or the structure of the aircraft. An "aircraft incident," in contrast, is any occurrence which results in an injury or damage to the aircraft, but which is not severe enough to qualify as an accident.

A "survivable accident" is one in which most, if not all, of the passengers survive the impact. Though passengers may survive the impact phase (and so the accident is termed "survivable"), fire or smoke may sweep through the cabin so swiftly that few of the passengers get out alive. Following a survivable water landing, passengers may not have time to get their life jackets on or get out of the aircraft quickly enough. The impact can be survivable, but the postcrash conditions may allow only a few, if any, to survive.

The determination of whether an impact is survivable is based on a number of criteria, such as estimated impact forces ("G" loads) inside the cabin, whether deformation of the aircraft cabin is severe enough to have precluded survival, and whether the seats and safety belts restrained the passengers during the impact.

An accident in which one or more people have died is a fatal accident, regardless of whether or not it was classified as survivable according to the criteria just given. Interestingly enough, most people believe that the majority of accidents are fatal. A survey of airline passengers revealed that the average passenger believes that 75 percent of the accidents involve some fatalities, whereas *only about 15 percent of actual accidents are fatal.*[7] And in most of these fatal accidents, the majority of the passengers survive (see Table 1.1).

This overestimation of the dangerousness of aircraft accidents may be explained by a greater media coverage of fatal accidents than of nonfatal

TABLE 1.1
Perceived and Actual Survivability Rates of Aircraft Accidents

	Passenger perception of the percent of accidents in which[a]	Actual percent of accidents in which[b]
None die	25%	86%
Some or all die	75%	14%

[a] From a survey conducted by the author for the FAA; also summarized in the *Proceedings of the International Conference on Ergonomics and Transport*, The Ergonomics Society, London, Sept. 1980.
[b] From *Monthly Aviation Diary* (Flight Safety Foundation), 11, no. 1 (1980).

accidents. Moreover, this kind of coverage could have an undesirable consequence in the event of an accident: a passenger who believes that nothing can be done because of the hopelessness of the situation will simply do nothing—when in fact there is something that can be done.

TYPES OF ACCIDENTS

This book will only cover survivable accidents. I will not look into the relatively rare nonsurvivable accident since there is obviously nothing the passenger can do to survive in such an instance. I will therefore discuss only the vast majority of accidents—those that are survivable.

Inflight Accidents

Many survivable accidents occur inflight. A pilot may perform an "evasive maneuver" to avoid hitting another aircraft. The plane may suddenly hit heavy turbulence, or the cabin may unexpectedly undergo a decompression at high altitude.

Evasive maneuvers to avoid another aircraft can occur as passengers walk down the aisle. On the night of November 26, 1975, an L-1011 with 103 passengers and a crew of 11 was heading west from Philadelphia to Los Angeles at 35,000 feet. At the same time a DC-10 with 192 passengers and a crew of 13 had taken off from Chicago's O'Hare International Airport and was cleared by air traffic control (ATC) to climb to 37,000 feet on an easterly course toward Newark, New Jersey. But in one of those rare instances, ATC had erred. As the DC-10 broke through the clouds, the pilots saw, directly in front of them, the approaching L-1011. The pilot of the DC-10 put the plane into an emergency, nose-down descent. He later estimated that the span of time between his first seeing the L-1011 and having passed within 100 feet of it was three to four seconds.

As the DC-10 went into its descent, dinner and beverages were being served in the cabin. Four passengers as well as the flight attendants and service carts were thrown against the cabin ceiling by the negative G forces. When the aircraft leveled out at 33,000 feet, all unrestrained people and carts, temporarily pinned to the ceiling, fell heavily, hitting the floor and other passengers. Ten flight attendants sustained minor injuries and 14 passengers were injured, 3 seriously. No one in the L-1011, not even the pilots, had any idea of what had happened until after they had landed.[8]

Turbulent air due to thunderstorm activity, or air moving in vertical columns (wind shears), causes an average of fifteen to twenty accidents a year, with each accident producing an average of four or five injuries. Most of the passenger injuries (72 percent) are minor whereas about half the flight attendant injuries (52 percent) are serious.[9] Reasons for these serious injuries, as well as how they can be avoided, will be discussed in a later chapter.

Another type of inflight hazard is decompression, which occurs when the air pressure inside of the plane is suddenly reduced. There are a number of reasons why this may occur. The pressurized portion of the aircraft, which includes the cabin and the cockpit, may be punctured by a piece of an exploding engine. Or a door leading from the inside of the cabin to the outside could blow out if not closed properly and a rapid decompression could occur. But if the opening were relatively small in relation to the volume of air in the cabin, a slow decompression would result.

Reduced air pressure can cause a loss of consciousness. It might even trigger a heart attack, or as a result of loss of oxygen, result in brain damage or even death.[10] Therefore anytime an aircraft flies over 15,000 feet, Federal Aviation Regulations (FARs) require that there be supplemental oxygen on board for each passenger.[11]

When flying at cruising altitudes, which could be as high as 42,000 feet, the air pressure in the cabin is equal to that at 6,000–8,000 feet above sea level. This "cabin altitude" is the altitude at which the plane would be flying if the cabin were not pressurized. If the plane were flying at 42,000 feet and the air pressure in the cabin was the same as it would be on a mountain 6,500 feet above sea level, then the cabin altitude is said to be 6,500 feet. During a decompression, air would escape, air pressure in the cabin would drop, and cabin altitude would increase. The cabin altitude might even reach the actual altitude of the aircraft. If this happened, and if the plane were flying at a high altitude, passengers might feel dizzy, experiencing a warm, tingling sensation of the skin; some could even lose consciousness.

Before the cabin altitude reaches 15,000 feet the passengers' oxygen masks should automatically deploy. If you had paid attention to the flight attendants' briefing you would probably know how to put the mask on and how to start the oxygen flowing. But most passengers assume that oxygen will flow automatically as soon as the masks deploy. Though this happens on a few airplanes, such as the L-1011, on most planes passengers must pull a pin free to start the oxygen flowing. This pin is attached either to the mask, or to its supply tube, by a small cord. Strangely enough, many passengers in actual decompressions have hesitated to pull the cord for fear of "breaking something." Consequently they have failed to get the additional oxygen that they needed.

Before using the mask, you should, of course, stop smoking. Once the oxygen is flowing you should know how to adjust the mask to your face. If you are able to do this within ten seconds, then you would not lose consciousness even in the worst situation—the very rare rapid decompression caused by a large opening in the wall of the aircraft cabin at a very high altitude.

In a severe decompression the cabin would probably fill with fog, which would dissipate within a few seconds. There would most likely be considerable noise from the air rushing out of the hole in the aircraft. Moreover, the aircraft would go into a rapid descent which might cause additional alarm. It's no surprise that many passengers do not respond well to these circumstances.

During one decompression aboard a wide-body aircraft, only 1 of the 53 passengers was able to get the oxygen flowing to her mask without the aid of a flight attendant.[12] Within a year another decompression occurred and only 2 of the 180 passengers were capable of starting the oxygen flowing without assistance.[13] To alleviate this disturbing situation, several airlines now use a unique televised passenger briefing, shown on board just before takeoff, which illustrates the use of the oxygen masks.

Death following a decompression on commercial aircraft is extremely rare. During fifteen years in the field of aviation I have learned of only five deaths associated with decompressions. Two separate incidents involved men over the age of sixty who apparently died of heart attacks during the descent of the aircraft following the decompressions, and both of these men had prior heart conditions. Reportedly, physicians traveling as passengers gave quick but unsuccessful emergency treatment.[14]

Another death occurred when a wing engine exploded, propelling metal fragments into the fuselage of an aircraft flying over New Mexico at high altitude.[15] One man, seated next to a window, had his safety belt connected but it had about eight inches of slack. The exploding engine ruptured the window with a piece of flying metal. He was lifted out of his seat and pushed by the rushing air out the window. For a moment he was lodged in the opening, and another passenger grabbed his legs and tried to pull him back inside, but the force pushing him out was too great. His body was never found. In an equally horrible accident, a tire exploded below the cabin floor of an aircraft flying at about 29,000 feet.[16] A piece of flying metal tore into the floor of the aisle and two children were blown out. Reportedly they too had their safety belts loosely fastened.

Survivable accidents during flight caused by turbulence, evasive maneuvers, and decompressions have caused few deaths, but a considerable number of injuries. Some of the injuries to the passengers could have been avoided had they learned what to do beforehand, and then done it.

Water Landings

There are two types of water accidents: water landings and ditchings. Most flights take off and land over water, and an unexpected emergency could force the plane down into the water. These unplanned water landings are far more common than "ditchings," which are water landings in which there is some warning time for the cockpit and cabin crew to prepare for the accident.

One ditching, involving a commercial jet aircraft, occurred in 1970 when a DC-9 ran out of fuel over the Caribbean. Water conditions were good, it was daytime, and there were five to ten minutes for the cabin crew and passengers to prepare for the ditching. But a poorly coordinated effort among the crew and apparent lack of knowledge among the passengers resulted in tragedy. Approximately one-third of the sixty-three occupants died—at least some of whom were standing in the aisle trying to put on their life vests.[17]

Water landings are more dangerous than ditchings since they are preceded by no prior warning or preparation. Yet in some instances the planes do not have life rafts on board. However, on long flights over water—where the plane is over fifty nautical miles from the nearest shore, and where a ditching is more likely—life rafts are required.

There are cases in which water landings were so extraordinarily smooth that the passengers thought they had landed on the runway. In one instance a DC-8 landed in the bay at San Francisco, coming to a halt with its wheels on the bottom and its wings above the water.[18] As unbelievable as it may seem, no injuries and very little damage to the plane resulted from this accident.

Though water accidents are rare, when they do occur they often terminate in some injury and death. Just as in land accidents, it is not the impact that accounts for all of the injury. In many cases the general lack of preparation by the passenger contributes to the problem. The passenger most likely to survive a water accident will have some idea of how his plane would float even before an accident. Some planes float level, others tail-down, and a few nose-down. (The flotation characteristics of various aircraft will be covered in a later chapter.) He would know not to head for an emergency exit in the rear of the plane if that exit was likely to be underwater. He would also know beforehand which types of water survival equipment—life jackets, seat flotation cushions, life rafts—were on board and where they were located. Furthermore, the survival-oriented passenger would make it his business to know how to put on a life jacket, as well as how to board and launch life rafts. The passenger least likely to survive would not concern himself with these matters, leaving everything to fate. Unfortunately, after landing on water he would have little if any time or ability to figure out what he should do.

Information currently available on planes includes the type and location of water survival equipment. The safety information cards usually indicate whether or not there are seat flotation cushions on board, the location of life rafts, and the location and operation of the life jackets. In addition, flight attendants usually demonstrate how to operate the life jackets as well as point out the locations of the life rafts.

Other potentially useful information includes: (1) how the aircraft is likely to float in the event of a water accident, (2) how a life jacket may be adapted to fit a small child, and (3) how to retrieve, inflate, board, and launch life rafts. Detailed information on these important points is provided in Chapter Nine.

Land Accidents

The great majority of land accidents are survivable because they usually occur during landing or takeoff, when the plane is near or on the ground and the speed of the plane is relatively low. Furthermore, they commonly occur near airports housing trained crews with emergency equipment.

Unlike an automobile, when a plane hits a stationary structure or vehicle, it usually does not stop. Thus the passengers are not subjected to the violent impact forces they would receive in an automobile. The rare exception is, of course, when a plane runs into steep terrain, such as a mountain, in which case, as you might imagine, the chances of survival are slim.

Some survivable land accidents result from aborted takeoffs, in which the aircraft runs off the runway, sometimes striking buildings, trees, or rough ground. Other survivable accidents occur while approaching the airport or upon landing. An approach accident occurs if the plane lands before reaching the airport surface. This could happen if it ran out of fuel, or flew too low and ran into a hilltop or trees. A landing accident can occur on the runway if the plane lands too hard, damaging the landing gear (that structure, including the tires, which supports the plane on the ground). Still other landing accidents have been traced to the pilot's difficulty in setting the plane down soon enough on the runway—in some cases the plane has run off the end of the runway. Other accidents have been attributed to excess water on the runway (which can cause the tires to hydroplane) or to ice, both of which reduce the braking effectiveness, making it difficult to stop the plane in time.

In about 20 percent of survivable land accidents fire occurs—usually caused by the ignition of spilled fuel. It often originates outside the aircraft but within a minute or two can spread to the interior. In some accidents the fire has penetrated the cabin before the plane has even stopped.

But the fire itself may pose less danger to the passenger than the smoke it creates. This smoke from the burning fuel, or from the burning materials inside the cabin, contains a number of toxic chemicals, such as hydrogen cyanide and carbon monoxide. Also, as mentioned earlier, smoke obscures the emergency lighting and illuminated exit signs located near the ceiling, since it concentrates most thickly toward the ceiling. The passengers' eyes become so irritated that their vision is greatly impaired.

Land accidents, as opposed to water accidents, are the most common cause of serious injury and death. They bring into question the crashworthiness of the aircraft. "Crashworthiness" is the ability of an aircraft to contain safely the passenger within the shell of the aircraft during an accident. This includes resistance to burning rapidly and to giving off toxic fumes, both of which are areas of considerable research in the aircraft industry. Just as important as the crashworthiness of a plane, however, are the passengers' knowledge and actions during an accident. Consider a well-publicized accident which took place on St. Thomas, in the Virgin Islands, on April 27, 1976. As the pilot attempted to land the plane, wind conditions prevented him from setting the plane down at the beginning of the runway. When it finally touched ground, the pilot realized that there was no longer enough runway left in which to stop. So he tried taking off again, but soon realized that he had neither enough runway nor speed to get back into the air. Futilely he tried to stop the plane before leaving the runway, but it smashed through a fence and finally came to a halt after crashing into a gas station and a rum factory. The plane split into three sections: the nose section, a center section, and the tail. Only a few seats were still attached to the floor. An extensive fire spread through the aircraft even before the plane had come to rest.[19]

John Horsfall, a young geophysicist form Cambridge University in England, had been sitting next to an overwing window exit. Prior to the flight he had, as was his custom, read the safety information card and listened to the flight attendant's briefing. As a seasoned traveler he made it his business to read the card and pay attention to the briefing.[20]

By the time the plane had come to a halt, Horsfall had lost his eyeglasses. But he didn't need them, since he had already read the instructions on operating the exit at the beginning of the flight. He reached over and pulled the handle down, pulled the window in, and then—stopped. Up to now he had not given thought to what he was supposed to do with the window. As the fire spread, he asked himself, should he throw the window out? Would it even fit through the opening or would it become jammed and prohibit his escape? Where else could he throw it in the close confines of the plane? On the floor, it would block the exit. Behind him, it would land on the laps of other passengers. Next to him, it would land in the laps of his neighbors. In front, it would hit the heads of others. As he later said, the photographs on the safety information card instructing him on what to do with the window were of "limited usefulness."

Finally, a passenger behind him took the window from him. Horsfall climbed out the opening leading to the wing, hurried to the tip, and jumped off to safety.

Some might say that his survival was luck, but he had taken some preparations in case of an emergency to save his life. He knew from the outset where the exit was and how to operate it. In contrast, many passengers seated near an exit are completely unaware of it, let alone know how to open it.

Horsfall's quick thinking, coupled with his prior knowledge of how to use the exit, saved the lives of at least some of his fellow passengers. While he was busy opening it, the fire spreading inside the cabin left less and less time for escape. Thirty-seven of the eighty-one occupants died, but of the forty-four who survived, many escaped through the exit Horsfall had opened.[21]

WHY CREWMEMBERS CAN'T ALWAYS HELP PASSENGERS

Flight attendants are the most knowledgeable and highly trained crewmembers in the area of cabin safety. To supplement their initial training, they are also given additional emergency training every six months. With so much training it's little wonder that flight attendants respond extremely well to cabin emergencies. But there are a number of factors that limit their capability of helping passengers during an actual crisis. Passengers who rely too heavily on them may simply not survive.

One factor hindering flight attendants is their own injury or entrapment. As many as 45 percent of the flight attendants who experience a survivable accident are reportedly incapacitated during that accident.[22] Flight attendant "stations," their seating areas during takeoff and landing, are sometimes located in areas which pose hazards during certain types of accidents. Flight attendants must be stationed in an area in which they can see an emergency exit. But since partitions and closets, which sometimes fall or shift position in a severe accident, are also located near the exits, flight attendants are occasionally injured or trapped during the impact.

Another station for the flight attendant is at the emergency door. In the B-727 and the DC-9, for example, the flight attendant seats are attached to a door in the rear of the aircraft leading either to stairs (B-727) or to an escape slide (DC-9). During some survivable accidents flight attendants in this location have received injuries which have impeded their ability to assist passengers. Moreover, not only are they helpless, but they also add to the problem by becoming obstacles between the passenger and the exit (see Figure 1.1). In many accidents passengers have had to open some of the emergency exits. In several accidents they have had to open *all* the exits, and assist the flight attendants to escape the aircraft (see Appendix).

In the event of certain inflight emergencies the flight attendant may have a greater chance of becoming a victim than a rescuer. During turbulence or an evasive maneuver, a greater percentage of flight attendants than passengers is injured because flight attendants spend much of their

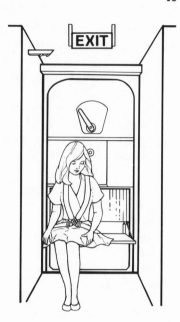

FIGURE 1.1. A flight attendant seat
attached to the door of an emergency exit.

time walking or standing unrestrained. Flight attendants may know better
than any passenger how to operate the oxygen equipment, but in a decompression they may be less able, from a physiological perspective, to
apply their knowledge. Being more active than passengers—preparing and
serving food in the cabin—their metabolic rates would be higher than that
of the passengers, subsequently reducing their time of consciousness in a
decompression.[23] Another point to consider about decompressions is that
verbal commands by crewmembers might not be intelligible. For one thing,
it is difficult to ennunciate clearly when wearing an oxygen mask. Furthermore, if the decompression were caused by a hole in the cabin wall,
such as in the case of a broken window, the ensuing noise could be
deafening.

Following accidents on land the primary duty of most flight attendants
is to open one of the exits. This entails checking outside the exit for fire,
and if there is none, opening and preparing the exit for passengers to
evacuate. This preparation usually includes inflating an escape slide if
inflation doesn't occur automatically, or at some exits, lowering stairs.

From that moment on the flight attendant's responsibility is to remain at that exit and assist passengers out of the plane. If there is a fire outside, or if a slide deflates, the flight attendant will need to direct passengers to other exits. It should be obvious by now that during an evacuation there is little or no time for the flight attendant to help each individual passenger.

Planning to rely solely on flight attendants for assistance is unrealistic. U.S. Federal Aviation Regulations require that there be only one flight attendant for each fifty passengers, or fraction thereof.[24] Depending on the type of emergency, the flight attendant may have too much to accomplish in too short a period to assist each passenger. Obviously passengers should know how to unfasten safety belts and where to find the closest exits. Moreover, when ditchings occur, passengers should know how to put on their life vests—a task which is not as simple as one might expect.

The need to acquaint yourself with these details is compounded by the fact that airplanes can fly legally with fewer flight attendants than there are emergency exits. On narrow-body aircraft—planes with only one aisle down the center such as the DC-9 or B-727—there are either two or four overwing window exits. The primary responsibility for opening them is seldom that of the flight attendant. If these exits are to be opened at all, it will likely be done by passengers. In some dramatic instances, as you might expect, these have been the only exits through which survivors have escaped.

On wide-body planes—planes which have twin aisles such as the DC-10 and the B-747—there may be more floor-level door exits than flight attendants. The number of flight attendants on board is not solely determined by the 1 : 50 rule. A B-747 with ten exits in the main cabin, for example, must carry at least seven flight attendants if there are any passengers aboard. On the other hand there is no legal requirement that more than seven flight attendants be on board if there are fewer than 351 passengers. This means that there will be three exits unattended with no flight attendant primarily responsible for opening them. The rationale for allowing fewer flight attendants than exits is that it must be demonstrated to the satisfaction of the FAA that the maximum number of passengers a particular aircraft can carry can be safely evacuated in a dark environment, using only half of the exits, in ninety seconds or less.[25] This means that five of the attendants on a B-747 could open half of the ten exits, leaving two additional flight attendants to assist individual passengers, and still get all passengers out in under ninety seconds.

Imagine a situation, however, in which one or two flight attendants are incapacitated and unable to make it to their assigned exits. To ensure a rapid escape in this case, some passengers would have to open the exits and make sure the escape slides are inflated, two challenging tasks on the spur of the moment for even the mentally prepared passenger.

There has been much written and said about air safety, and about how problems in the air traffic control system, the manufacture of the aircraft, and pilot performance have caused passenger injury and death. The position taken here is that while problems in these areas may exist, you still have some control over your own well-being. If an accident does occur, then you may find yourself in a situation where your survival and the survival of others depends on your knowledge of the safety equipment on the plane. If you find yourself in that situation, some of the facts on the following pages may be useful to you.

REFERENCES

1. *Accident Report, Boeing 707–321 B, N454PA, American Samoa, Jan. 30, 1974*, Report no. AAR–77–7, National Transportation Safety Board, Washington, D.C.
2. *Special Study, Safety Aspects of Emergency Evacuations from Air Carrier Aircraft*, Report Number AAS–74–3, National Transportation Safety Board, Washington, D.C., 1974.
3. Daniel A. Johnson, "Effectiveness of Video Instructions on Life Jacket Donning," *Proceedings of the Annual Human Factors Society Meeting*, Human Factors Society, Santa Monica, Calif., Oct. 16, 1973; Daniel A. Johnson, *Oxygen-Use Placard Evaluation*, Report no. MDC J6752, Douglas Aircraft Company, McDonnell-Douglas Corporation, Long Beach, Calif., 1974.
4. "100 More Might Have Lived, Says Survivor," *Long Beach* (California) *Press Telegram*, April 1, 1977.
5. Daniel A. Johnson, "Behavioral Inaction under Stress Conditions Similar to the Survivable Aircraft Accident," *SAFE Journal* (1st quarter, 1972); N. H. Pronko and W. R. Leith, "Behavior under Stress: A Study of Its Disintegration," *Psychological Reports*, no. 2 (1956): 205–22.
6. Chapter 7 of Title 49 of the *Code of Federal Regulations*, part 830.
7. Daniel A. Johnson, "Emergency Safety Instructions: Who Attends and Why?" *Proceedings of the International Conference on Ergonomics and Transport*, The Ergonomics Society, London, Sept. 1980; *Monthly Aviation Diary* (Flight Safety Foundation, Inc.), no.1 (1980): 4.
8. *Aircraft Accident Report, Near Midair Collision, Douglas DC-10, N124 and Lockheed L-1011, N11002, near Carleton, Michigan, November 26, 1975*, Report no. AAR–76–3, National Transportation Safety Board, Washington, D.C., 1976.

9. *Special Study, In-flight Safety of Passengers and Flight Attendants Aboard Air Carrier Aircraft,* Report no. AAS–73–1, p. 5, National Transportation Safety Board, Washington, D.C., 1973.

10. James G. Gaume, "Factors Influencing the Time of Safe Unconsciousness (TSU) for Commercial Jet Passengers Following Cabin Decompression," Douglas Aircraft Company, McDonnell-Douglas Corporation, 1969, Paper no. 5628, p. 2.

11. *Federal Aviation Regulations,* vol. 7, part 121.329.

12. M. W. Eastburn, Dallas/Ft. Worth Airport, Texas. Personal communication about a decompression aboard a wide-body jet aircraft on Oct. 3, 1974, between Dallas and Mexico City.

13. M. W. Eastburn, Dallas/Ft. Worth Airport, Texas. Personal communication about a failure to compress which occurred aboard a wide-body jet aircraft flying between New York and Chicago in May 1975.

14. William Collins, investigator for the National Transportation Safety Board, Washington, D.C. Personal communication following a decompression aboard a B-707 over the Atlantic in May 1975; "747 Cabin Pressure Loss Kills Texan," *Los Angeles Times,* Nov. 11, 1977.

15. "Board Details Overspeed Accident," *Aviation Week and Space Technology,* April 21, 1975, pp. 63–66.

16. "2 Children Sucked out of Jetliner over Qatar," *Daily Olympian,* (Olympia, Washington), Dec. 23, 1980, p. 1.

17. *Special Study, Passenger Survival in Turbojet Ditchings (A Critical Case Review),* Report no. AAS–72–2, National Transportation Safety Board, Washington, D.C., 1972.

18. "All 107 Escape as Japanese Jetliner Crashed in S.F. Bay," *Los Angeles Times,* Nov. 11, 1968.

19. "Accident Report, Boeing 727, St. Thomas, V.I., on April 27, 1976," Human Factors Group Chairman's Factual Report, National Transportation Safety Board, Washington, D.C., Docket Number SA–453, p. 7.

20. John Horsfall, R. B. Hawkins & Associates, Limited, Cambridge, England. Personal communication, 1980.

21. "Accident Report, Boeing 727, St. Thomas, V.I., on April 27, 1976," p. 7.

22. Del Mott, testimony given in *Hearings before the Subcommittee on Investigations and Review of the Committee on Public Works and Transportation,* United States House of Representatives, 94th Cong. 1st sess., Feb. 3–5, 1976 Washington, D.C., p. 7.

23. Douglas Busby, E. Arnold Higgins, and Gordon Funkhouser, "Effect of Physical Activity of Airline Flight Attendants on Their Time of Useful Consciousness in a Rapid Decompression," *Aviation, Space, and Environmental Medicine* 47, no. 2 (1976): 117–20.

24. *Federal Aviation Regulations,* vol. 7, part 121.391.

25. Ibid., part 121.291.

Chapter Two

HOW PEOPLE BEHAVE IN EMERGENCIES

There are only a few alternatives open to a person in the face of an emergency. These include making quick preparations, combatting the threat directly, fleeing from it, or as happens too often, sitting and waiting for the "inevitable."

How well a passenger prepares for an emergency depends on whether the crew has issued a warning, how it has been given, and the experience and expectations of the passenger.

Most aircraft emergencies occur so quickly that there is no time to warn the passenger. If the pilot suspected that a particular takeoff would be aborted, or a particular landing would be short of the runway, he wouldn't have attempted that maneuver in the first place. Since the emergency is usually unexpected, little or no time is left for preparation. The first major accident at Los Angeles International Airport (LAX) occurred on the night of January 13, 1969, when a DC-8 on approach in the rain to LAX made an unexpected water landing about eight miles from the shore. The plane broke into two sections. The forward section remained afloat for the entire night while the section aft of the wing sank, lowering fifteen passengers to their deaths. But two passengers in the tail section lived.

Mats Hellstrom, age thirty, an electrical engineer from Sweden, explained that he was sitting at the rear of the plane waiting to see the lights of the city when the craft hit the water, and his section of the plane broke away and started to sink. Struggling free of his seatbelt, he dove to escape from the tail section. This required a quick, almost automatic, reaction. Safety belts in automobiles differ from those in aircraft in the way they are opened. Because of this, some passengers may have trouble unfastening the safety belts aboard airplanes. Hellstrom, however, with little or no light, managed to unfasten the belt and escape from the sinking craft. The following day he recalled that, as he surfaced:

> The main fuselage was 60 feet away by this time, the wings high in the water. I was holding onto an English woman. She kept yelling "Don't let go! Hang onto me!" And then there were five of us clinging to a piece of wreckage—a Swedish girl and two men. . . . We were so busy trying to keep above the surface—that we didn't have time to get frightened. We kept calling to each other to keep our spirits up. . . . [We] lost track of the main section of the plane and were afloat for about an hour before a tug caught us in its light and pulled us to safety.[1]

Since there is limited time to respond to an unexpected emergency, some of the preparation must be done beforehand. Airlines attempt to have passengers prepare in advance for possible emergencies by showing them how to fasten, tighten, and unfasten the safety belts; pointing out the location of the exits; teaching them how to use the oxygen system; and encouraging them to read the safety information cards.

When an unusual situation arises in flight, most pilots will give a warning to the passengers, or will instruct a flight attendant to do so. But at least in one case the pilot reportedly could not warn the passengers or flight attendants because the emergency itself required his complete attention.[2] In another instance the warning was so ambiguous that the cabin crew and passengers did not realize the seriousness of the situation.[3] One important determinant of how people will behave in an emergency is the type of preparation they have made prior to the emergency, and this preparation is affected by whether or not they have received a warning. If a warning is not given, or if it is ambiguous, then a person's behavior will be less adaptive than if a clear warning had been given.

In the event of a warning, passengers may be more responsive to the warning if they have experienced a similar emergency before. If a disaster has not occurred before, then people will be less likely to respond to the warning; also, if the threat is slow in coming, the immediate response to the warning will not be to flee.

This latter response is evident in communities in the paths of oncoming floods. Dozens of reports from both the United States and abroad indicate that many people in doomed communities are reluctant to flee.[4] This resistance to escape a doomed community may be based on the hope that the flood will not occur, or will not be as dangerous as the authorities have predicted. Warnings given by crewmembers aboard planes, however, are not resisted by passengers probably because most passengers believe plane accidents are dangerous[5]—even more dangerous than they actually are, as will be discussed later.

BEHAVIOR IMMEDIATELY BEFORE AN EMERGENCY

Assume that a warning of a possible emergency is given and passengers are told when and where it will occur. Suppose the captain announces that the plane will make a wheels-up landing in half an hour. One question is how accurately the crew and passengers will perform any of the required tasks as "Time Zero" approaches. Psychological theory, backed up by empirical research, indicates that behavior is affected by the increase in "stressors"—those things in the environment that bring on stress. (Stress is dealt with in more detail in Chapter Ten.) Sometimes the stress improves performance, especially when the tasks are easy and well practiced. But many times the stress adversely affects memory as well as performance.

One of the effects of increasing stress is the reduction in a person's ability to remember instructions, especially if those instructions were poorly presented in the first place. In one study, army recruits examined passenger safety information cards prior to a flight. They were told that the purpose of the flight was to rate certain characteristics of the aircraft. After the plane had taken off they heard over the public address system, as if "by accident," the pilot telling air traffic control that the aircraft had engine problems and an emergency was in progress. The pilot then shut down one engine and circled the landing field, allowing the recruits to see fire trucks lining up along the runway. The recruits were asked to fill out a "Next of Kin" form, which ostensibly was to be dropped from the aircraft prior to landing, just in case the landing wasn't successful. As the plane circled, the recruits were tested by one of their military leaders on the emergency instructions.

Another group of recruits was taken on a similar flight, the ostensible purpose of which, again, was to rate certain characteristics of the aircraft. On this flight, though, no emergency was simulated. During this flight the second group of recruits was also tested on emergency instructions. A third group was given the passenger safety information card, and after a comparable period of time was also tested. But this third group did not fly.

The results showed that the first group (aircraft emergency) performed significantly worse on recall of the emergency instructions than the other groups, even though the first group's perceived need to remember the information was greater. The second group (flying but no emergency) answered 55 percent more of the questions correctly than did the first group. But the third group (the group that stayed on the ground) answered 28 percent more of the questions correctly than did the second group.[6] One implication of this study is that the stress of simply flying can reduce the memory for safety instructions, and the additional stress of a possible emergency can reduce the memory for those instructions even more.

Just as memory can be adversely affected by stress, performance can also be affected. As the time to an anticipated emergency draws closer, one would expect that the performance of a task would either improve or worsen. In one study, navy and marine pilot cadets performed a relatively easy task—selecting one of four keys in response to the presentation of one of four colors. Each pilot was instructed to work as quickly as possible. During the study each pilot was to consider himself as being on a series of five-minute "missions" over enemy territory. Subjects in the experimental group were informed that they might receive "a hit" from the enemy, simulated by a painful electric shock. The probability of the hit (high or low probability of shock) as well as the severity of the hit (high or low intensity of shock) was displayed on the instrument panel. On the most stressful missions a pilot was told he would have a 90 percent chance of being "hit" and that the severity of the hit (intensity of shock) was also high. The subjects had no control over the probability or intensity of the shock. Subjects in the control group simply flew each mission without threat of a hit. Each subject performed the task of matching the keys to the colors, which were presented on a display on the instrument panel, for several five-minute missions.[7]

The experimental subjects did better on this task than the control group, but *only* in the early phase of the first mission. As the anticipated shock approached, however, performance decreased. Also, the higher probability of a hit resulted in worse performance. In addition, on subsequent missions the experimental group's performance was worse throughout the mission because of the psychological stress produced by the anticipated pain associated with a hit.

In a similar way, passengers have tasks that must be performed during some emergencies. One of the most difficult is putting on life jackets, since most passengers have little or no experience with the type found aboard aircraft. And putting them on is probably made even more difficult because of the psychological stress associated with the unpleasant prospect of having to land in the water. Other tasks the passenger may have to perform, and which could be made more difficult because of the stress of the situation combined with lack of prior experience, include using oxygen masks, opening emergency exits, and launching and inflating life rafts.

In a ditching of a DC-9 in 1970, passengers had trouble putting on their life jackets even though they had between five and ten minutes to put them on before the plane struck the water. Although the plane was equipped with life rafts, none was launched. One was accidentally inflated inside the plane and the others were not taken from their stowage locations.[8]

BEHAVIOR DURING AN EMERGENCY

Performance and Stress

Performance under stress is related to the complexity of the task and the individual's level of anxiety. The effect of task complexity and stress on ability to perform a task was established early in the behavioral sciences; it is probably one of the closest approximations to a true scientific principle that has emerged in this field.[9] This relationship, called the Yerkes–Dodson Law, was formulated in 1908.[10] It holds that the relationship between stress or fear and learning or performance* is curvilinear. Increasing stress improves performance up to a point, whereas increasing stress further degrades performance.

A low level of stress facilitates learning only slightly if at all, presumably because the motivation it provides is inadequate to affect performance. This could explain, for example, why some passengers apparently pay little attention as the flight attendant gives the pretakeoff briefing. The situation produces little stress and the briefing is not designed to increase stress or fear. (This absence of stress found during the standard pretakeoff

---

* Learning is many times defined in terms of performance since it is a mental behavior which cannot be easily observed except through the performance of a physical task.

briefing would not be evident, or course, if the flight attendant were instructing passengers on what to do in an anticipated emergency.)

At the other extreme, a very high level of fear interferes with the learning process so that the performance may be similar to that under a low level of fear. The optimal level lies somewhere in between.

The Yerkes–Dodson Law further states that the difficulty and complexity of the task also affects performance. The optimal level of stress is higher for simple tasks than for difficult ones; in other words, the optimal stress for doing the relatively simple job of opening an overwing emergency exit would be higher than for doing something more difficult, such as putting on a life jacket. So the Yerkes–Dodson Law states that there is an "inverted U" relationship between amount of fear and task performance; performance increases as fear increases—up to a point—and then with further increases of fear, performance decreases. Furthermore, difficult tasks can be done well only under relatively low levels of stress as compared to easy tasks. (See Figure 2.1.)

Related to the Yerkes–Dodson Law is a theory set forth by Kenneth Spence regarding what he calls "habit hierarchy."[11] He says that the response highest in the habit hierarchy is the one a person is most likely to

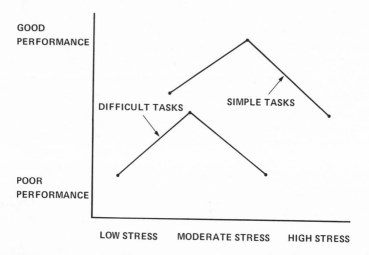

FIGURE 2.1. The relationship between levels of stress and performance for both simple and difficult tasks.

perform in a given situation. A number of reasons exists why one response is the highest in the hierarchy: it may be the only response that the person can physically make. Or the person may have practiced that response so often that it becomes "second nature" in a particular situation, a response that is said to be "overlearned."

Spence's theory is that as drive increases, the response highest in the habit hierarchy is the most likely to be performed. Fear acts like a drive. When the correct response is the one that is highest in the hierarchy, then increases in fear will result in a greater likelihood of the correct response. However, when the most likely response is not correct, then under the stress of an emergency the probability of the incorrect response increases.

An instance in which the overlearned response is the incorrect response, and results in loss of time in an emergency, involves safety belts. For many people who use their automobile safety belts, the overlearned response in unfastening the safety belt is to push a button on the outward surface of the release mechanism. In an aircraft, however, the safety belt is released by lifting up on the top metal surface (see Figure 2.2). In the stress period following an accident people could have problems releasing their aircraft safety belts with which they are far less familiar than their auto safety belts. Passengers in numerous instances have been reported to have problems in releasing their safety belts after accidents.[12]

It is not possible to determine from these reports whether the trouble was overfamiliarity with auto safety belts or ignorance of operating any

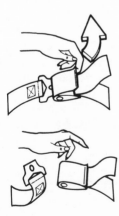

FIGURE 2.2. How to unfasten a safety belt on most aircraft.

safety belt. As of September 9, 1978, Federal Aviation Regulations require flight attendants to demonstrate how to fasten and unfasten the safety belt prior to taking off in a commercial aircraft.[13]

Panic

This section will examine the phenomenon called panic. An attempt will be made to define it in terms of how people behave, and discuss how it affects passenger safety. As mentioned before, there are three basic ways a person can respond to a physical threat: fight it, attempt to escape from it, or do nothing. A person aboard an aircraft could fight a physical threat, such as a fire, by using a fire extinguisher. It is not, however, something most passengers will have the opportunity to do. Flight attendants are usually the first to notice fires. Since they know where the extinguishers are kept, and have regular training in firefighting, they will likely be the ones to use the extinguishers.

Nonetheless, if a plane were to crash and extensive fire erupted, then the most adaptive behavior would be to escape. It is in this situation that panic could occur.

The term "panic" has been used to describe many kinds of human behavior, from the buying or selling of stock on Wall Street, to extreme anxiety, to a mass stampede out of a burning building. According to the *Oxford English Dictionary,* panic derives from the mythological god Pan: "Sounds heard by night on mountains and in valleys were attributed to Pan, and hence he was reputed to be the cause of any sudden and groundless fear." In more recent times panic has come to imply an overwhelming fear that is contagious insofar as it can spread throughout a crowd, creating chaos. Furthermore, it is commonly thought that whatever a panicky person does is counterproductive, which would result in either greater danger for that person or for others.

As will be shown later, these common ideas related to panic are not always true. Panic may mean fear and flight, but one person in a crowd can panic without the others necessarily becoming fearful. Also, panic flight may not necessarily be counterproductive; indeed panic flight may be the best thing that a person can do in some dangerous situations. This response, therefore, may have had considerable survival value to the species. Under certain circumstances panic flight in large groups may have disastrous consequences, however, as illustrated in this "classic" case of panic which occurred in 1942.

Over 800 people filled a nightclub in Boston called the Coconut Grove, when

> . . . a girl, her hair ablaze, hurtled across the floor screaming "Fire!" That shriek heralded catastrophe. Some 800 guests, insane with panic, lunged in a wild scramble to get out the only way they knew—the revolving door exit. Flames flashed with incredible swiftness. . . . Smoke swirled in choking masses through hallways. The revolving doors jammed as the terror-stricken mob pushed them in both directions at the same time. Blazing draperies fell, setting women's evening gowns and hair on fire. Patrons were hurled under tables and trampled to death. Others tripped and choked the 6-foot-wide stairway up from the Melody Lounge. Those behind swarmed over them and piled up in layers—layers of corpses. . . . The fire was quickly brought under control, but the fatal damage was done.[14]

Of the 100 people who escaped unhurt, half were employees of the club who were familiar with the alternative exits.

Although panic stampedes do occur, they are much less frequent than one might think. Some aircraft passenger safety information cards tell passengers not to panic, as if panic were something under conscious control, and I remember one intriguing safety briefing card which instructed passengers to remain calm and to keep their clothes on.

One thing that does not occur as often as one might imagine—even when a life-threatening emergency is imminent—is large numbers of people running around looking for the nearest escape route. A case in point: Civil defense organizations commonly believe that before the breakout of war, the police and military will be needed to control the populace who supposedly will be flooding every escape route. The authorities fear that once the bombing begins police will be needed in order to keep the people from stampeding over each other.[15]

But what really happens in war? During World War II the authorities in both London and Berlin were ready for the panic stampede of the people out of the cities. But the stampedes never took place. In fact authorities spent much time getting such city occupants as nonworking mothers and their children, as well as others who were not dependent on the city for a living, out to the countryside. But they kept streaming back to the cities.[16]

Why responsible officials are under the false impression that panic flight is inevitable in these situations is not known. One writer, Morgan Martin, believes there are two likely explanations of why the "panic myth" exists:[17] first is that the mass media require such exciting material to sell novels, newspapers, movies, and so on. Panic is just what is needed to grab the audience's attention. More common human behavior is not so dramatic and lacks the appeal for maintaining the attention of television viewers. Martin further maintains that each of us has strong inner fears which we strive to control: "Probably few of us have complete confidence in this inner control. This being the case, it may be that we doubt the ability of others to control their inner impulses, especially under severe and sudden stress. We continue to believe that most people in a disaster will panic. Fortunately, we have the disaster research evidence to combat this false expectation. Unfortunately, there is little effective dissemination of this evidence."[18]

Even if panic may not be common in cities being bombed, there are obvious differences between this situation and one involving passengers aboard a burning or sinking aircraft. In researching this field I tried to find out how common panic was during aircraft accidents. One of the first problems that arose concerned the different connotations of the word "panic." If panic refers only to the subjective, hidden emotion of terror, then it is dubious whether a person can state that panic is widespread without actually having questioned everyone present about whether they are terrified. We can only guess at another person's emotions; one person, very fearful of fire, may fight it rather than run away, while another person, experiencing less intense fear, may run away. We would be hard-pressed to ascertain the internal feelings of a person simply through observing his behavior, especially if we ourselves were in the same stressful situation. Is screaming an indication of panic? If so, can a person in a threatening situation accurately differentiate between "a panicky scream" and a person's yelling commands or crying for help?

I found that virtually no experimental studies on panic had been conducted until some research was sponsored in the early 1950s by the U.S. government, apparently in anticipation of a possible nuclear attack from the Soviet Union. There was concern that the behavior of people in the cities would be just as devastating as the bombs themselves. The most comprehensive studies on how people behave in disasters were conducted in the 1950s by the National Opinion Research Center (NORC), which interviewed hundreds of people after such disasters as plane crashes, earthquakes, tornados, mine explosions, hotel fires, and plant explosions.[19] From these investigations, a definition of panic evolved which takes into account not only the internal feelings but also the outward behavior which invariably involves flight.

Characteristics of Panic Flight

According to Quarantelli, one of the NORC investigators, panic flight has the following characteristics:[20]

Panic Flight Is Always in a Direction Away from the Danger. There is no attempt to deal with the danger or to control it. This does not mean, however, that panic flight is maladaptive, since it frequently is the most effective action possible, especially when the danger is overwhelming. Though panicky people usually run, they may also drive, swim, or crawl. Little coordination is lost, permitting flight to be expressed in a number of ways.

The fact that flight from danger, including panic flight, can be a rational, adaptive form of behavior is expressed by an old Chinese saying: "Of the thirty-six ways to escape danger, running away is best."[21]

Panic Flight Is Not Random. The person does not run every which way. There is always some direction. At least two factors help determine the specific direction: (1) habit or recently performed behavior, such as aircraft passengers heading toward the door through which they boarded the aircraft, and (2) the direction others are taking.

Panic Flight Is Nonsocial in Nature. The strongest social bonds may be temporarily broken. Mothers have left their infants; husbands have left their wives. Some may injure or even kill others in order to survive.

It is this feature—lack of social bonds—that distinguishes panic flight from normal escape behavior. Panic flight, though, is not antisocial but "nonsocial," in that the person, who may hurt others or leave them behind, does not do this to cause injury but simply to escape. It may never occur to the panicky person that another may be injured or killed by his actions.

The Panicked Person Always Believes the Situation Is Highly Dangerous. A panicked person always feels that he will be killed unless he escapes. Therefore the danger is thought to be in the future, and not what has already happened. Also, the danger is seen as very imminent so that survival depends on very rapid escape. Panic flight generally ceases when the person believes he is out of the danger area.

The Panicked Person Is Capable of Conscious Thought. The person keeps evaluating the situation, and if danger remains imminent he continues to flee from it. The person is also at least partially aware of what others are doing.

The Panicked Person's Thinking Is at a Low Level, But It Is Not Irrational. Flight from the danger seems appropriate to the panicked person though the consequences of what he does may not be thought out in detail. A person may inadvertently kill himself running through a wall of flame, or jumping from too great a height, in order to escape a threat. The panicked person does not seek different solutions, such as searching for alternative exits.

Reducing the Chance of Panic

Certain conditions must exist before a mass panic flight will erupt aboard an aircraft during an emergency. Being aware of these conditions could reduce the chances that panic will occur.

Being Informed. Before a person will panic he must believe the situation is extremely dangerous, and believe he knows the specific time and source of the danger. Whenever possible, crewmembers should give passengers adequate and believable explanations of suspicious occurrences so that passengers would not interpret these occurrences as portending disaster—especially if they do not. For instance, an L-1011, a wide-body aircraft carrying 260 passengers, was starting to take off from La Guardia Airport in New York on December 17, 1982, when some passengers saw a burst of flame come out of one of the wing engines. This occurrence during takeoff is caused by excess fuel in the engine, and though somewhat unusual, is not dangerous. But the passengers did not know this. "Unfortunately a couple of passengers noticed it and nervous types started yelling and screaming," an airline spokesman said. "A couple of passengers got everybody else so concerned that they brought the plane back to the gate." Later, airline officials tried to reassure the passengers that there was no danger, but even so, thirty decided to stay behind.[22] It seems obvious that if these passengers had been forewarned of such an occurrence, their reaction to the flare from the engine would have been quite different.

If there is an actual danger that could affect passenger safety, then you, the passenger, should be made aware of it so that the probability of panic and other maladaptive behavior is reduced. How to warn people of dangers so that they react in an appropriate manner has been studied by Drs. Irving L. Janus and Leon Mann.[23] According to them, the person giving the warning should be perceived as being credible; he must appear to know what he is talking about and that he is telling the truth. The person to whom the message is intended—the passenger—should conclude that he needs to take the suggested protective action to avoid the risk, and that if he doesn't, then the risk to him will be serious. The effective warning must inform the passenger that a means of escape is possible and that there will be sufficient time to perform the necessary measures to effect that escape.

Responsibility. People who are responsible for the welfare of others, or for performing some specific job, are less likely than others to display maladaptive behavior, including panic flight, in an emergency.[24]

Occasionally situations occur in flight which will result in a possible emergency landing minutes, or even hours, later. For instance, the flight crew realizes that the landing gear may not fully extend, and so the wheels will not be down and in the locked position for landing. This could result in a wheels-up landing. Where adequate time exists between recognition of the possible emergency and its occurrence, the chance of mass panic could be reduced if each passenger was assigned a task. Some passengers could be given special instructions on opening an emergency exit, and each pair of passengers not involved in performing a specific task could be given the responsibility of assisting each other during the emergency.

Availability of Escape Routes. Panic flight can occur if a person believes there is a way out but fears that he could be trapped before getting out. On the other hand, panic flight reportedly has not occurred in situations where no escape appears possible, such as with navy crews trapped in submarines at the bottom of the ocean and miners trapped under the earth.[25]

It is those passengers who do not think they will reach an exit in time who are more likely to initiate a panic flight. If each passenger knew there were enough exits so that he could reach one in time, knew where they were, and knew how to operate them, the chance of panic flight following an accident would be very low.

Although panic flight may increase the chances of survival in very dangerous situations, it may not be desirable since its occurrence can adversely affect the escape of a large number of people through a limited number of exits. Yet it is not necessarily the worst thing that can happen during an accident. If it should occur while the plane were on fire, then at least some passengers might escape. Another reaction, which is poten-

Behavioral Inaction

Less spectacular, but probably more common and dangerous than panic flight, is what I have called "behavioral inaction." Others who have noted it in disasters have called it by such names as "freezing" and "negative panic."[26] Specifically, behavioral inaction is said to occur when a person does little or nothing to escape from, or resist, a threatening situation. A person may just sit in a burning airplane without trying to escape. It's not that he is unaware of the danger. On the contrary, he knows that if nothing is done, severe pain and even death will probably occur—but still he does nothing.

Compared to panic, there has been little written about this strange reaction. But aboard aircraft after accidents it probably occurs more frequently than panic flight.

As a B-747 was taking off in the fog at Los Rodeos Airport at Tenerife, Canary Islands, on March 27, 1977, it struck another B-747 which had been ordered by air traffic control (ATC) to taxi down the runway. As the first aircraft unsuccessfully tried to lift off at the last instant, its undercarriage sheared off a large section from the top of the taxiing aircraft. After passing overhead, it crashed farther on down the runway, killing all 248 people aboard. Even though 61 of the 396 people aboard the taxiing aircraft survived, more people were killed in this accident than in any previous aircraft accident; altogether, 583 of the 644 passengers and crew aboard the two planes died.[27]

I interviewed several of the passengers a few months after the accident. Mr. and Mrs. Able,* both around seventy years of age, were seated in the middle of the taxiing aircraft, on the left side of the plane, several rows behind the exit that led onto the wing. They were traveling with a group touring the Mediterranean, many of whom were over sixty. During the long wait before the flight took off, Mr. Able walked around the aircraft with his wife, pointing out where the doors were located. He listened carefully to the preflight briefing given by the flight attendant and studied the safety information card. Since paying such close attention to safety procedures is unusual I asked him why he was so concerned. He told me that when he was about eight years old he was in a theater when a fire had broken out and the audience panicked. He was caught in the rush for the exits, an experience which left a lasting impression. Afterward, whenever he went into a building he automatically checked the locations of the emergency exits.

Prior to the accident, both airplanes, along with several others, had been diverted to Tenerife, since terrorists had exploded a bomb at the

* Although the parties referred to in this incident were actual people, the names I am using here are fictitious.

original destination of the two planes, Las Palmas. After several hours of waiting for ATC clearance before takeoff for the short flight from Tenerife to Las Palmas, the cockpit crew was finally told to start taxiing down to the end of the runway where they would turn around, and after receiving clearance from ATC, they could start their takeoff. The pilots knew there was another B-747 already at the end of the runway, awaiting clearance to take off, but they couldn't see the other plane through the fog. As they slowly moved down the runway, the cockpit crew suddenly saw the other B-747 break out of the fog, heading toward them at high speed. Somehow the captain of the other plane had mistakenly thought ATC had given him clearance to take off. But clearance had not been given.[28]

The taxiing aircraft swerved to the left in an unsuccessful attempt to get out of the path of the other plane. To the Ables the impact did not feel too severe. They remember being thrown forward and to the right, but like everyone else they had on their safety belts. The impact was not even hard enough to throw them against the seats in front, yet right after the impact they remembered "columns of fire" dropping down inside the cabin. (This fire could have sprung from fuel lost by the aircraft that passed overhead.) The Ables had not seen the other plane, nor did they know what had happened. Someone screamed "We've been bombed!" After a moment Mr. Able got up and started toward the exit. As he left his seat he told his wife "Follow me!"

At first Mrs. Able sat in her seat, doing nothing. She later remembered thinking "This is it." She thought she was going to die but she was not afraid. And though religious, she did not pray. Nor did she have any thoughts of escaping. She says she was in a daze, but after Mr. Able yelled "Follow me!" she got out of her seat and moved into the aisle. The Ables were traveling with another couple, the Hansens, who were seated directly across the aisle from them. As Mrs. Able left her seat, she remembers seeing Mrs. Hansen sitting, hands folded in her lap, mouth slightly open, looking straight ahead. She doesn't remember looking at Mr. Hansen, although she knows he was there. But neither of them moved. She thinks that if she had yelled she could have roused her friends, but it never occurred to her to do so. As they headed toward the door they saw most of the other passengers sitting in their seats, just as the Hansens were. Apparently many of the people, at least in this section of the aircraft, were behaviorally inactive.

The Ables believe they went a few feet past the door that led onto the wing and went to a large opening in the left side of the fuselage. They couldn't explain why they didn't go out the exit which was open; it may have been blocked by rubble or fire, but they couldn't remember what it looked like or why they didn't use it. Mr. Able pushed aside some burning material that was partially blocking the opening in the fuselage and went out onto the wing with Mrs. Able following.

Once outside, Mr. Able ran straight to the tip of the wing and jumped off. He landed hard, injuring his back so that he couldn't get up. He rolled over onto his side and looked up for his wife but he couldn't see her on the wing. As he started to crawl away he heard three explosions, the last one being very loud. He was in pain, and he thought that even if his wife was still on the wing, she was beyond his help.

Mrs. Able followed her husband through the fuselage opening. But for some reason she couldn't explain, she turned to her left instead of following him straight out to the wing tip. She slid down the flaps at the rear of the wing. (Since this was the direction of escape that was shown on the safety briefing card, she may have been following its instructions without realizing it.) She was momentarily dazed because she hit her head as she slid down the wing flap. She also sprained muscles in her back and legs. Because of the pain she couldn't stand up, and like her husband, had to crawl away from the burning aircraft. Neither of them found out that the other was alive until several hours later.

The Ables said that many more people could have survived this accident had they simply moved from their seats and gone to the exits. Mrs. Able felt that she would have died had it not been for her husband telling her to follow. They both agreed that a major reason for their survival was the attention they paid to the flight attendant's briefing and the safety information card before the accident.

Another passenger, Mrs. Charles, was seated farther back, also on the left side of the plane. In an interview, she said that she always paid attention to the flight attendant's briefing, though she seldom read the safety cards.

Before takeoff she sat chatting with the Wallaces, a couple seated next to her, between her aisle seat and the window. After the planes collided she sat for several moments without doing anything, apparently in a state of behavioral inaction. She remembers thinking "This is the way it feels to die in an airplane accident." Suddenly the thought came to her: "God damn it, Joan, get out of the plane!" She remembers this very clearly because she doesn't usually swear, but she swore to herself then. She looked around. The whole top of the fuselage was gone. She remembers looking up and seeing the sky. There wasn't any ceiling in this section of the plane because the whole top of the aircraft had been torn off, down to the window sills.

And this was lucky for her. She and the Wallaces stood up after unfastening their safety belts. Mr. Wallace helped his wife, and then Mrs. Charles, to step up on the seat next to the window and over the sill onto the wing outside. She went to the forward edge of the wing (she said there was burning debris in back of the wing, where Mrs. Able said she got off), slid off between the two engines, and quickly got away from the aircraft.

It is apparent from the above reports that a number of instances of behavioral inaction occurred in this accident. Mrs. Able experienced it prior to being ordered to get up by her husband. Their friends, the Hansens, and quite a number of others seated inside the plane also experienced it. Moreover, Mrs. Charles remembers distinctly that it happened to her. And she remembers the instant she overcame it, when she commanded herself to escape.

Instances of behavioral inaction in ditchings have also occurred, as indicated in this account of one that took place near San Juan, Puerto Rico, on April 11, 1952:

> Passengers had not been briefed on location or use of life vests, and were not told when ditching was about to occur. After the airplane was on the water, cabin attendants shouted to the passengers the location [of the life vests] and told them to put on the vests. The second officer brought a life raft into the cabin and launched it through the forward overwing exit. The first officer and a passenger tried unsuccessfully to loosen another raft (they were stowed in the cockpit), and because of rapidly rising water, were forced to leave through the right-side cockpit window. The Captain went to the main cabin door, ordered passengers to abandon ship, but received little response. He and a passenger opened the door, and he began forcibly evacuating passengers. A wave slammed the door shut. The Captain pushed the door open but as he did so, another wave pushed it violently outward, throwing him into the sea. He could not return in the heavy seas.

Of the sixty-nine aboard, fifty-two passengers went down with the craft.[29]

Behavioral inaction can also occur on the part of only a few people in an emergency. Jack Carroll, who was with the National Transportation Safety Board, relayed the following incident.[30] The fire department at a large airport was alerted by ATC that an aircraft was coming in for a possible emergency landing. As they waited next to a runway, a B-747

touched down and a momentary flame belched out of an engine, an occurrence which is unusual but not dangerous.

The fire department contacted the pilot by radio and told him the
aircraft was on fire and that he should evacuate the passengers as soon as
he could stop the plane. The pilot quickly stopped the aircraft, and ordered
the evacuation over the public address system.

As it turned out, the aircraft with the actual emergency was landing
on another runway. When the fire department crew realized their mistake,
they told the B-747 pilot that the aircraft was not on fire after all. One of
the cockpit crewmembers went into the cabin to see if he could stop the
evacuation. (He couldn't use the public address system since the engines
had been shut down.) To his astonishment he observed a number of passengers seated when they should have been evacuating the aircraft. One
passenger was lying in the aisle in such a rigid, trance-like state that when
she was lifted she retained her muscular rigidity.

Behavioral Inaction in Other Species

Apparently behavioral inaction is not unique to humans. Other animals
also exhibit it. One example is "playing possum," a behavior Darwin felt
might represent a form of feigning death.[31] He thought that some predators
would pass over a dead prey, and so by feigning death an animal could
increase its chances of survival. The response, of course, is not a volitional
act; the animal does not think "Perhaps by just lying still, maybe I won't
be eaten." Rather, the response has probably evolved as an automatic
defensive reaction against predators. In the case of a cat's attacking a
mouse, if the mouse remains motionless after the initial attack the probability of additional attacks is reduced. A number of predators are highly
sensitive to movement on the part of the prey, and unless the prey continues
to move, the predator loses interest. Laboratory and field research has
shown that if animals, even of quite diverse species, become behaviorally
inactive the chances of predation are reduced.[32]

Behavioral inaction seems to be associated with a novel, fear-pro-
voking situation. Numerous published reports confirm that when an animal
not accustomed to handling by humans is held down firmly for fifteen to
twenty seconds, after a few frantic moments the initial struggling will
subside. When let loose, the animal will retain this position. In one laboratory, the record duration of behavioral inaction occurred when a chicken

was let loose after being restrained; it didn't move for three hours and forty-seven minutes. Many animals will show this response if they have not had much prior contact with humans.[33]

Behavioral inaction in animals is sometimes called "animal hypnosis," which may be a misleading term insofar as the method of induction, and the physiological reaction itself, are quite different from hypnosis in humans. The physiological symptoms of behavioral inaction in animals (and probably in man too, though it has not been studied in detail with humans) include increased heart and respiration rates, altered electrical brain patterns, Parkinsonian-like tremors in the extremities, reduced body temperature, apparent analgesia, and waxy flexibility—a condition in which the limbs and trunk remain relatively rigid though they can be moved, and when moved they retain the new position. Onset of the inactive state is sudden, as is its termination, which is commonly followed by an aggressive reaction. There is no loss of consciousness despite a lack of responsiveness. Some animals have actually been trained in this condition.[34] Hypnosis, on the other hand, is quite different. Neither fear nor physical restraint is required for inducing hypnosis. In fact trust in the hypnotist is more likely to result in an hypnotic state than is fear. In hypnosis, respiration rates tend to decrease rather than increase, and waxy flexibility and tremors are not common physiological responses, although they can certainly be induced under hypnosis. Moreover, a state of deep physical relaxation generally occurs in hypnosis but apparently does not occur in behavioral inaction.

The length of inactivity during behavioral inaction has been increased by many things which increase fear, such as a loud noise or an electrical shock. Of particular interest is the potential effect of prior learning on behavioral inaction. Pavlov, in his early research, felt that this reaction was due to inhibition of cortical activity, meaning that for some reason the animal couldn't think at as high a level as usual, and so became inactive. Pavlov believed the animal became inactive because it was incapable of deciding whether to fight or to escape.

More recent research indicates, however, that the cortical activity in the brain may interfere with behavioral inaction. It seems that behavioral inaction is a response initiated from a control center located somewhere deep within the primitive brainstem,[35] and that animals which are able to "think" (that is, have an intact cerebral cortex) experience shorter periods of inactivity.

A connection has been made between the tonic immobility in animals and a paralysis reported by rape victims. During emergency room interviews, twenty-two of thirty-four rape victims reported physical paralysis during the episode.[36] Two researchers, Susan Suarez and Gordon Gallup, Jr., report that the reactions of rape-induced paralysis include an inability to move, body shaking, inability to call out or scream, numbness and insensitivity to pain, a sensation of feeling cold, both a sudden onset and a sudden remission of the paralysis, and occasional attempts to attack the rapist following the remission from the paralysis.[37]

EXPERIMENTAL STUDIES PRODUCING BEHAVIORAL INACTION IN HUMANS

There has been little experimental research on behavioral inaction involving humans. In one study the experimenters, Pronko and Leith, seated subjects before a console containing a number of unusual knobs and switches. A confusing situation, induced by a noisy environment, was established, and the subjects were threatened with painful electrical shocks for making mistakes. Some subjects were in a "sink-or-swim" group, so named because they received no practice or leadership during the test. This group had the poorest performance. Other subjects were given some leadership during the test and performed much better, while those subjects who were able to practice with the knobs and switches before the test performed best. Pronko and Leith reported that "frozen reactions," or what I have been referring to as behavioral inaction, only occurred with subjects in the sink-or-swim group. This study indicated that both leadership and practice prior to an emergency could increase the incidence of quick and correct actions, and that without practice or leadership behavioral inaction could occur.[38]

After an aircraft accident on takeoff or landing, one in which fire makes rapid escape of utmost importance, the passenger may need to do a number of unusual things. Locating and operating an emergency exit and inflating an escape slide are certainly things most passengers have never done before. And the interior of a plane after an accident can be an extremely confusing environment, with flight attendants yelling commands, passengers talking, and perhaps even the roar of fire. At one time I believed that this environment could be so confusing that passengers might not be able to perform the correct actions to get out of the plane. I also believed that some passengers might have the idea that if they didn't find an exit and get out of the plane, they would probably suffer a painful death. So I tried to incorporate into a study these three important factors: need to perform novel tasks, a confusing environment, and a painful consequence for not performing the tasks correctly and quickly.[39]

I was curious about what effects confusion and threat of pain might have on the ability of someone to perform an unusual task. I set up a laboratory situation similar to the one used by Pronko and Leith. My study differed from theirs, however, in that no subjects were given leadership or were allowed to practice with the unusual switches and knobs. In other words, all the subjects were in a sink-or-swim situation. In a way this is similar to passengers aboard an aircraft who have never used the emergency equipment before, who haven't paid attention to the safety briefings, and who don't receive any leadership during an emergency. In some emergencies passengers must perform unusual actions (putting on life jackets, opening emergency exits), and must do so quickly and correctly, or receive the painful, if not deadly, consequences.

I had four groups: no confusion or threat (electric shock); confusion only; electric shock only; and both confusion and electric shock. I supposed that the incidence of behavioral inaction would be greatest in the confusion and shock group, and least in the group that received neither confusion nor shock. But, surprisingly, some subjects in *each* group were behaviorally inactive. Apparently neither confusion nor threat of shock, nor the combination, had a measurable effect on the number of mistakes made, or the incidence of behavioral inaction. The proportion of the subjects in each group who became behaviorally inactive for thirty seconds or more ranged from 37 to 56 percent—and there were no significant differences between the groups.

Based on this study, as well as Pronko and Leith's study and the anecdotal information provided by Jack Carroll, it seems that the amount of danger or confusing aspects following an accident are less important than the novelty of the situation and the lack of leadership, as far as contributing to behavioral inaction. Reducing the novelty of the actions, and/or increasing leadership, should reduce the incidence of inaction.

THE PANIC–BEHAVIORAL INACTION RELATIONSHIP

Panic and behavioral inaction, as we have seen, appear to be quite distinct. But it is not quite obvious exactly how these behaviors are related to each other and under what situations they occur.

Animals apparently behave in ways similar to humans when threatened. At a safe distance from a possible predator the potential victim does not take any protective action. Similary, the person aboard an aircraft about to take off may not pay attention to the safety briefings since no emergency is anticipated. This person is far removed psychologically from the actual threat of an aircraft accident, and so no "unnecessary" safety precautions are taken. But according to Gallup, the behavior of a prey changes as distance from the predator decreases. If the predator comes too close, but the prey "feels" that it is still unseen, it may not move in order to avoid detection.[40] This inactivity has no counterpart aboard the aircraft, since there is no predator from which hiding will provide safety.

As the distance between predator and prey continues to decrease, the animal will take flight. At first the flight may be almost leisurely, but as the threat increases, and as the predator closes the distance, the animal will break into all-out flight. The counterpart aboard the aircraft is that normal escape flight may occur if the danger does not appear too imminent. But as the threat increases and the perceived availability of escape decreases, panic may ensue. Gallup does not differentiate panic flight from normal escape flight on the part of animals. Such a differentiation could be possible, I suppose, if the breaking of normal social bonds between animals could be easily measured, though I know of no study of this phenomenon.

If flight from the predator is unsuccessful and the prey cannot be successfully fended off, behavioral inaction commonly occurs. The prime illustration of this is when an animal not used to human handling is restrained; struggling to no avail, it finally ceases to move. This represents the terminal defensive reaction.[41] If the prey does not move, the predator may lose interest and go away. If a threatening situation seems overwhelming aboard an aircarft and the person does not think that escape is available, then behavioral inaction could very likely set in.

Therefore normal escape flight, panic, and behavioral inaction are seen as occurring under similar conditions; either may occur when a threat is perceived as life-threatening, overwhelming, and immediate. I believe it is possible that a person may exhibit all three of these responses in succession in a given situation, from normal escape flight through panic to behavioral inaction. The situation would have to be one in which the person perceives the situation as becoming more and more dangerous, until it is seemingly obvious that no escape is possible. The following is one set of possible reactions which a passenger might experience in a large aircraft filled with passengers during an accident:

An accident has occurred following an aborted takeoff in which the plane has run off the end of the runway. A fuel fire starts outside. One man hears the flight attendants open the doors and start yelling to the passengers to evacuate the aircraft. At first there doesn't appear to be much of a problem and he doesn't notice any fire, though he sees some smoke outside. He thinks he may have at least four or five minutes to get out. (In reality he has only a minute and a half.)

As he moves down the aisle with the rest of the passengers he notices smoke starting to fill the cabin—it becomes more difficult to see and breathe. People are coughing and movement almost comes to a halt. Suddenly it dawns on him that if the line doesn't hurry, he won't get out. So he starts pushing the person in front, trying to get him to move faster. But the person in front can't move faster since there is someone in front of him. Then, behind him, he is startled to see that the fire has burnt through into the cabin and is spreading down the aisle, giving off a thick, black smoke which rises to the ceiling. He is closer to the exit now, but it is one of the small window exits through which people cannot move very quickly. Suddenly he feels terror welling up in his chest. If he doesn't get to that exit in a few seconds, the fire will consume him. He starts to push people out of the way, but they push back. And those right by the exit become so jammed up against it that they aren't even able to bend over in order to climb out. The passengers are yelling at each other and no one is getting out. They are in a state of panic.

At this point he gives up hope of getting out. The fire is too close. The smoke is thick, and it stings his eyes and burns his throat. He sits down and waits, and never gets up again.

This type of situation is survivable, at least for the survival-oriented passenger, as Chapter Seven will show. In the meantime, though, let's analyze the behavior of the passenger in this hypothetical example. He made a transition through three stages: from normal escape flight, to panic flight, to behavioral inaction. This does not always occur. A person may go directly to behavioral inaction without panicking, as shown by some of the passengers aboard the B-747 at Tenerife. It is also possible that a person could panic, after which he would start showing normal escape flight. It is probably also true that a person can go directly from behavioral inaction to either panic flight or normal escape flight. Therefore I believe that these three behaviors are not true stages, in the sense that one must start with one and pass through each in a given order. Any of the three may be a person's first response in an emergency situation. The above example, however, may be used to illustrate how easily one state can slip into another.

Knowing what to do before an emergency occurs and receiving some leadership from a crewmember during the emergency are key factors in determining whether normal flight, panic, or behavioral inaction will occur. The passenger who has had the chance to think about what he would do if he had to get out of the aircraft in a hurry, and who has paid attention to the safety information available to him, would be better able to handle an emergency situation than one who had blithely carried on as if the safety information were completely useless.

The passenger who examines the safety information card, even if only for a moment, will learn where the exits are located so that he would be less likely to panic or become behaviorally inactive in case of an unexpected emergency. Mr. Able had mentally reviewed what he would do in an emergency, and indeed he had even walked over to the exits, behaving in a manner similar to the subjects in the Pronko and Leith practice group mentioned earlier. When the accident occurred, he was one of the first to move to the exit.

The importance of leadership is illustrated as well in this same accident. Mrs. Able had not given as much thought as her husband had to what to do in an accident. And when it occurred she initially experienced behavioral inaction. But Mr. Able provided the necessary leadership when he gave her the command "Follow me!" She reacted much as did the subjects in the group that received leadership in the Pronko and Leith study—she followed him.

Mrs. Charles also experienced behavioral inaction. Just as with Mrs. Able, she wasn't mentally prepared to escape from the aircraft. But, interestingly, she experienced a command every bit as effective as the one Mrs. Able received from her husband. The difference was that Mrs. Charles's command emanated from her own mind. This appears to be a good example of how cortical activity interferes with the behavioral inaction response. In other words, the thinking process itself had somehow overridden the response of behavioral inaction. Unfortunately, it doesn't occur soon enough or often enough to save the lives of many people in such situations. Why it occurred as quickly as it did with Mrs. Charles, and not with the Hansens or with many of the others who remained seated aboard the aircraft, is not known.

In summary, then, it seems that if you were to prepare yourself for what to do in an emergency—to practice mentally what steps to take—then the chance that behavioral inaction or panic will occur would be reduced. Mental practice can be facilitated by the simple steps of studying the safety information card, paying attention to the briefing, and simply looking about the plane and noting where you are seated in relation to the exits.

REFERENCES

1. Art Berman and Susan Stocking, "Survivors of Crash Unaware of Death and Tragedy in Sea," *Los Angeles Times*, Jan. 15, 1969, part 1, p. 3.
2. *Aircraft Accident Report, Convair 580, N4825C, Kalamazoo, Michigan, July 25, 1978*, Report no. NTSB–AAR–79–4, National Transportation Safety Board, Washington, D.C., 1979, p. 10.
3. *Special Study, Passenger Survival in Turbojet Ditchings (A Critical Case Review), April 5, 1972*, Report no. AAS–72–2, National Transportation Safety Board, Washington, D.C., 1972.
4. Enrico Quarantelli, "Images of Withdrawal Behavior in Disasters: Some Basic Misconceptions," *Social Problems* 8, no. 1 (Summer 1960): 69.
5. See, for example, *Aircraft Accident Report, McDonnell-Douglas DC-10-10, N68045, Los Angeles, CA, March 1, 1978*, Report no. NTSB–AAR–79–1, National Transportation Safety Board, Washington, D.C., 1979.
6. M. Berkun, H. M. Bialek, R. P. Kern, and K. Yagi, "Experimental Studies of Psychological Stress in Man," *Psychological Monographs: General and Applied*, 76, no. 15 (1962).
7. P. M. Curran and R. J. Wherry, "Some Secondary Determiners of Psychological Stress," Report no. A.D. 635–205, U.S. Naval Aerospace Medical Institute, Pensacola, Fla., May 1966.
8. "Human Factors Group Chairman's Factual Report, Flight 980, May 2, 1970," Report no. DCA–70–A–7, National Transportation Safety Board, Washington, D.C., 1970; *Special Study, Passenger Survival in Turbojet Ditchings (A Critical Case Review), April 5, 1972*, Report no. AAS–72–2, National Transportation Safety Board, Washington, D.C., 1972.
9. Eugene Levitt, *The Psychology of Anxiety* (New York: Bobbs-Merrill, 1967), p. 117.
10. R. M. Yerkes and J. D. Dodson, "The Relation of Strength of Stimulus to Rapidity of Habit-Formation," *Journal of Comparative Neurology and Psychology* 18 (1908): 459–82, as cited in Levitt, *Psychology of Anxiety*, p. 117.
11. Kenneth Spence, *Behavior Theory and Learning* (Englewood Cliffs, N.J.: Prentice-Hall, 1960), as cited in Levitt, *Psychology of Anxiety*, p. 112.

12. "Human Factors Group Chairman's Factual Report, B727–81, N124AS, Ketchikan International Airport, Ketchikan, Alaska, April 5, 1976," National Transportation Safety Board, Washington, D.C., 1976, pp. 38, 39, 43, 49; "Summaries of Human Factors Group Survivor Interviews, B727–95, N1963, Harry S Truman Airport, St. Thomas, U.S. Virgin Islands, April 27, 1976," National Transportation Safety Board, Washington, D.C., 1976, pp. 2, 3, 7, 8; Horsfall's statement, in "Survivors Statements, B727–95, N1963, Harry S Truman Airport, St. Thomas, U.S. Virgin Islands, April 27, 1976," National Transportation Safety Board, Washington, D.C., 1976.

13. *Federal Aviation Regulations,* vol. 7, part 121.571.

14. *Newsweek,* Dec. 7, 1942.

15. Quarantelli, "Images of Withdrawal Behavior in Disasters," p. 69.

16. Ibid.

17. Morgan Martin, "The True Face of Disaster," *Medical Times* 92, no. 2 (Feb. 1964): 165.

18. Ibid., p. 166.

19. Eli Marks and Charles Fritz, "Human Reactions in Disaster Situations," (3 vols.), unpublished report, National Opinion Research Center, University of Chicago, June 1954.

20. Enrico Quarantelli, "The Nature and Conditions of Panic," *American Journal of Sociology* 60 (1954): 267–75.

21. Carlton Culmsee, "Tight Little Island off China," *New York Times Magazine,* (Aug. 19, 1956), p. 66, as quoted in C. E. Fritz and H. B. Williams, "The Human Being in Disasters: A Research Perspective," *Annals of the American Academy of Political Social Science,* 309 (Jan. 1957): 42–51.

22. "Near-Riot Halts Takeoff of 260 on Jetliner," *Seattle Post-Intelligencer,* Dec. 19, 1982.

23. Irving L. Janus and Leon Mann, "Emergency Decision Making: A Theoretical Analysis of Responses to Disaster Warnings," *Journal of Human Stress* 3, no. 2 (June 1977).

24. Marks and Fritz, "Human Reactions in Disaster Situations."

25. Quarantelli, "Nature and Conditions of Panic," p. 274.

26. John Carroll, *Emergency Escape and Survival Factors in Civil Aircraft Fire Accidents,* Federal Aviation Administration, Washington, D.C., July 1968, p. 3.

27. "Spaniards Analyze Tenerife Accident," *Aviation Week and Space Technology,* Nov. 20, 1978, pp. 113–21; ibid., Nov. 27, 1978, pp. 67–74.

28. Ibid, p. 74.

29. R. L. Paullin, *Summary of Civil Transport Aircraft Accidents Involving Ditching, Collision with Water, and Lost at Sea (Unknown); Jan. 1950 to Oct. 1962,* Federal Aviation Administration, Washington, D.C., 1963.

30. John Carroll, Mt. Jackson, Va. Personal communication, 1971.

31. Gordon Gallup, Jr., "Hypnosis in Animals," *New Scientist,* April 10, 1975, pp. 68–70.

32. Ibid., p. 70.

33. Ibid., p. 68.

34. Ibid.

35. Ibid., p. 69.

36. A. W. Burgess and L. L. Holstrom,"Coping Behavior of the Rape Victim," *American Journal of Psychiatry* 133 (1976): 413–17.

37. Susan Suarez and Gordon Gallup, Jr., "Tonic Immobility as a Response to Rape in Humans: A Theoretical Note," *The Psychological Record* 29 (1979): 315–20.

38. N. H. Pronko and W. R. Leith, "Behavior under Stress: A Study of Its Disintegration," *Psychological Reports,* 2 (1956): 205–22.

39. Daniel Johnson, "Behavioral Inaction under Stress Conditions Similar to the Survivable Aircraft Accident," *SAFE Journal* (1st quarter, 1972).

40. Gallup, "Hypnosis in Animals," p. 69.

41. Ibid.

Chapter Three

DECOMPRESSIONS

Each of the next several chapters is devoted to a particular type of emergency. Each chapter provides guidelines on how to behave in the various emergencies as well as a description of the emergency equipment which may be available. This information, I hope, will be useful should you find yourself in one of these unfortunate situations.

If you have flown on a commercial aircraft you probably have seen the flight attendant give the oxygen mask demonstration; even so, you may have some of the following misconceptions:

1. In case of a decompression—a loss of air pressure in the cabin— the oxygen mask will automatically fall from the ceiling. Wrong. The mask may fall from a ceiling compartment, but it may instead drop out of a compartment located in the seat in front of you. Or if there is a partition rather than a seat in front of you, the mask compartment may be in that partition.
2. After the decompression you have at least a minute in which to get oxygen. Wrong. You may have as little as fifteen to twenty seconds of consciousness if the decompression has occurred rapidly at a high altitude.
3. You can tell if you need oxygen. Wrong. Unless you have had special training you will probably be unaware of the symptoms of hypoxia, the lack of sufficient oxygen.
4. If you are with a child, an elderly person, or someone else who needs assistance, you should help that person get the oxygen mask on before putting on your own mask. Wrong. If you hesitate or fumble getting that other person's mask on you may both lose

consciousness. But if you put your own mask on quickly enough, you will then be able to help someone else.

5. The oxygen will automatically flow from the mask once you put it to your face. Wrong. Aboard most aircraft the passenger must start the flow of oxygen to the mask by pulling the mask until a pin, attached by a cord to either the mask or the oxygen-supply tube, is pulled free of a mechanism which governs oxygen flow.

6. You will always be able to tell when the oxygen is coming out of the mask. Wrong. Oxygen is odorless, and it can come out of the mask at such a slow rate that you may not feel it against your face, and the bag attached to the mask may not inflate.

7. The oxygen mask has a strap but it is unnecessary to put it over your head since you can hold the mask to your face. Wrong. After you get the oxygen mask to your face you could still lose consciousness from hypoxia, as will be explained later in this chapter. If this happened, the mask would fall from your face unless it was held there by the strap.

8. If necessary, the flight attendant will help you in getting your mask on during the decompression. Wrong. Flight attendants may try to help every passenger, but you could lose consciousness before help arrives.

In this chapter I will examine the various factors which affect the severity of aircraft cabin decompressions, the physiological reactions which occur, and how people actually behave compared to how they should behave when a decompression occurs.

First, however, is an excerpt from a newspaper article written by a passenger aboard a wide-body jet which decompressed at a high altitude when an engine exploded and ripped several holes in the cabin:

After routine stops in New Orleans and Houston, we were cruising at 39,000 feet and were approximately one hour out of Las Vegas. The flight was smooth, peaceful, and uneventful.

Suddenly a very loud explosion snapped us out of our relaxed state of mind. Simultaneously, the huge DC-10 shuddered as if it had struck an object in mid-air.

Instantly, the sound of air rushing through and around the cabin area filled our ears. Within a split second, the plane banked severely, and it was obvious that this big bird was headed downstairs in a heck of a hurry. The big question was, "Was it headed downstairs on purpose or accidentally?" Everything took place so quickly it's difficult to timetable the sequence of events, but approximately three seconds after the explosion, the entire cabin area filled with a very toxic gas . . . .

The first reaction was to not breathe the foul mixture, but how long can you hold your breath? A lot of people were coughing and gasping, including yours truly. Whatever this stuff was, it will never replace oxygen. As bad as it was to breathe, it became even worse when it became necessary to swallow. Our throats stung just as if we were swallowing acid.

All the time this was taking place, that big bird was doing the hoochie coochie and let me tell you that it's just not natural for a DC-10 to be vibrating the way that it was at this particular time.

Within ten or twenty seconds, the stewardesses attempted to collect themselves and be of assistance to the people. Unfortunately, they just weren't ready for this kind of emergency. They shouted instructions to the passengers both individually and over the P.A. system, but their voices were hysterical. Needless to say, the passengers felt the stewardesses knew more about what was going on than they did. It was clear that the stewardesses felt we had "bought the farm."

Fortunately for everyone on board, most of the passengers adopted on a "wait and see" attitude and did not panic.

Approximately 3 minutes after the explosion, the compartments in the seat backs snapped open and the oxygen masks popped out. At least some did.

Paul and I were astounded to see that the couple sitting next to him had no masks in the oxygen compartment. They immediately got up to take another seat and found the same situation occurred in other seats. They ended up splitting up and taking separate seats in order to find locations where masks were available.

Can you imagine what would have happened if the plane had been full? The real clinker to this story is the fact that the oxygen wasn't working anyway, or at least so little as to be of very little help. We were never really quite sure whether there was a small amount of oxygen coming out of the masks or not. I felt there was not, but Paul indicated there was a small amount.

Every minute the plane kept flying, I felt better about the situation. After approximately 8 to 10 minutes, the captain came on the P.A. system to announce that he was headed back to Albuquerque for an emergency landing.

The captain sounded cool as a cucumber, and his voice was most reassuring. It was unfortunate that he could not have gotten on the P.A. system before to help reassure the people, but I am positive that his hands were more than full taking care of more important matters. . . .

Fifteen minutes after the explosion took place, the captain brought the jet into one of the smoothest landings that we have ever experienced, but it wouldn't have mattered if it had of been the roughest; we were down and rolling [on the runway].[1]

This article illustrates several problems that are common in high-altitude decompressions, with the exception of the choking smoke in the cabin, which is unusual (it turned out to be hydraulic fluid which was sucked into the air-conditioning system when the engine exploded). Most of the other problems, however, are more common during decompressions. To understand why they occurred requires a little background on how people react, both physically and psychologically, to decompressions.

Jet aircraft fly at high altitudes where the jet engines are more efficient than in the denser air at lower altitudes. Additional advantages include less air turbulence, adverse wind, and icing conditions at high altitude.[2] But it has long been known that high altitude can adversely affect a person's physiological functioning. In 1862 a balloon flight was sponsored by the British Association for the Advancement of Science. The Englishmen, Glaisher and Coxwell, ascended to approximately 29,000 feet to study the effects of high altitude. During this flight Glaisher noticed a series of unusual symptoms, notably loss of visual acuity and hearing, and paralysis of the arms and legs. He finally lost consciousness. Fortunately, even though Coxwell's arms were also paralyzed, he managed to pull the valve rope with his teeth and start the balloon downward. Both men recovered as the balloon descended, but this marked the first practical encounter with the dangers of high-altitude flight.[3]

At altitudes above 10,000 or 12,000 feet a person requires more oxygen than is available in the ambient air. Actually, at high altitudes the percentage of oxygen in the air remains about the same as it is at sea level; that is, about four-fifths of the air is the inert gas nitrogen, while the remainder is mostly oxygen. Air is not weightless, however, and because the blanket of atmosphere surrounding the earth is miles thick, it exerts considerable pressure on us living at sea level. But the higher up we go, the lower the pressure. As a jet aircraft takes off and climbs to its cruising altitude, the cockpit crew allows the air pressure inside the cabin to decrease, but at a slower rate than the external air pressure. At cruising altitude, which is usually between 35,000 and 41,000 feet on long flights, the cabin pressure is the same as it would be if you were flying in an unpressurized cabin at between 6,000 and 8,000 feet.

There are a number of reasons why this pressurized container, the cabin of your aircraft, might lose pressure, or might not even become pressurized in the first place. The rubber seal around the door may give way, thereby resulting in a relatively slow loss of air pressure. Or problems may occur in the air-exchange system. You would not be very happy if you landed in New York with the same cabin full of air that you left Los Angeles with five hours earlier. So the air in the cabin is replaced every few minutes during flight. The air is pumped into the cabin under pressure, and the air pressure in the cabin is adjusted upward or downward by opening or closing an outflow valve. As the aircraft ascends after takeoff the opening of the outflow valve is decreased, but it is not closed completely. It is left partially open to allow stale air to leave the cabin as the fresh air is pumped in.

One problem occurs when cigarette smoke in the cabin air coats the outflow valve, causing it to stick so that the valve does not close. As the aircraft ascends the air in the cabin rushes out the outflow valve faster than it should, and the air pressure in the cabin may not be maintained at a safe level. This occurrence is normally referred to as a "failure to compress," though in reality it is a slow decompression.

An unusual cause of depressurization is an explosion, either inside or outside the cabin, which could result in a hole in the cabin wall. For instance, an exploding engine or tire could send pieces of metal into the cabin, allowing the air to escape and the pressure to fall.

There have been instances when doors actually blew out because they were not completely closed prior to takeoff, thereby causing rapid decompressions. In each of two cases involving an early model of the DC-10, a door blew out in the cargo compartment below the cabin floor. The pressure in the cargo area immediately dropped while the air pressure above, in the passenger cabin, decreased but at a slower rate. The result was that the pressure in the passenger compartment became relatively greater than in the cargo compartment. This pushed the floor of the passenger cabin downward into the cargo area.

In the first such decompression, which occurred on June 12, 1972, during a flight from Detroit to Buffalo, some cargo was blown out of the cargo door and a portion of the cabin floor was depressed downward into the cargo area. This was potentially catastrophic because cables between the cockpit and the tail, used to control the direction of the airplane's flight, are strung through the floor of the cabin. All of these cables, luckily, were not severed when the floor was deformed, so the pilot successfully landed the aircraft.[4]

The manufacturer made several modifications to prevent this from occurring again, but unfortunately one particular DC-10 did not receive these modifications. Just before the plane's takeoff from Paris in March 1974, an airline worker thought he had closed the cargo door tightly. But it wasn't completely closed, even though it appeared to be. Several minutes after takeoff the door blew out at an altitude of about 12,000 feet. The floor was deformed downward, but this time it completely severed or jammed the control cables. Minutes later the aircraft crashed in a field killing all 346 persons aboard, making it the worst single aircraft accident in history.[5]

Several procedures have since been instituted to stop this from happening again. Partial closing of the cargo door to the point where it looks as if it is closed is no longer possible. Moreover, vents have been put in the floor throughout the cabin so that if a decompression were to occur, either in the top half or the bottom half of the airplane, the pressure between the compartments would equalize without deforming the floor and severing the control cables.

Whenever you fly you are subjected to some decompression. Even a relatively mild decompression may produce some significant, though usually unnoticed, physiological effects, which we will examine later on.

FACTORS AFFECTING PASSENGER SAFETY

Important factors affecting passenger safety during decompressions are the speed of the decompression, the highest cabin altitude reached, how long the cabin altitude remains at that altitude, the total time the cabin altitude is above 25,000 feet, the rate of descent, and the final altitude at which the aircraft levels off.[6] The speed of decompression depends on several factors, such as the size of the opening and the volume of the cabin: the bigger the opening the faster the decompression; also, the smaller the cabin the faster the decompression.

It is common to refer to a decompression as either being slow, rapid, or explosive. While these are not officially recognized categories, they are useful in describing decompressions. By an explosive decompression I am referring to a decompression which is completed almost instantaneously, say, within two seconds. By rapid decompression I mean one which is completed within about a minute or two, and a slow decompression takes longer to complete.

PHYSICAL AND PHYSIOLOGICAL DANGERS OF DECOMPRESSIONS

There are three types of problems associated with decompressions. First, there are the blast effects of the decompression, whereby a passenger may be injured by the movement of air as it escapes the cabin. Second, there are problems caused by the actual loss of pressure, which are due to the sudden expansion of air within the cabin and within the body itself. Third, there are problems caused by the low air pressure, the most important of which is hypoxia.

Blast Effects of an Explosive Decompression

If a large enough opening occurs in the wall of a pressurized cabin, someone nearby may be injured or actually blown out through the hole. The term "blown out," rather than "sucked out," is used because a vacuum is unable to exert a force, and thereby cannot pull a person out of the aircraft. It is the movement of air inside which forces objects, or a person, out through the opening. While a person's actually being blown out of the aircraft is a very rare event, it has occurred on both the DC-10 and the L-1011.

In the DC-10 accident a man was sitting next to a window when it was fractured by an exploding engine. Although he had his seatbelt on, it was loosely fastened and he was blown through the window opening. In the L-1011 accident two children were blown through a hole in the aisle caused by an exploding tire.[7]

The blast effect, while severe near the opening, is very localized. People seated more than two or three feet away from an opening the size of a broken window will probably suffer no adverse effect as the air moves through the opening.[8]

Gas Expansion within the Body

At sea level the blanket of air under which we live produces a pressure of 14.7 pounds per square inch (psi). This is also the force that it takes to raise a column of liquid mercury (Hg) in a vacuum tube to a height of 760 millimeters (mm). (Millimeters of mercury [mm Hg] is the usual measure of air pressure in physiological studies.)

Everyone is familiar with the phenomenon of bubbles' forming in a bottle of soda when the cap is removed. In these drinks the gas, carbon dioxide, has been dissolved under pressure and is held in the liquid by the high pressure in the capped bottle. When the cap is removed, the pressure in the bottle is reduced and the dissolved gas forms into bubbles and escapes.

In daily life nitrogen and oxygen are absorbed in the blood and tissues. If pressures were suddenly reduced, gas bubbles could form in various parts of your body. If they form in areas from which they cannot escape, such as in the abdomen, the sinuses, underneath the teeth, or within the inner ear, they could cause considerable pain.[9] The gas bubbles may also form within the tissues, and around the joints, causing a painful condition known as "the bends".[10]

During very rapid decompressions the air within the lungs expands and forces its way out through the nose and mouth. People can undergo sudden decompression without adverse effect as long as the trachea, the airway which leads from the lungs to the mouth, is open. The resting lung can easily withstand a sudden doubling of volume. But if the lungs expand too quickly the surface of the lungs can be torn, allowing air bubbles to enter the blood through the torn vessels. This causes a condition known as "burst lung" or vascular air embolism.[11] Burst lung is an extremely rare condition. The only reported cases have occurred when people have tried to hold their breaths during decompressions.[12]

Actually the tolerance of the lungs to rapid or explosive decompressions, when the trachea is open, is very great. Experimental subjects have been decompressed from 8,000 feet to 50,000 feet in 0.2 seconds with no injury.[13] The chances that a situation worse than this would occur aboard a commercial aircraft causing lung damage are very small.

Hypoxia

Air is composed principally of two gases, nitrogen (79.02 percent) and oxygen (20.95 percent). The remainder (0.03 percent) is made up of other gases, primarily carbon dioxide. Water vapor can occupy up to 4–5 percent of the total air volume, so when the humidity is high the amount of nitrogen and oxygen will each be reduced by one or two percentage points. The amount of oxygen in the air is referred to as the partial pressure of oxygen, P_{O_2}. At sea level in dry air the P_{O_2} is 20.95 percent of the 760 mm Hg, or 159.2 mm Hg.[14] A decrease in the P_{O_2} in the atmosphere can result in hypoxia. Even at altitudes as low as 5,000 feet above sea level, where P_{O_2} has dropped from 159 to 120 mm Hg, a person experiences a slight decrease in sensitivity to light—the eyes are one of the most sensitive organs to reduced oxygen levels. Normally, when you go from a bright room to a dark room you have some difficulty seeing a dimly lit object in the dark room. At an altitude of 5,000 feet or higher you would have even more difficulty seeing the object unless you happened to be adapted to living at that altitude.[15]

Although it may be more difficult to see dimly lit objects at the relatively low altitude of 5,000 feet, it would be erroneous to conclude that flying at this altitude is necessarily dangerous. It is certainly no more dangerous than driving an automobile at the same altitude on a mountain road in Denver, Colorado, a city which is 5,000 feet above sea level. But even though this reaction is slight it does occur, and can be more serious at higher cabin altitudes. This is one reason why the air pressure in the cabin and cockpit of airliners is kept at safe levels, even though the plane may be flying at very high altitudes.

Two other factors which can increase symptoms of hypoxia at a given altitude are smoking and drinking alcohol. Breathing just a small amount of carbon monoxide, a component of cigarette smoke, can deactivate a large amount of hemoglobin, the component in the blood that carries oxygen. A heavy smoker at sea level may be physiologically affected in the same way that a nonsmoker is affected at 12,000 feet above sea level.[16] When cabin altitude goes up to 6,000–8,000 feet, the heavy smoker will experience symptoms associated with altitudes even higher than 12,000 feet. In other words, the detrimental effects of carbon monoxide and of altitude are additive. Similarly, the combined effects of alcohol and altitude may also be additive. Alcohol slows down the cells' ability to use oxygen. At high altitude there is less oxygen available in the air, and if you drink alcohol your body has less ability to use the available oxygen. This can be a deadly combination in the event of a decompression.

In 1979 a man thirty-six years of age died on a charter flight between Mammoth and Palm Springs, California, after getting aboard the small aircraft intoxicated. He was one of five passengers who boarded the Cessna Turbo Centurion bound for Palm Springs. The pilot said the man was so drunk that the other passengers had to carry him aboard, whereupon he immediately went to sleep. During the flight the pilot had to climb to 19,000 feet to clear a cloud cover. Sometime during the flight the passenger stopped breathing.[17] Though there may have been other reasons contributing to the man's death—he could have suffered a heart attack even before boarding—the combination of high altitude and intoxication could well have been the primary cause.

"Cabin altitude" is a term which describes the relative altitude of the cabin of the plane as far as air pressure is concerned. A plane may be flying at 30,000 feet but have a cabin altitude of only 5,000 feet because the air within the cabin is kept at the same pressure as it is found, say, at Denver, Colorado, 5,000 feet above sea level. The pilot controls the cabin altitude so that it does not rise over about 8,000 feet even if the plane is flying at 40,000 feet or more. In an emergency it is probably not dangerous for the cabin altitude to rise to 15,000 feet without passengers receiving any additional oxygen. Even at this cabin altitude you should remain conscious for an indefinite period. But unless you received additional oxygen, after ten minutes or so you might experience some symptoms of hypoxia, such as temporary memory impairment, dizziness, and headache.[18]

At higher altitudes the severity of these symptoms increases, as does the chance of unconsciousness. On any jet flight exceeding 200 or 300 miles the pilot will probably fly at 30,000 feet or more. On transcontinental flights altitudes of 35,000–41,000 feet are usual. At these heights cabin altitudes of 6,000–8,000 feet are common. If the aircraft experienced an explosive decompression at 30,000 feet, then the cabin altitude would climb to 30,000 feet and you would probably remain conscious for about a minute. If your plane was higher and the cabin altitude were to reach 40,000 feet, you would remain conscious only about eighteen seconds.[19]

The "time of useful consciousness" (TUC) is the period from onset of decompression to failure to perform a purposeful act; at 40,000 feet TUC is about fifteen seconds.[20] The reason for the rapid loss of consciousness at high altitudes involves the process by which oxygen gets into the blood. In the lungs the atmospheric oxygen moves across the tissue of the small lung sacs, called the alveoli, and into the blood because the P_{O_2} in the air is greater than the P_{O_2} in the blood arriving at the lungs. The blood arriving at the alveoli is not devoid of oxygen; it has a P_{O_2}, but one that is normally much lower than the P_{O_2} in the air. This is the case until an altitude of about 33,000 feet is reached. Above this altitude the P_{O_2} in the air is *less* than the P_{O_2} in the blood.[21] So the blood that arrives in the lungs to be oxygenated actually loses oxygen and is pumped to the brain with less oxygen than when it arrived at the lungs. This oxygen-poor blood travels to the brain in about five or six seconds if the person is seated and resting—faster if he is working. The brain has a high oxygen consumption but stores very little, so that when this oxygen-poor blood reaches the brain only a few seconds of consciousness remain.

Physical activity decreases the time of useful consciousness because activity increases the circulation rate, thereby reducing the time it takes for the blood to reach the brain. A study of physical activity and its effect on TUC was conducted by the FAA. It involved twenty men and women, all of whom were in their twenties or early thirties and who were also airline flight attendants.[22] Each of the flight attendants was decompressed twice in a manner simulating actual conditions aboard. The decompression chamber was first brought to a cabin altitude of 6,500 feet. Before one decompression test, each flight attendant rested at this 6,500-foot altitude, simulating the seated passenger aboard an aircraft flying at high altitude. The chamber was then decompressed to an altitude of 34,000 feet in twenty-six seconds, followed by a descent rate (recompression) of 5,000 feet per minute.

Prior to another decompression test each flight attendant performed mild physical activity at the 6,500-foot level, to simulate a flight attendant when working during flight. Again the chamber was decompressed to 34,000 feet in twenty-six seconds, followed by recompression at a rate of 5,000 feet per minute. Table 3.1 summarizes the results of the study.

There were no statistically significant differences between men and women in this study. Working, however, reduced the TUC by about 39 percent. If the time of decompression had been faster, say five seconds instead of twenty-six seconds, and the cabin altitude had gone to 40,000

TABLE 3.1
Effect of Physical Activity on Time of Useful Consciousness[a]

	At rest			At work		
	Average TUC (sec.)	Range for the group (sec.)	Standard deviation (sec.)	Average TUC (sec.)	Range for the group (sec.)	Standard deviation (sec.)
Men	54	45–71	7.1	34	25–40	4.4
Women	54	40–68	8.1	32	26–38	4.0

[a] The average TUC for the men decreased from 54 seconds at rest to 34 seconds while performing work. The average TUC for the women decreased from 54 seconds at rest to 32 seconds while working. There was no significant difference between men and women at rest, nor between men and women at work.

feet rather than 34,000 feet, the TUC would undoubtedly have been shorter for both the resting person and the working flight attendant.

THE IMPORTANCE OF ADDITIONAL OXYGEN

One way of increasing the P_{O_2} in the lungs is to increase the total air pressure. After a rapid or explosive decompression the only practical way to increase the air pressure in the cabin is to descend to a lower altitude where the pressure is greater. But this takes time. Even though an aircraft can descend quickly (e.g., 10,000 feet per minute) it will still take three minutes to go from 40,000 feet to 10,000 feet. But you would not have several minutes of consciousness after an explosive decompression at 40,000 feet.

Another way of increasing P_{O_2} is to increase the percentage of oxygen in the air. This is the purpose of the "supplemental oxygen system," which requires using the oxygen masks demonstrated by the flight attendants prior to takeoff. In this system oxygen masks are automatically presented to passengers before the cabin altitude exceeds 14,000 or 15,000 feet. By using these masks you can receive up to 100 percent pure oxygen, which should be sufficent even in an unpressurized cabin up to 41,000 feet. Above that altitude a pressurized oxygen system would be needed to remain conscious.[23] No aircraft is equipped with pressurized oxygen systems for passengers. Not only are pressurized oxygen systems needed above 45,000 feet, but some kind of pressure suit would also be required. Since a supersonic transport such as the Concorde, which flies up to 65,000 feet, is equipped only with the standard, nonpressurized oxygen mask, we must assume that either the aircraft will not decompress at this altitude, or that if it does, it will be able to descend to 41,000 feet or lower before passengers will require oxygen under pressure.

The speed with which a passenger puts on an oxygen mask is very important. The same researchers who conducted the study of TUC among resting and working flight attendants also conducted a follow-up study to find out, among other things, how long a flight attendant could safely wait before putting on an oxygen mask. The study duplicated the decompression profile used in the preceding study: a waiting period at a 6,500-foot cabin altitude, decompression to 34,000 feet in twenty-six seconds, followed by a descent rate of 5,000 feet per minute.

Results showed that a flight attendant could safely wait only about fifteen seconds before putting on an oxygen mask without losing consciousness. Fifteen percent of those who waited twenty seconds lost consciousness, and of those who waited twenty-five seconds, 55 percent lost consciousness. In faster decompressions, or ones to higher altitudes, there would be less time to get the mask on.

One obvious question: If the working flight attendant has only fifteen seconds or so to get on an oxygen mask, what about the pilot? If the flight attendants and passengers lose consciousness they can still recover when the pilot brings the plane to a lower, safer altitude. This depends, though, on the pilot's remaining conscious.

I know of no case involving a commercial passenger-carrying aircraft where the pilot has lost consciousness during a decompression. There are several reasons for this. First, the flight crew, which is comprised of the captain, first officer, and on some aircraft a second officer, have experienced decompressions during training. In altitude chambers they have learned to recognize the subtle physical sensations associated with a decompression, such as warmth and tingling of the skin. Faster decompressions, of course, are more easily recognizable. Second, there are alarms in the cockpit which should warn the cockpit crew of the reduced air pressure. Third, the cockpit crew have "quick don" oxygen masks within easy reach, and have practiced getting the masks on quickly, usually within five seconds. So even if an explosive decompression occurred and the cabin altitude went to 40,000 feet, the pilot would not lose consciousness if he or she could put the mask on and started breathing 100 percent oxygen within five seconds.[24]

HOW TO RECOGNIZE A DECOMPRESSION

Explosive and rapid decompressions are easily recognized. They usually start with a loud noise as the air rushes out of the cabin. Dust from the floor, seats, and ceiling fills the air. A fog may occur for a few moments as the decrease in air pressure causes the water vapor in the air to condense. Even after the plane has decompressed there will probably be a loud noise as the outside air rushes past the hole in the fuselage.

The compartments holding the oxygen masks will automatically open if the cabin altitude reaches 14,000 or 15,000 feet. You will probably notice air rushing out of your lungs, a process you shouldn't try to stop. You may also notice pressure and perhaps some pain in your ears, sinuses, or intestinal areas due to gas expansion in your body. There will be confusion in the cabin. Don't expect any immediate announcements from the cockpit crew because they will be very busy determining the cause of the problem and its effect on the rest of the flight, and bringing the aircraft down to a safer altitude.

The flight attendants may try to make some announcements, as well as try to help some passengers. But they should be putting on their own masks, and since the mask covers the nose and mouth, it makes speaking almost impossible. The flight attendants may not be able to help more than a few passengers in those first critical moments. So you must know how to put your own mask on and how to get the oxygen flowing, because your time of useful consciousness may be very short without additional oxygen.

Failures to compress are different, however, from rapid or explosive decompressions. There may not even be any warning that the plane has a problem. In one instance aboard a wide-body aircraft, the plane took off and climbed steadily on the beginning of a flight from New York to Chicago with 182 passengers. But before takeoff a mechanic had inadvertently left a small door open in the nose of the plane so that as the aircraft ascended it didn't pressurize.[25] Two alarms in the cockpit, a light and a horn, are normally triggered when the cabin altitude goes above 15,000 feet. But as luck would have it, a wire to the lightbulb was broken and the warning horn was inoperable. As the aircraft ascended through 12,000 feet a flight attendant called the cockpit crew and told them that the oxygen mask compartments had opened. One of the cockpit crewmembers misinterpreted the message and thought the compartment at only one seat location had opened, a minor occurrence. Apparently no one aboard the aircraft was aware that the cabin altitude was as high as it was and increasing.

Several minutes later the flight attendant again called the cockpit and said that all the oxygen mask compartments had opened and also that he was feeling hot and dizzy. The pilot looked at the aircraft altimeter, which registered 33,000 feet, and at the cabin altimeter which read 18,000 feet and rising. Suddenly realizing that they were in an emergency situation, he put the plane into an immediate and rapid descent.

In the cabin, while this was going on, all but two of the passengers simply sat and looked at the open oxygen compartments. A man and a sixty-five-year-old woman, who both said later that prior to the decompression they had read the passenger safety information cards, had put on their masks and had started the oxygen flowing by the time the flight attendants got to their seats. The flight attendants had to help the other passengers get oxygen to their masks. Luckily there were no injuries, and the plane landed without further incident.

What I found interesting from this account was that only 2 of the 182 passengers responded as they were supposed to. The others didn't behave as the designers of the supplemental oxygen system predicted they would. Each passenger was expected to take a mask and pull it to the face. In so doing, he would start the oxygen flowing to the mask. Instead most passengers just sat and looked at the masks, and except for the man and woman, those who took hold of a mask did not pull it hard enough to start the oxygen flowing.

In checking through other reports of decompressions on passenger-carrying aircraft, I found that incorrect or nonuse of the oxygen masks by passengers was not so unusual. On October 3, 1974, an aircraft with fifty-three passengers and a crew of twelve was descending from 35,000 feet, prior to landing at Mexico City, when a pressurization problem caused the cabin altitude to go to 25,000 feet.[26] The oxygen masks automatically deployed as the cabin altitude reached 14,000 feet, and one of the flight attendants instructed the passengers to put on their masks. But again only two passengers correctly put their masks on and started the oxygen flowing. The flight attendants had to assist the other passengers. Luckily, everyone aboard except one flight attendant remained conscious.

The reports of these incidents are intriguing. The demonstration on how to use the oxygen mask is probably the most often seen and remembered instruction on aircraft emergency equipment. And yet just a few of the passengers who saw these demonstrations were able to use the oxygen mask correctly in actual decompressions. Was there a problem with the oxygen mask itself, or was there a problem in the instructions to the passengers? Would better instructions help? Should instructions be given during the decompression itself, or just at the beginning of the flight?

Other researchers have recently studied this problem and found that even in the laboratory some test subjects failed to put on an oxygen mask during a decompression. In each of two similiar studies a test subject sat in a decompression chamber after receiving a briefing on oxygen mask use. The chamber was sealed and the altitude was brought up to "cruise" level (5,000–8,000 feet). Suddenly the chamber was decompressed to 20,000–30,000 feet. In each study most of the passengers were able to get their masks on and the oxygen flowing. In one study seventy-seven (96 percent) of the eighty subjects (all male, between eighteen and twenty-five years of age) got their masks on and the oxygen flowing within twenty seconds.[27] In the comparison study, twenty males and twenty females between the ages of nineteen and seventy-eight were tested. Thirty (75 percent) of these subjects got their masks on, started the oxygen flowing, and had started breathing oxygen within eighteen seconds.[28] The investigators did not find that age or sex were significant factors affecting performance.

It was after these studies were published that the reports came out that passengers were having difficulty in using the oxygen systems during actual decompressions. Why were the subjects in the test situations doing so well compared to actual passengers? It may have had something to do with safety precautions taken in the test situation which were not present in the aircraft. The subjects were briefed on why they were there, and instructed specifically on how to use the oxygen system. During the test a monitor, who had an oxygen mask on, was in the decompression chamber with each subject. It could be that test subjects were more likely to use the masks than passengers because of the briefing directed solely at each subject. Furthermore, because a test official with the subject in the chamber also had on an oxygen mask, the likelihood of the subject's putting on a mask may have been increased.

I conducted a test using 101 subjects, about half of whom were male and whose ages ranged from twenty to sixty. They had no experience with oxygen masks, though nearly all had flown before and all were familiar with the flight attendant's oxygen mask demonstration.[29] One purpose of the study was to see if an instructional placard would increase the percentage of passengers who could use an oxygen mask correctly after a decompression. The placard was designed to be attached to the inside of the oxygen compartment door aboard DC-10s, and would be seen by the passengers when the compartment door opened during a decompression. The test was to find out how effective the placard instructions were as compared to no instructions.

This test differed from those conducted earlier in that a decompression chamber was not used. Subjects were seated, and in front of them was an aircraft-type passenger seat containing an oxygen mask compartment. The subjects were instructed to play the role of passengers aboard an aircraft flying at a high altitude. The test subjects were not briefed on the purpose of the test nor were they given an oxygen mask demonstration, and there was no one else in the room wearing a mask. This ensured that they would not be mentally set to respond to a decompression—aboard an airplane there is no warning of imminent decompression. So, going into the test, most of the subjects were familiar with oxygen mask demonstrations from previous flights, but they were not aware of the purpose of the test.

The results were surprising in several ways. First, there was a group of twenty subjects whose compartment doors had no placard attached to them. The performance of this group, the control group, was compared to that of another group of twenty subjects, the experimental group, to see what effect, if any, the placard had. The first surprise was that the placard had no effect on performance. The second surprise was that the behavior of the subjects in each group was abysmal. Only two to five subjects (10–25 percent) were able to put the mask on and start the flow of oxygen, reacting nearly as poorly as passengers did during the actual decompressions.

The placard was analyzed in light of these errors and revisions were made. Actually the placard was revised several times, being tested after each revision. We finally ended up with a placard which resulted in most (94 percent) of the test subjects' being able to use the mask correctly (see Figure 3.1). The average combined time for putting the oxygen mask over the face and for pulling the cord to start the oxygen flowing was a relatively slow 40 seconds (range, 12–122 seconds; standard deviation, 26 seconds).

This time is certainly longer than desirable. Consequently I set about to find out if the subjects could be induced to put the mask on and start the oxygen flowing more quickly. Some aircraft, such as the L-1011 and the DC-10, have the capability of automatically playing a taped recording over the public address system in case of a decompression. But this device is optional, so not all airlines use it.

A taped recording could benefit many passengers. For one thing, in a decompression you can't rely on seeing or reading a placard. It could occur at night so the lighting levels might be low. Also, the temporary fog could obscure the placard. Furthermore, vision is more susceptible to hypoxia than is hearing.[30] Therefore I devised the following message to be given over the public address system in a laboratory test:

A decompression is occurring. Quit smoking. Pull the yellow mask until the green

FIGURE 3.1. A placard passengers would see on the inside of the open door of an oxygen compartment on some airplanes. This placard was associated with a high percentage of subjects' being able to use the mask.

cord breaks loose. Take the plastic bag out and put the mask over both nose and mouth. Put the strap overhead and pull the ends snug. If no mask is available, go to another seat. Do not help others until your mask is on and adjusted. Don't touch the metal box in front of you for it may be hot. Don't be alarmed for the plane will descend rapidly. Tighten seatbelts and don't remove your mask until told to by the crew.[31]

Now one problem with spoken instructions is that they cannot be understood by people who don't know the language. So I had the instructions recorded in Spanish by a male speaker. The English message was recorded using a woman's voice (which another study had found to have been better understood against aircraft noise than other voices).[32]

The purpose of using two voices that were different in pitch was this. Since putting the oxygen mask on quickly is important, it would take too long to give the message in one language, then repeat it in the other language. A more practical method would be to give each sentence or two in one language, then to repeat them in the alternate language. The problem with this approach is that it would take twice as long for a passenger to hear the entire message. My hunch was that the message could be understood even though it was given in two languages simultaneously. A test subject might be able to understand the message given in the language he or she spoke if the two voices were different in pitch.

In this study, 92 percent of the seventy-two subjects had flown commercial jet aircraft and 35 percent of them had been on DC-10 flights; 75 percent of them were men. As before, they were told only that they were to play the part of a passenger aboard a commercial jet flying at high altitude, and that "an event will occur which is like one that could actually happen aboard a commercial jet flying at high altitude." Each subject was seated behind a seat containing an oxygen mask compartment. Suddenly the sound of a decompression, taped earlier in a decompression chamber, filled the laboratory. The recorded message started playing several seconds after the decompression noise started and at the same time as the oxygen compartment opened up.

I had set up the test so that some subjects saw the instructional placard which had been developed in the previous test, and others did not. Some subjects heard the message in one language, others in two languages (alternating phrases), and still others heard the message spoken simultaneously in two languages. Table 3.2 summarizes the results of the study.

TABLE 3.2
Effects of Spoken Instructions and Placard on Oxygen Mask Use

Group	Number of subjects	Time to get oxygen (sec.) Mean	Time to get oxygen (sec.) S.D.	Percent getting oxygen
1. Placard only	10	36	30.6	80
2. Placard plus verbal message— English only	10	23.5	6.9	100
3. Placard plus verbal message—2 languages, alternating	10	36.3	13	100
4. Placard plus verbal message—2 languages, simultaneously	17	37	31	94
5. No placard: verbal message—2 languages, simultaneously	15	36.5	30.3	80
6. Control group: no placard, no verbal message	10	84	71.9	40

The instructions, whether in the form of spoken instructions or a placard, were effective in significantly increasing the proportion of subjects who were able to don the mask and activate the oxygen flow. Compared to the 40 percent in the control group, 90 percent of the subjects in the experimental group were able to perform the task. There were no significant differences within the experimental groups in the proportion of subjects who were able to perform the task.

As far as performance time is considered, the only statistically significant difference was between Groups 2 and 3: Group 2 was faster than Group 3. While the performance time of the control group was much longer than that for the experimental groups, there were so few subjects who were able to complete the task in Group 6 that no statistical test could be made.

Incidentally, a small number of the subjects were bilingual in these two languages and seemed not to perform any better or worse than others. In posttest interviews they claimed they had no difficulty understanding the message because they would switch from listening to one language to the other. This was possible, however, because the messages were recorded so that a "skip" from one language to another wouldn't result in a loss of information.

From these test results it appears that instructions given at the time of decompression can significantly increase the percentage of people who quickly and accurately respond. Since the crewmembers will probably not be able to help each and every passenger at the time of a decompression, the instructions should either be given automatically over the public address system or as printed instructions—in the clearest form possible—available to the passenger when the decompression occurs. Of course, passengers who knew beforehand what to do in the decompression would need neither recorded messages or printed instructions.

WHAT TO DO IN A DECOMPRESSION

First, remember to act quickly. Don't wait for help. If you are standing up, quickly sit down and buckle your safety belt. The captain will put the plane into a rapid descent and anyone not buckled in could be injured. Also, if smoking, put your cigarette out.

There are several ways that oxygen masks are presented to passengers. On most Boeing aircraft, as well as on the Lockheed L-1011 and the Airbus

A-300, the oxygen masks drop out of ceiling compartments and hang within arm's reach of the seated passenger (see Figure 3.2). On Douglas aircraft the oxygen mask remains attached either to the oxygen compartment door or it remains clipped within the compartment itself.

On Douglas DC-9 aircraft, the compartments are located overhead, and the passenger must remove the mask from the wire clip attached to the compartment door (see Figure 3.3). On the DC-10 the oxygen masks are usually attached to the compartment door or in a special location inside the compartment; these compartments are located in some of the seat backs in front of the passengers. If you are aboard a DC-10 and there are no seats in front of you, then the oxygen masks will either be located in an overhead compartment or in a partition in front of you (see Figure 3.4).

All lavatories are supplied with oxygen masks which, as a rule, are located in an overhead compartment, and which you can reach even if seated.

You should be mentally prepared to react to the opening of an oxygen compartment by quickly taking hold of the closest mask. Don't try to figure out if it's the right thing to do, and don't follow the lead of others. Most

FIGURE 3.2. Oxygen masks usually fall from ceiling compartments on Boeing aircraft.

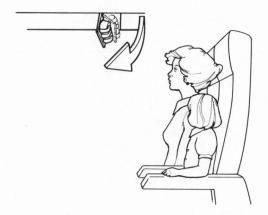

FIGURE 3.3. On DC-9 aircraft the mask remains attached to the door of the ceiling compartment.

people won't do anything right away, so you should act. If there is no
decompression, then the worst that can happen is that you will have inhaled
some oxygen. But if a decompression is occurring, then you'll be ahead
of the game.

Take the mask closest to you and pull it to start the oxygen flowing.
This is necessary on all commercial jet aircraft except the L-1011. On
Douglas aircraft, such as the DC-9 and the DC-10, there is a cord attached
to the mask itself (see Figure 3.5). This cord is in addition to both the
strap that goes over the head and the tube that supplies oxygen to the
reservoir bag. When this cord is pulled, a pin is pulled loose from the
mechanism which regulates oxygen flow. Only by pulling this pin loose
will oxygen flow through the tube and into the bag.

On Boeing aircraft, such as the B-747, the cord that must be pulled
to start the oxygen flowing is attached to the oxygen-supply tube rather
than to the mask (see Figure 3.6). But just as with the Douglas system,
pulling the mask toward you results in the pin being pulled loose and starts
the oxygen flowing to the mask.

When the oxygen masks are packed into the compartment, the strap
that goes over your head, and a plastic bag called the reservoir bag, are
packed inside the mask. The bag and the strap should come out of the
mask when you pull it toward you, but in some cases they may stick inside.

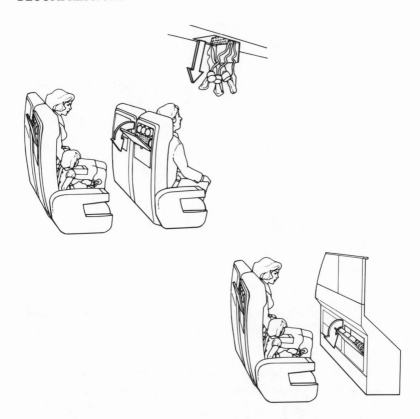

FIGURE 3.4. On DC-10 aircraft oxygen masks usually are in one of the seat backs in front of the passengers. If there is no seat in front, the masks will be in a ceiling compartment or in a partition in front of you.

If so, pull them out before putting the mask over your face (see Figure 3.7).

Put the mask over your nose *and* mouth. Don't make the common mistake of putting it over your mouth and breathing through your nose.

Probably the major problem of the Boeing and Douglas systems is not with the materials themselves, or with the systems, but with the passengers who haven't paid attention to the safety instructions, and who, as a result, are unsure of what to do. They are hesitant and fail to pull the

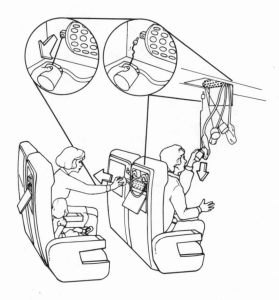

FIGURE 3.5. On Douglas aircraft a pin attached to the mask by a lanyard must be pulled to start oxygen flowing.

mask hard enough to start the oxygen flowing. In posttest interviews of subjects in the control groups, those who had not been instructed on how to use the masks, many said they were afraid that pulling the mask would "break the system," and so they would put their faces to the mask rather than pulling the masks to their face.[33] However, though some force is needed, the passenger should not pull the mask *too* hard or *too* far, or it could be pulled free from the oxygen supply.

It only takes about a one- to four-pound pull force to get the oxygen flowing. And it doesn't have to be pulled very far—just to your face. Usually two or three oxygen masks are stowed in a compartment so that one compartment can supply oxygen for the two or three passengers in that row. On some aircraft, pulling one mask will start the oxygen flowing to the other masks in the compartment—on others, each mask must be pulled before oxygen will flow to it.

The L-1011 system certainly would appear easier to use because all you must do is put the mask on and start breathing. This is close to a

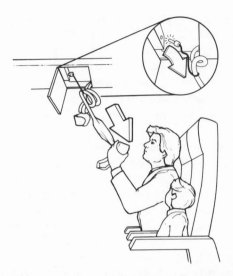

FIGURE 3.6. On Boeing aircraft a pin attached to the oxygen-supply tube must be pulled to start the oxygen flowing.

FIGURE 3.7. You may have to remove the plastic bag from the mask.

problem-free method, except in the rarest of circumstances when a cockpit crewmember inadvertently hits the wrong switch, thereby deploying the masks and depleting the oxygen.

Once you have put the mask to your face, placed it so it covers both your nose and mouth, and started the oxygen flowing, your next step is to breathe normally. Some people actually hyperventilate (breathe too fast) when breathing oxygen during a decompression, and as a result lose consciousness.[34]

The next step is to put the strap overhead and adjust it, if necessary, so that the mask will stay on your face (see Figure 3.8). Don't assume that the strap is there just for convenience. It isn't. If you experience a very rapid or explosive decompression at a high altitude, the oxygen-poor blood leaving the lungs will take ten or fifteen seconds to reach your brain. Even if during this period you get the mask to your face and start breathing 100 percent oxygen, you could still lose consciousness. If the mask were not strapped to your face, you would drop it.

The mask must fit snugly enough so that the oxygen doesn't escape around the edges, and so that you don't inhale ambient air. This could be a problem for those with beards since the edges of the mask would not fit tightly against the cheeks and jaw, thereby allowing oxygen to escape. Also, the mask must be adjusted to fit the faces of children.

FIGURE 3.8. Put the mask over both your mouth and nose, and the strap overhead. Make sure the strap does not slip below your ears.

A problem with adjusting the mask is that you must find and pull the ends of the strap, which are located only three or four inches from your eyes when the mask is on your face. Unfortunately, most people cannot focus on objects less than six to eight inches from their eyes. So people have problems finding the ends of the strap. If you can't find them right away, you may have to take a deep breath of oxygen and then pull the mask away from your face for a better look. Once you see the strap ends, take one in each hand, and with the mask back on your face, pull both ends of the strap until the mask feels tight against your face (see Figure 3.9). Remember to breathe only the air coming out of the mask. Don't breathe the ambient air.

Only after you have your own mask on, and adjusted if necessary, and the oxygen is flowing, should you help other people seated near you (see Figure 3.10). Children and some handicapped passengers may not be able to reach an oxygen mask or put one on. Others, unable to understand the nature or urgency of the situation, will simply not respond.

But don't try to help someone else first, even if it's your own child. It should be obvious by now that helping another person first is not advisable because if you try to help someone before you get your own mask on, you could lose consciousness. And if the person you tried to assist wasn't able to help himself in the first place, he won't be able to help either himself or you should you lose consciousness.

The steps outlined above for putting on the oxygen mask and getting

FIGURE 3.9. Adjust the strap, if necessary, to hold the mask on your face.

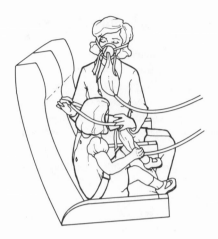

FIGURE 3.10. Help others only after putting on your own mask.

the oxygen to flow are important, but there are other things which you should be aware of which could cause problems. One problem is how to tell if oxygen is actually getting through to the mask. The flow of oxygen will seem relatively slow if there is moderate air pressure in the cabin. At 14,000 feet, oxygen comes through the mask at between 0.5 and 1.0 liters per minute (L/min).[35] A liter is equivalent to about one quart of air; at this rate you may not feel it on your face. Furthermore, since it's odorless, tasteless, and colorless you may think you're not getting any oxygen.

Also, the reservoir bag probably will not expand at a low level of oxygen flow. It will look deflated even though there is adequate oxygen coming through it. In the words of one researcher, "Unfortunately, the public has been deluged with fictional medical and emergency popular entertainment media programs depicting oxygen masks, resuscitation equipment, etc., in use. These devices normally employ rebreathing bags, have high flow rates, waste oxygen, and are inefficient and impractical for use on aircraft carrying large numbers of passengers. This indoctrination by the media has conditioned the public to expect the gas bag attached to an oxygen mask to expand and contract with each breath. The reservoir of the [oxygen] mask does not respond in this manner and, consequently, passengers and crewmembers complained that these systems did not function properly."[36]

At 14,000 feet, the flow of 0.5 L/min would only partially inflate the reservoir bag once every minute. At a 25,000-foot cabin altitude the flow of oxygen would be equivalent to 1.6 L/min, thereby inflating the bag about every fifteen seconds. Of course, if you were breathing from the mask and bag at these altitudes, the bag would not inflate because you would be inhaling the oxygen before it could fill the bag. Nevertheless, at a higher altitude, such as 35,000 feet, the oxygen flow rate would be 3.2 L/min, thereby filling the bag every five seconds. At this rate the bag would expand and contract at each inhalation.

Up until now it has been difficult for you to tell if, after a decompression to a moderate cabin altitude (25,000 feet), oxygen is getting into the mask. But there has been a new device designed to help the passenger, the oxygen-flow indicator. There are two types of oxygen-flow indicators used on some commercial aircraft. One, produced by Scott Aviation, makes use of a small area of the reservoir bag. (See Figure 3.11.) The oxygen-supply tube leads into this small area which is filled with oxygen before the gas moves into the larger section of the bag. This small area is colored green and has the words "Green Inflated—Oxygen O.K." printed on it. If

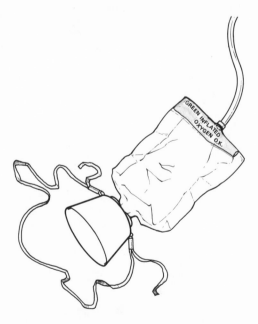

FIGURE 3.11. Some masks have a green portion at the base which inflates to indicate that oxygen is flowing.

the bag attached to your mask has this flow indicator (known in the industry as the "green weenie"), then right after the oxygen starts flowing the small area balloons up. If it doesn't expand then you probably are not getting oxygen.

Another type of indicator, produced by Puritan, is built into the oxygen-supply tube which leads into the reservoir bag (see Figure 3.12). This indicator is normally opaque white, but inside is a small green cylinder which you can't see unless oxygen is flowing through the tube. When it is flowing, this small green inner cylinder becomes visible through a transparent section.

Another recent improvement in the oxygen system, called the chemical oxygen generator, has solved some major problems but has created some different, though mostly minor ones. The older system, and the one still

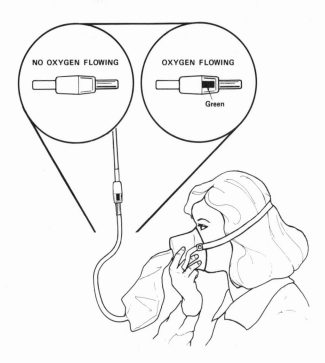

FIGURE 3.12. In some cases a flow indicator in the oxygen-supply tube will show green when oxygen is flowing.

on many aircraft, is called the gaseous oxygen system. It consists of oxygen stored in the gaseous form in high-pressure oxygen tanks, similar to the ones you've probably seen in hospital rooms. The tanks are connected by distribution lines to each oxygen mask compartment. These oxygen tanks are heavy and expensive to fly around year after year. And there is always the fear that following an accident the tanks could explode, or the gas could escape and fuel a fire.

The new chemical oxygen generator, however, now used on many new planes such as the DC-10, A-300, and the Boeing 757 and 767 has several advantages. Besides being lightweight, it won't explode in a fire. Following an accident on the ground there is little chance that it could fuel a cabin fire. Located right in the compartment with the masks, it doesn't need long supply tubes from a central area as does the gaseous system. Chemical oxygen generators contain a solid material, a chlorate-fuel composite chemical that is stored in metal cylinders two to three inches in diameter and six to eight inches long (see Figure 3.13).

During a decompression the chemical in the generator is ignited, burning to produce oxygen, which, after being filtered, travels through the supply tube to the mask.[37] One problem with the chemical oxygen generator is that the metal casing heats up as the chlorate burns. There is no chance that the heat might cause the oxygen to explode—oxygen doesn't explode, but it does increase the rate at which something else is burning, which is the reason why you should put out your cigarette in the presence of oxygen.

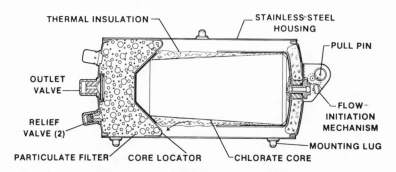

FIGURE 3.13. Increasingly common are chemical oxygen generators, located in seat backs or overhead compartments, which burn on the inside to produce oxygen. The generator will get hot to the touch while it is producing oxygen.

When the metal casing heats up it can reach a temperature of up to 500°F, high enough to burn someone's fingers, were he to touch it. Because of this the generator has been shielded, though on some airplanes I'm sure that if a person really tried he could still touch the generator and get burned.

Following a decompression, the aircraft may make an emergency landing because the incident which caused the decompression might also increase the chances of a landing accident. On some aircraft the oxygen compartments are located in the seat backs rather than in overhead compartments. About half of the seat backs in these planes have compartments which contain two or three oxygen masks. After a decompression, and before landing, make sure that the oxygen compartment in front of you is closed. You won't need oxygen below 10,000 feet, and if there were an accident during landing you could be injured if you struck the exposed metal surfaces in the compartment. Closing the compartment will require the assistance of a flight attendant because the complicated latch mechanism must be reset in order to keep the compartment door shut.

REFERENCES

1. Frank Glindmeier, "From the Flying Bridge," *Meadview Monitor* (Meadview, Arizona), Jan.-Feb. 1974.
2. Ross Armstrong McFarland, "Human Factors in Relation to the Development of Pressurized Cabins," *Aerospace Medicine* 12 (1971):1303–18.
3. Ibid., p. 1304.
4. *Safety Information,* Report no. SB 73-27/878C–D, National Transportation Safety Board, Washington, D.C. April 24, 1973.
5. Peter S. Greenberg, "Aftermath to Disaster," *Los Angeles Magazine,* Aug. 1979, p. 159.
6. James G. Gaume, "Factors Influencing the Time of Safe Unconsciousness (TSU) for Commercial Jet Passengers Following Cabin Decompression," *Aerospace Medicine* 41 (1970):382–85.
7. "Human Factors Group Chairman's Analysis Report, Accident LAX 74–A–L031, Nov. 3, 1973," Federal Aviation Administration, Washington, D.C., 1973; "2 Children Sucked out of Jetliner over Qatar," *Daily Olympian* (Olympia, Washington), Dec. 23, 1980, p. 1.
8. J. Ernsting, "The Physiological Effects of Failure of the Pressure Cabins of Passenger Aircraft Flying at Altitudes between 35,000 and 65,000 Feet," IAM Report no. 313, RAF Institute of Aviation Medicine, Farnborough, Hants, England, Feb. 1965.
9. McFarland, "Human Factors"; Ernsting, "Physiological Effects."
10. MacFarland, "Human Factors."
11. Ernsting, "Physiological Effects."

12. Ibid., p. 2.

13. Ibid.

14. *Bioastronautics Data Book,* 1964, NASA, Washington, D.C., sect. 1, p. 2.

15. MacFarland, "Human Factors," p. 1310.

16. Ibid., p. 1311.

17. "Man Believed Drunk Dies in Flight," *Los Angeles Times,* March 6, 1979.

18. Ernsting, "Physiological Effects," 35.

19. Ibid., p. 33; Gaume "Factors Influencing the TSU," p. 1.

20. Douglas E. Busby, E. Arnold Higgins, and Gordon E. Funkhouser, "Effect of Physical Activity of Airline Flight Attendants on Their Time of Useful Consciousness in a Rapid Decompression," *Aviation, Space, and Environmental Medicine* 47 (1976):117.

21. Gaume, "Factors Influencing the TSU."

22. Busby et al., "Effect of Physical Activity."

23. Gaume, "Factors Influencing the TSU"; Ernsting, "Physiological Effects."

24. Charles I. Barron and Thomas J. Cook, "Effects of Variable Decompression to 45,000 Feet," *Aerospace Medicine* (May 1965):425–30; Charles A. Bryan and Wilson G. Leach, "Physiological Effects of Cabin Pressure Failure in High Altitude Passenger Aircraft," *Aerospace Medicine* 31 (April 1960):267–75; A. Peter Holm, T. Freedman, and A. Puskas, "Accidental Decompression: A New Philosophy for the Transports of the 1970's," *Aerospace Medicine* 11 (3) (March 1970):277–282.

25. *Special Study: Chemically Generated Supplemental Oxygen Systems in DC-10 and L-1011 Aircraft,* Report no. NTSB–AAS–76–1, National Transportation Safety Board, Washington, D.C., 1976, p. 4.

26. Ibid., p. 3.

27. G. W. Hoffler, H. S. Turner, R. L. Wick, Jr., and C. E. Billings, "Behavior of Naive Subjects during Rapid Decompressions from 8,000 to 30,000 Feet," *Aerospace Medicine* 45 (2) (1974):117–22.

28. D. M. Chisholm, C. E. Billings, and R. Bason, "Behavior of Naive Subjects during Decompressions: An Evaluation of Automatically Presented Oxygen Equipment," *Aerospace Medicine* 45 (1974):123–27.

29. Daniel A. Johnson, "Oxygen-Use Placard Evaluation," Report no. MDC J6752, Douglas Aircraft Company, Long Beach, Calif., Dec. 1974.

30. McFarland, "Human Factors."

31. Daniel A. Johnson, "Effectiveness of Spoken Instructions on Passenger Use of Oxygen Masks," Report no. MDC J7098, Douglas Aircraft Company, Long Beach, Calif., Feb. 1976.

32. David M. Zamarin, "Intelligibility Testing for Synthetic Speech Voice Model Selection," Report no. MDC J6757, Douglas Aircraft Company, Long Beach, Calif., Dec. 1974.

33. Johnson, "Oxygen-Use Placard Evaluation."

34. Chisholm et al., "Behavior of Naive Subjects during Decompressions," p. 125.

35. E. R. McFadden, "Human Respiratory Considerations for Civil Transport Aircraft System," Report no. FAA–AM–78–9, Office of Aviation Medicine, Federal Aviation Administration, Washington, D.C., March 1978.

36. Ibid., p. 6.

37. *Special Study,* NTSB, 1976.

Chapter Four

INFLIGHT EMERGENCIES

Besides decompressions there are several other types of inflight emergencies. One is the evasive maneuver wherein the pilot causes the plane to climb, dive, or bank sharply to the left or right to avoid a mid-air collision. Injuries to passengers and flight attendants during such episodes, though rare, have occurred.

A passenger-carrying airplane, an Electra, was a few miles north of Dodger Stadium on a flight from Lake Tahoe to Los Angeles on July 22, 1977, when the pilot put the plane into a steep dive to avoid a smaller plane. Some of the passengers were thrown from their seats and struck the ceiling of the plane's cabin.[1] Twenty-three passengers and three flight attendants, out of the ninety-seven passengers and six crew aboard the propeller-driven aircraft, had to be hospitalized, three for potentially serious fractures. "It all happened so fast that I didn't know what happened," said one of the passengers, Ruth Katsof, of Studio City, California. She said she had her seatbelt fastened, but "The man in front of me didn't. He really went flying in the air and he fell back and hit me."[2]

Another passenger, Ronald Mason, a theatrical agent from North Hollywood, California, said he thought for an instant that the plane was going to crash. "It seemed for a moment we were going down," he was quoted as saying. "Everything in the racks [baggage racks located over the passengers' heads] came tumbling down. It sounded like a collision."[3]

Passengers who do not wear their safety belts when seated, or who are out of their seats even though the safety-belt signs are lit, stand a greater chance of being injured during turbulence or evasive maneuvers. A woman was returning to her seat from the lavatory on a B-707 which was descending into Phoenix, Arizona, on December 10, 1974. Suddenly the large aircraft veered to avoid another aircraft, and the lady fractured her ankle.[4]

However, less than 10 percent of inflight accidents occurred as a result of evasive maneuvers during 1968–1971, according to a National Transportation Safety Board (NTSB) study.[5] By far the most common cause of inflight accidents was air turbulence. Even in the early days of flying, turbulence produced by visible cloud storm systems was a concern to those who built and operated aircraft. Not only was passenger discomfort during bumpy flights common, but severe storms could destroy an airplane in flight.

The advent of jet flight at high altitude has revealed a new hazard, clear-air turbulence, commonly referred to as CAT. As its name implies, CAT is turbulence in air where no clouds are visible. It is associated with the high-altitude jet stream, a broad band of fast-moving air that runs in a west-to-east direction across the United States. According to John Enders, formerly with NASA, "unexpected encounters [with CAT] at high cruise speeds have resulted in injury to passengers and crew, damage to aircraft, and in rare instances fatal injuries."[6] Although Enders says that not all scientists agree on the cause for CAT, it appears that waves in the jet stream become unstable and some of the air is diverted downward in columns. An aircraft flying below the jet stream could suddenly enter one of these downward-moving columns of air, and occupants not strapped into their seats could find themselves pressed up against the ceiling. As the aircraft passes through the column and reaches the other side, its downward movement suddenly ceases and the unstrapped occupants fall to the floor, or onto passengers below them.

If an aircraft encounters CAT, the pilot generally notifies ATC so that other aircraft can avoid the turbulent area. Also, several methods are being evaluated which could allow the pilot to scan several miles ahead for CAT. Regardless of the advances in detection and avoidance, however, it may be a number of years before CAT can be dismissed as a potential threat. NTSB records show that in the United States, between 1964 and 1975 turbulence caused 183 accidents in which injuries occurred. While most of the accidents were associated with visible storm systems, sixty-eight (37 percent) were associated with CAT; of these sixty-eight accidents, more than half (61 percent) occurred during the normal cruise phase of the flight. In fact, the most common altitude for CAT occurrence was between 31,000 and 35,000 feet.[7]

Because of CAT and evasive maneuvers, both of which can unexpectedly cause violent movement of the aircraft, captains on some commercial aircraft in the United States will inform you that even after takeoff you should keep your safety belt fastened when seated.

Thunderstorms, nonetheless, are still the most common cause of inflight accidents resulting in injuries.[8] While jet aircraft can fly at altitudes above 41,000 feet, they still may not be able to get above all thunderstorm activity. According to the FAA there are approximately 45,000 thunderstorms on earth each day, and every state in the United States experiences some thunderstorms each year. On a state-by-state basis, central Florida has the greatest number, about 100 per year, while the west coast of California, Oregon, and Washington have fewer than 5 per year. Furthermore, thunderstorms bring about hazards other than turbulence that can affect the aircraft, among them hail, lightning, sudden wind shifts, wind shear, and heavy rain.[9]

Webster Todd, former chairman of the NTSB, wrote a letter to the heads of forty-two airlines that warned of the dangers of flying in storms. He indicated that between 1972 and 1976 nine airline accidents occurred during flights through thunderstorms, resulting in 251 injuries.[10] One accident occurred on June 24, 1975, when a B-727, on approach to New York's JFK Airport, passed through a thunderstorm. The strong winds forced it into the ground short of the runway, killing all 112 people aboard.

A DC-9 was flying from Huntsville, Alabama, to Atlanta, Georgia, on April 4, 1977, when it encountered very heavy thunderstorms at about 15,000 feet. To the misfortune of the crew and passengers, the aircraft was on a route which took it through the center of one of the thunderstorms. A flight attendant stationed in the front of the plane stated that suddenly the aircraft was engulfed in hail.[11] It was very loud, lasting about one minute. The engines, located in the rear of the DC-9, ingested a large amount of hail and water which caused them to fail. When the flight attendant in the rear of the plane realized what had happened, she started preparing the passengers in the rear of the plane for an emergency landing. Following her lead, the other flight attendant, though unsure of what had happened, started to brief the passengers in the front of the plane for an emergency landing. Later, the rear flight attendant called her and told her the engines had quit operating. According to a discussion I had with the forward flight attendant several months later, when she opened the door of the cockpit she saw that one of the windshields had been cracked, probably as a result of the hail. The pilot yelled at her to sit down.

Because of the failed engines the plane was unable to reach an airport, and therefore about eight minutes after its encounter with the thunderstorm the pilot attempted to land on a highway in New Hope, Georgia. Of the eighty-five passengers aboard, sixty-two were killed and twenty-two were seriously injured. The flight attendant in the front of the plane was extremely fortunate: she was in a small section of the forward cabin which was not destroyed, and she escaped with just minor injuries.

Whenever your aircraft must fly in the vicinity of a thunderstorm, or whenever CAT has been reported en route to your destination, the captain will illuminate the seatbelt signs. When this happens, you should return to your seat if you are not already there and fasten your seatbelt snugly, because a loose seatbelt is inadequate. During violent vertical movements of the aircraft, passengers have been injured, and some have even been thrown out of their seats, when their safety belts have been connected but just loosely fastened.[12]

FORCES INVOLVED IN TURBULENCE AND EVASIVE MANEUVERS

The most common cause of injury in these accidents is the result of vertical movements of the aircraft. Sideways movement is of little consequence unless the pilot banks the aircraft to the left or the right. Also, the aircraft is not likely to accelerate or decelerate in the longitudinal (forward or backward) direction to a significant degree.

The forces involved in these accidents are measured in "Gs." One G is the force exerted by gravity at the earth's surface. If you weigh 150 pounds, this means that the gravitational pull of the earth is exerting a force of 150 pounds, or 1 G, on your body. If you were sitting aboard an aircraft and it suddenly experienced a downward movement of 1 G, this would mean that the aircraft would start moving downward at the same rate that gravity would exert on your body and you would experience a sensation of floating. Even without a seatbelt on, you would remain in the general vicinity of your seat. This is the same experience the astronauts have when in orbit about the earth. Conversely, the plane could also move upward at a high rate of acceleration, and if you were standing the force could be enough to throw you to the floor.

It is possible, whether you are aboard a large or small aircraft, for the plane to move suddenly downward or upward at a very high rate of acceleration as a result of evasive maneuvers or turbulence. Forces as high as ±2 Gs have been recorded,[13] meaning that a 150-pound person would have the experience of suddenly weighing an additional 300 pounds or alternatively being pushed against the ceiling with a force of 150 pounds. And these forces have been known to alternate back and forth very quickly.

INFLIGHT INJURIES

Passengers sustained fewer serious injuries (29 percent) than minor injuries between 1968 and 1971, according to NTSB.[14] On the other hand flight attendants sustained more serious injuries (51 percent) than minor injuries during the same period. One plausible explanation for this difference is that flight attendants were more likely than passengers to be standing in the galley, where turbulence or an evasive maneuver could throw them against hard surfaces. Apparently, no cockpit crewmembers were injured during these accidents. Table 4.1 gives a summary of the passenger and flight attendant injuries as they are related to location in the aircraft for the years 1968–1971. As a result of this work the NTSB compiled a hierarchy of risks for potential injury as related to activity and area of aircraft (see Figure 4.1).

TABLE 4.1
Occupant Injuries as a Result of Location in the Airplane

Location	Passenger		Flight attendant		Total	
	Serious	Minor	Serious	Minor	Serious	Minor
Forward cabin	1	2	4	1	5	3
Mid cabin	8	35	4	7	12	42
Rear cabin	9	37	10	14	19	51
Galley/buffet	11	5	42	37	53	42
Lavatory and area	14	12	3	1	17	13

Source: NTSB.

FIGURE 4.1. Relative risks of areas inside a plane as far as injuries sustained during flight are concerned (NTSB).

The farther a person is located from the aircraft's center of gravity, which is usually forward of the wings, the higher the potential for injury during inflight disturbances. Passengers in the rear of the aircraft experience greater vertical movement than in the front, accounting for some of the increased injuries in that part of the plane.[15]

Injury reports indicate that some seated passengers experienced rib fractures from striking the armrest of the seat, and facial injuries from striking the seats in front. These injuries were much less severe for those wearing safety belts snugly fastened. Abdominal bruising and internal injuries were more likely to occur to those passengers who had seatbelts loosely fastened.[16]

Many aircraft have lavatories, as well as galleys, in the rear of the aircraft where vertical movement may be greater than in other locations. During turbulence, the most common injuries sustained in lavatories were fractures of the arms and legs, internal injuries, facial and head lacerations, abrasions, and contusions.[17]

In summary, the rear of the aircraft is a somewhat less safe area to be in during turbulence and evasive maneuvers unless you are seated with your safety belt snugly fastened. If you have your belt loosely fastened, the potential for injury is greater than if it were snugly fastened. However, when turbulence strikes or the pilot makes an evasive maneuver, the greatest injury potential is in the galley or lavatory. Whenever a "Return to Seat" or "Fasten Seatbelt" sign is illuminated, follow these instructions as quickly as you can, and stay seated until the signs are turned off.

REFERENCES

1. "Near-collision over L.A. Injures 26 on Airliner," *Los Angeles Times,* July 23, 1977, part 1.
2. Ibid.
3. Ibid.
4. R. G. Snyder, *Advanced Techniques in Crash Impact Protection and Emergency Egress from Air Transport Aircraft,* AGARD–AG–221 (available through NTIS, Springfield, Va.), June 1976, pp. 12.
5. *Special Study, In-Flight Safety of Passengers and Flight Attendants Aboard Air Carrier Aircraft,* Report no. NTSB–AAS–73–1, National Transportation Safety Board, Washington, D.C., March 1973.
6. John H. Enders, "NASA Technical Advances in Aircraft Occupant Safety," Technical Paper no. 780020, presented to the SAE, Warrendale, Penna., March 1978.
7. Alan I. Brunstein, "Clear Air Turbulence Accidents," *Proceedings of the 1977 SAFE Symposium,* available from SAFE, Canoga Park, Calif.
8. *Special Study,* 1973.
9. Frank V. Malewicz, Arthur Hilsenrod, James H. Muncy, and Raymond Colao, "Characterization of the Thunderstorm for Safe Aircraft Operations," *Proceedings of the 1978 SAFE Symposium,* available from SAFE, Canoga Park, Calif.
10. "U.S. Warns Airlines on Flying in Storms," *Los Angeles Times,* Aug. 29, 1977, part 1.

11. Human Factors Group Chairman's Factual Report, "National Transportation Safety Board Aircraft Accident Report, DC-9-31, New Hope, Georgia, April 4, 1977," Docket No. 458.
12. *Special Study,* 1973.
13. Ibid.
14. Ibid.
15. Ibid., p. 11.
16. Ibid., p. 19.
17. Ibid., p. 20.

Chapter Five

SAFE SEATING LOCATIONS

Many people believe the safest area of an aircraft in the event of an accident is the rear of the plane—and for good reason. If an aircraft strikes something head-on, the people in front are more likely to be injured than those in the rear. Some accidents, however, occur in which this is not the case. In fact you can't be absolutely sure of the safest area of an aircraft before an accident because the safest area on one plane is not the safest on another. In addition, the safest area in one type of accident may not be the safest area in another type of accident. Nonetheless there are some general guidelines (which will be given later) that can increase your margin of safety if you happen to be in an accident.

In researching the problem of safe seating areas I looked at over ninety accidents on which I have records. Most of the accidents involved large passenger-carrying aircraft, though a few involved the smaller commuter planes. From these accident reports I looked closely at just those in which passenger injuries seemed to be related to the location of the seats. I selected accidents ranging from those which had as few as one passenger seriously injured or killed, to those more serious accidents in which only a small number survived. I also selected only those accidents in which the injuries or deaths occurred while the passengers were inside the aircraft. In some accidents, injuries and death occur during or after evacuation from the aircraft and are not related to seating location. Therefore these accidents were not considered.

From my analysis I found reports of twenty-one accidents between 1965 and 1982 which indicated that some areas of the plane were safer than others. Fourteen of the accidents occurred on approach and landing, four occurred on takeoff, and three occurred when the aircraft landed in the water (see Table 5.1). In two-thirds of these accidents, the rear of the aircraft was safer than the front.

A rather typical approach accident—one which happens while the aircraft is approaching the airport but is still short of the runway—occurred

TABLE 5.1
Safe Seating Areas

Type of accident	Date	Type of aircraft	Safest area
Approach and landing accidents			
	11/11/65	B-727	Rear
	11/20/67	CV 880	Rear
	1/6/69	CV 440	Rear
	12/28/70	B-727	Front
	12/8/72	B-737	Rear
	1/30/74	B-707	Mid
	9/11/74	DC-9	Rear
	4/5/76	B-727	Rear
	4/27/76	B-727	Front
	6/23/76	DC-9	Front
	12/12/77	DHC-6	Rear
	2/11/78	B-737	Rear
	12/28/78	DC-8	Rear
	6/12/80	METRO	Rear
Accidents on takeoff			
	11/27/70	DC-8	Front
	8/7/75	B-727	Front
	6/26/78	DC-9	Rear
	7/25/78	CV-580	Rear
Water landing accidents			
	1/13/69	DC-8	Front
	5/2/70	DC-9	Rear
	1/13/82	B-737	Rear

Summary of Safe Seating Areas

Number (%) of accidents in which the safest area was:

Front	6	(28.5%)
Mid	1	(4.7%)
Rear	14	(66.8%)

on the evening of December 28, 1978, when a DC-8 crashed into a wooded, populated area of suburban Portland, Oregon.[1] The aircraft had delayed landing for fifteen to twenty minutes while the cockpit crew checked a landing gear malfunction. During this period the flight attendants prepared the passengers for an emergency landing.

The cockpit crew was so preoccupied with the landing gear problem that they failed to correlate the amount of fuel left in their tanks with the fuel required to reach the airport. They were eighteen to twenty miles from the airport when one of the four engines on the large jet quit because of lack of fuel. They tried to reach the airport, but crashed six miles short. Of the 181 passengers and 8 crewmembers aboard, 8 passengers and 2 crewmembers were killed. Another 21 passengers and 2 crewmembers were seriously injured. A number of fortunate occurrences accounted for the relatively low loss of life considering the severity of the accident. The first was that the passengers and crew had adequate time to prepare for the accident. They were in the emergency brace positions when the aircraft touched down, and this undoubtedly saved a number of lives.

Second, the aircraft collided with a number of things which slowed it down without destroying it. It struck two unoccupied homes and several trees before sliding under thick high-tension power lines. These lines caught the vertical stabilizer, that section of the tail which rises above the rest of the plane, thus slowing it down much the way arresting cables on aircraft carriers stop jet fighters when they land. Moreover, no fire ensued, probably because there was little if any fuel in the tanks.

There was extensive damage in the front of the plane, however, from the nose to seat row number 5. All the fatalities, along with the most seriously injured, were seated in this area. Some less seriously injured passengers sat farther back in the cabin, near the trailing edge of the wing. Both of these areas, the front of the plane and the area near the wing, were penetrated by trees which caused the injuries and deaths.

One of the passengers, Kim Campbell, age twenty-seven, seated in the rear of the plane, played a major role in assisting other crash survivors to escape. He was seated near an exit and so could have been one of the first off, but he stayed inside and helped lift passengers down to the ground, eight feet below the door sill. This had to be done since the trees outside prevented the use of the inflatable escape slide. According to a corrections officer seated beside him before the accident, Campbell believed there was a possibility of an explosion, yet he stayed on the plane until all the passengers were off before getting off himself. After he was out of the plane, he somehow persuaded the corrections officer to get back on to make sure no other passengers were aboard. Then he disappeared into the crowd before anyone could thank him, much to the chagrin of the corrections officer who was escorting him back to the prison from which he had escaped.[2]

The rear of the plane is not always the safest area to be seated in, however. A DC-9-31 was attempting to land in rainy weather at Philadelphia International Airport on June 21, 1976, when it encountered wind shear—unpredictable changes in wind direction—just prior to touchdown. As it approached the runway, ATC told the pilot there had been a shift in wind, so he decided to "go around," to abort the takeoff.[3] He raised the wheels, applied power to the engines, and raised the nose of the aircraft. But the winds were such that the plane could not gain altitude. In fact, a pilot in another airplane sitting on a taxiway said that he saw the DC-9 come out of the clouds at about 100 feet above the runway. Suddenly it fell to the ground, still in a slightly nose-up attitude, and slid for about 2,000 feet. None of the 107 people aboard was killed, though 36 suffered serious injuries.

Most of the passengers (81 percent) in the front of the plane, compared to 54 percent in the rear, suffered either minor injury or none at all. Apparently the people in the rear of the plane, which was the first to strike the ground, experienced greater impact forces than those in the front.

Another accident which may shed some light on the safest area in a plane occurred on November 11, 1965, when a B-727 made a hard landing at Salt Lake City. Of the eighty-five passengers only forty-four survived, even though the impact forces were mild. The problem was that fire broke out in the cabin when the aircraft touched down, and smoke rapidly built up during the thirty to fifty seconds it took to stop the plane. There was no usable exit in the rear of the plane, and passengers had to use the overwing exits and the two front doors. Even so, thirty (60 percent) of the fifty passengers in the rear of the plane survived, compared to fourteen (40 percent) of the thirty-five passengers in the forward half.

This particular accident involved fire and smoke, which decreased the time that passengers could survive in the cabin. An analysis showed that nine of the forty-four passengers who escaped received no injuries.[4] These people were seated near exits and were the first ones off. After an accident the first people out of an aircraft have a better chance of surviving than those who leave later. And the people seated closest to the exits are usually the first to use the exits.

In another accident the only surviving passengers were seated in the middle of the plane. This accident involved a B-707 which crashed on approach to Pago Pago on January 30, 1974. All of the 101 people aboard the aircraft survived the impact, but only 4 passengers survived the post-impact fire. These passengers were seated in the middle of the plane. They all stated later that before the unexpected accident occurred, they had read the safety information card and listened to the flight attendant briefing. When the plane landed short of the runway that night, most of the passengers went to either end of the plane where the doors are located. But for some reason the doors were never opened. The fire and the smoke must have moved quickly, for these 97 people who had lived through the impact could not get out.

The four survivors, instead of moving toward the doors, used the nearby overwing exits. The NTSB speculated that if more passengers had used the overwing exits, they might have survived. Many of the passengers seated in the middle of the plane may not have realized they were right next to overwing exits. Perhaps they were just following the lead of other people, or maybe their only thought was to get to the door through which they had boarded the aircraft.

This accident, however, does not really demonstrate which area of the plane is the safest since all the passengers survived the impact. Those who were seated in the middle lived not because the middle was necessarily safer, but because they were near an exit and they *knew* they were near it.

I cannot determine from available accident reports which section of a plane is safest if it lands in water. I found only three water-landing reports in which it was possible to relate seating location to injuries or deaths. When a DC-8 crashed unexpectedly on approach to Los Angeles International Airport, the section of the plane rear of the wing broke off and sank, resulting in a number of drownings.[5] But when a DC-9 ditched in the ocean, it did not break apart—the entire plane stayed afloat for a period of time. In this accident, which is elaborated on in Chapter Nine, the greatest loss of life occurred in the front of the plane.[6] A B-737 struck a bridge and landed in the icy Potomac River on January 13, 1982. The accident report indicates that the plane was descending with a nose-high attitude of about 15° when the tail struck vehicles on the bridge. This first impact caused the nose to plunge downward and the front of the plane to strike the ice-covered river with about three times the force as that received by the tail.[7] There were only a few survivors and they were seated in the rear of the plane. But since everyone else died from the impact (except for one passenger who drowned) and not from any factor related to landing in water, any conclusions drawn from this accident about safe seating locations in water landings would be tenuous.

It seems obvious that passengers seated in those sections of the plane which stay afloat longest will have the greatest chance of survival. Probably the strongest section of the plane, and the section that will float longest, is the section directly over the wings. The wings act as pontoons, and can help keep an aircraft afloat for a considerable length of time. If the tail were to break off and sink, as happened with the DC-8, then the floating portion of the plane will tend to take on water and the nose will go under water. In general, then, the safest section of the plane in a water landing would seem to be at the overwing area.

Where to sit if the plane does not break apart in a water landing depends on the flotation characteristics of the aircraft. Aircraft manufacturers usually calculate the flotation characteristics of an aircraft before it ever flies. Assuming that no major damage occurs when the aircraft lands in the water (which is not always the case), it is possible to determine about how long the plane will float, which exits will be underwater, and what attitude it will be in when it does sink. Based on this information, one can figure in advance which exits will probably be usable. You wouldn't want to open an exit if the door sill were underwater; this would increase the rate at which the aircraft sinks.

Generally, those aircraft which have all engines mounted on the tail (e.g., DC-9, B-727) are tail-heavy, and so the exits in the rear of the aircraft should not be opened. Aircraft with all the engines on the wings (DC-8, B-707, B-737, B-747), and those aircraft with one tail-mounted engine and two wing-mounted engines (L-1011, DC-10) will remain relatively level so that all of the exits should be usable. Unfortunately, there are exceptions to these guidelines, for different models of a given aircraft type may float differently from other models. Some B-737 aircraft may float in a wings-level attitude while others will float tail-down. A number of airlines show the flotation attitude of the aircraft on the passenger safety information card.

The safest area of the aircraft in case of turbulence has been reported to be the front of the aircraft, and the least safe area the rear.[8] Keep in mind, though, that most passenger injuries that occur in turbulence are minor, and passenger death as a result of turbulence is very rare.

Therefore, since the majority of severe but survivable accidents occur on takeoff and landing, and since most serious passenger injuries and deaths occur in these accidents, you can increase your margin of safety by sitting at the overwing section or in the rear of the plane. In addition, a seat closer to an exit, wherever it may be located, will be safer than one farther away. If you will be flying over water, and if the aircraft has all tail-mounted engines, then sitting at the overwing area could increase your chance of surviving a water landing.

REFERENCES

1. *Accident Report, McDonnell-Douglas DC-8-61, Portland, Ore., Dec. 28, 1978,* Aircraft Accident Report no. AAR–79–7, National Transportation Safety Board, Washington, D.C., 1979.
2. "Convict on Jet Helped Others Out—Then Fled," *Los Angeles Times,* Dec. 30, 1978.
3. "Safety," *Aviation Week and Space Technology,* Sept. 4, 1978, p. 229.
4. C. C. Snow, C. Hayden Leroy, and E. B. McFadden, "A Survival Study of a Modern Commercial Jet Aircraft (Boeing 727) Landing Accident with Subsequent Interior Fire: II. Injury and Fatality Analysis," paper presented at the Aerospace Medical Association 38th Annual Scientific Meeting, Washington D.C., April 11, 1967.
5. *Accident Report, McDonnell-Douglas DC-8-62 in Santa Monica Bay, Near Los Angeles, Calif., Jan. 13, 1969,* Aircraft Accident Report no. AAR–70–14, National Transportation Safety Board, Washington, D.C., 1970.
6. *Special Study, Passenger Survival in Turbojet Ditchings,* Report no. AAS–72–2, National Transportation Safety Board, Washington, D.C., 1972.
7. *Aircraft Accident Report, Boeing 737-222 Collision with 14th Street Bridge, Near Washington National Airport, Washington D.C., Jan. 13, 1982,* Report no. NTSB–AAR–82–8, National Transportation Safety Board, Washington, D.C., 1982.
8. *Special Study: In-Flight Safety of Passengers and Flight Attendants Aboard Air Carrier Aircraft,* Report no. AAS–73–1, National Transportation Safety Board, Washington, D.C., 1973.

Chapter Six

HOW TO PREPARE FOR THE UNEXPECTED CRASH ON LANDING OR TAKEOFF

All takeoff accidents, and most landing accidents, are unexpected. Those things that you have to do to increase your chances of survival must be done before each takeoff and landing, because you will have little or no warning of the accident. These things are easy to do and can be done without attracting attention. So whether a warning is given or not, by following these rules you will increase your chances of walking away from that rare, but still possible event, the aircraft accident.

COATS

Wear your coat. Following an accident a fire may occur and a coat can give you some much-needed protection. A DC-9 had lost power from both engines after flying through a thunderstorm, but before it crashlanded on a Georgia highway, one of the passengers had taken his leather coat from the overhead rack. As the plane skidded along the ground, he heard the noise of the fire—like a "giant blowtorch, popping and crackling." When the aircraft came to a stop, he was surrounded by fire. As he released his safety belt, melted plastic dripped onto his head from the burning ceiling panels. He pulled his coat up over his head, but the burning material was so hot it even made his coat smoulder. But if it weren't for the coat he could well have suffered severe burns which could have so incapacitated him that he might not have been able to escape the plane. As it was, he was the last person out.[1]

Unfortunately, not all coats give equal protection from fire. Many synthetic materials burn or melt quite readily when touched by a flame, and this could lead to severe burns. But some natural fibers, especially wool and leather, can give good protection against fire.

If you are not comfortable wearing a coat on long flights, at least keep it on until after takeoff and then remove it. Then a few minutes before landing, put it back on. Most passengers wait until the plane has landed and taxied to the terminal, when nearly all of them stand up to put their coats on at the same time. Putting your coat on before landing would not only give you some added protection, but would also help you avoid some of the congestion in the aisles.

SHOES

Plan on wearing your shoes in an emergency evacuation unless they have high heels, or unless the safety information card or the flight attendant specifically instructs passengers to remove their shoes prior to escaping. Some airlines tell all passengers to remove their shoes in order to protect the inflatable escape slide, or life raft, from damage. Others tell passengers only not to wear high-heeled shoes, and some airlines allow all passengers to wear shoes. The major reason for this is that older escape slides, some of which are still in service, were made with relatively thin material which could be easily punctured, even by men's shoes. However, more recent escape slides and rafts are made from a stronger material, one that is more resistant to puncture.

But some shoes can puncture virtually any material. Women's high-heeled shoes may have spikes with surface areas as small as 0.5 square inches. The average American woman weighs about 140 pounds, while 5 percent weigh over 208 pounds.[2] If a relatively heavy woman in high heels jumped onto a slide or raft from a height of just a couple of feet, and landed on the heel of one foot, she could exert a force of many hundreds of pounds per square inch. There are few materials which could withstand forces of this magnitude.

But you may need your shoes to protect your feet after the accident.

The same passenger who wore his leather jacket during the DC-9 accident in Georgia suffered severe foot injuries during his escape. He had taken off his shoes, as he was instructed by a flight attendant prior to landing.[3] The twisted and torn metal of the cabin floor, burning fuel on the ground, and pieces of metal strewn outside the aircraft can cause severe foot and leg injuries to someone who must jump and run from the plane, especially in the dark. Because foot and leg injuries can hamper escape, many airlines now recommend that you keep your shoes on unless they have high heels. If you are wearing high heels, I suggest that you carry the shoes with you and put them on after you're off the escape slide.

Some passenger safety information cards show removing the high-heeled shoes at the doorway, as shown in Figure 6.1. I would strongly urge that passengers not wait until they arrive at the doorway before removing their shoes, for if many passengers did this it could slow down the evacuation of those waiting to get out. If you're wearing high-heeled shoes, step out of the way of other passengers while you take them off, or take them off before getting to the doorway—don't block others trying to escape.

Passengers should keep their shoes on, whether they have high heels or not, if the escape route does not require using an inflatable slide or if

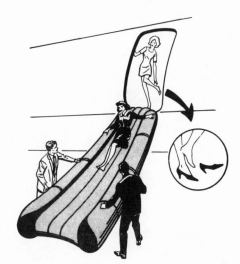

FIGURE 6.1. Some safety cards seem to instruct passengers to remove shoes at the doorway. This is probably not a good practice since it could slow the evacuation.

they will not be entering a raft. Most narrow-body aircraft have overwing window exits which lead directly onto the metal surface of the wing. Keep your shoes on when using these exits. But some wide-body aircraft, including the B-747 and DC-10, have inflatable escape slides which extend out over the wing and these slides can be damaged by high heels.

Also, some planes, such as the B-727 and certain B-737s and BAC 1-11s, have stairs you can use in an emergency evacuation which would not be damaged by high-heeled shoes. If you find that you will be using an overwing window exit, or stairs, then keep your shoes on. But if you will be using an inflatable device, such as an escape slide or life raft after a ditching, plan on carrying your shoes.

SAFETY BELTS

Pull your safety belt tightly about your hips before each takeoff and landing. The more slack there is in your safety belt, the greater your chance of injury. If you were sitting upright, as you would be on a normal takeoff or landing, but your safety belt were loosely fastened about your waist, you could slide under the belt in an accident, as shown in Figure 6.2. This movement, which is called "submarining," can cause severe internal injuries.

FIGURE 6.2. If a safety belt is loosely worn, a passenger could slide under the belt during an accident.

The safety belt should fit as low as possible about your hips. This is especially true for pregnant women. The belt should not be allowed to ride above your hip bones for it could cause internal injuries in a high-impact accident.

If you were in the brace position but there was slack in the safety belt, you could slide forward and hit your head and legs on the seat in front of you with greater force than if the belt was snug about your hips. Also, you could suffer internal injuries as your safety belt suddenly tightened about your waist. These injuries would be minimized if your safety belt was pulled tightly about your waist.

BRACE POSITION

Know the best brace position to reduce the severity of injury during an accident. Even if your safety belt was pulled tightly about your waist in a high-impact accident, you could still receive unnecessary injuries to your arms and legs, as well as to your head and neck, by being thrown against the seat in front, or even against the armrests of your own seat. Let's assume that you're sitting in an upright position with your safety belt on, and suddenly your aircraft has an accident which exerts the relatively mild force of 1.5 or 2 Gs in the forward direction. An FAA study indicates that even in an accident with such a low impact, your body would jackknife forward.[4] Your head and arms, as well as your legs, would strike the seat in front of you. However, if you had been in a brace position the chances of your being injured would be lessened.

One NTSB report illustrates the importance of brace positions in reducing injuries during crash landings. A helicopter carrying fifteen passengers and three crewmembers crashed at Newark Airport, New Jersey, on April 18, 1978. Three passengers were killed and ten others, along with the crewmembers, were seriously injured. But two passengers bent over in a brace position before the crash. Even though they were seated in the forward cabin where all of the fatalities and most of the severe injuries occurred, they sustained only minor injuries.[5]

The same NTSB report cited three other accidents, all involving the Twin Otter, a commuter-type aircraft which carries up to twenty passengers. One of the aircraft crashed on approach to Cape May County Airport, New Jersey, on December 12, 1976. Of the eight passengers and two crew on board, three passengers and one crewmember died. There had been no warning before the crash, but one nineteen-year-old man, seated in the second row of seats, had lowered his head between his legs because he was airsick. He suffered only minimal injuries even though the three passengers seated beside him and in the row in front of him died from head and chest injuries received during the impact.

Another accident occurred on December 4, 1978, when a Twin Otter crashed into some snow-covered mountains near Steamboat Springs, Colorado. Of the twenty passengers and two crewmembers on board, one passenger and one crewmember died, while fourteen others received serious crash injuries. Again no warning was given, but a twenty-six-year-old woman, seated in the center of the cabin, took a brace position because she was frightened. She suffered only minor injuries, although several others seated nearby were seriously injured.

Sixteen passengers and two pilots were in the third Twin Otter, which crashed on the approach to the Knox County Regional Airport, near Rockland, Maine, on May 30, 1979. One of the passengers was a sixteen-year-old boy seated near the rear of the plane. There had been no warning of a problem and most passengers were sleeping or reading. Suddenly the boy, who was looking outside, saw that the aircraft was going to crash into trees. He quickly lowered his head and braced his arms and knees against the seat in front of him. And although his seat, along with most of the other seats in the plane, was torn from the floor during the tremendous impact, he suffered only a fractured wrist and leg, as well as a scalp wound. The other seventeen people were killed.

Even though three of these accidents involved the Twin Otter, the NTSB was not implying that the Twin Otter was less safe than other aircraft, but that people who are in brace positions increase their chances of surviving an accident. There is no consensus in the airline industry as to the best brace position for all passengers. In fact there may not be a single brace position that would give maximum protection for everyone. Passengers range in size from the infant carried by his parent, to small children who have their own seats and safety belts, to pregnant women, to very obese or tall people. Some have no trouble bending over and putting their heads on their knees, but others are unable to do this because of some physical condition, such as decreased flexibility associated with aging or obesity.

It used to be common for flight attendants to cry "Grab your ankles!" just prior to an accident. But this may not be the best position for every passenger to attempt. Many passenger seats are spaced closely together, so that there is a space of only a couple of inches between your knees and the seat in front. Even if you have the flexibility to bend over and grab your ankles, the seat in front may stop you from doing this if you are tall. And if you were to turn your head and neck to the side so that your hands could reach your ankles, a sudden stop of the airplane might result in a neck injury. As a result the FAA has recommended alternative brace positions.[6] Probably the best brace position for most passengers is shown in Figure 6.3. After fastening your safety belt and pulling it tight, lean forward and place your crossed arms on the seat in front. Press your head against your arms. Put your feet as far forward as they will go, but try not to put them underneath the seat in front of you, for if the seat collapsed it could injure your feet.

A brace position will most effectively reduce injuries if you place your head, arms, and legs as closely as possible to where they would be forced in the accident. In most high-impact plane accidents you will be thrown forward and probably downward. In some accidents a considerable sideways force is exerted on the passengers if the plane slides sideways and then suddenly stops. Few accidents have exerted significant upward or backward forces on passengers. Therefore putting your head against the seat in front, cushioned by your arms, keeps your head from being thrown into that seat. Putting your legs forward before the accident keeps them from being thrown forward and striking the bottom of the seat.

If there is no seat in front of you, then bend over and hold your arms

FIGURE 6.3. A brace position recommended by the FAA if there is a seat in front of you.

tightly together under your knees. Your head should be down to your knees, or at least as far down as you can place it. And your legs should be on the floor, as far forward as they will reach (see Figure 6.4). This position will keep your arms and head from flailing about and striking your seat armrest, or another passenger.

Airlines commonly allow parents to hold small children on their laps. Although this is convenient for parents since the airlines don't charge fare for the children, it poses risk for the child.[7] Until mid-1982 none of the systems developed for use in automobiles was approved for use on aircraft. However, in April 1982 a car seat designed to hold a child up to forty pounds or forty inches in height (this includes most children up to four years of age) was certified by the FAA for restraining children on takeoffs and landings in commercial aircraft. This device is called the Safe-T-Seat and is produced by Cosco/Peterson of Columbus, Indiana. In the future it is possible that other car seats will be certified for use on planes,[8] but these car seats will need to display a notice so stating.

The risk of injury to a child in a seat without an appropriately sized restraint system is great in case of an accident. Just as it is not safe to hold an infant on the lap while riding in an automobile, it is not safe to do so in a plane. In an impact producing 4 Gs or more, a fifteen-pound infant could suddenly "weigh" in excess of sixty pounds, making it virtually impossible for a parent to hold. And there is no FAA-approved method for restraining the infant or small child held on the lap.

If there were a warning of a potential accident and a certified child

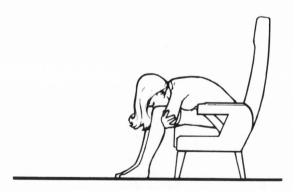

FIGURE 6.4. A recommended brace position if there is no seat in front of you.

safety seat was not available, then a child one year of age or more should be placed on the standard passenger seat by itself, if one is available, and strapped in using the safety belt. If the safety belt could not be tightened enough so that the child was held securely to the seat, a pillow or some other type of padding should be placed behind the child. To reduce the chances of abdominal injury there should be *no* padding between the child and the safety belt.[9]

A pretoddler, or a child younger than one year, would probably not be restrained by the safety belt. The infant's center of gravity is well above its hips, and in an accident it could fly forward over the top of the safety belt. There is no consensus on the best method of holding or restraining an infant during an aircraft accident. This is because there is no adequate, safe way of holding a child during an impact. If there were a warning period, the procedure some airlines use is to wrap the infant in a blanket and place it on the floor against the partition in front of the parent. In this way the infant will already be in the position he would be thrown to in most accidents, forward and downward (see Figure 6.5). This method was used in the DC-8 accident which crashed in Portland after running out of fuel.[10]

Another brace position some airlines suggest is for the infant to be laid across the lap of the adult, as shown in Figure 6.6. Another position

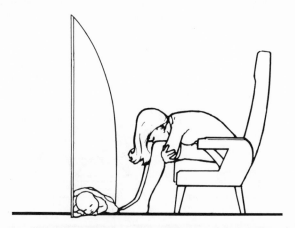

FIGURE 6.5. Some airlines will wrap an infant and place it on the floor, next to a partition, if time allows.

FIGURE 6.6. An infant may also be held across the lap by the parent.

other airlines suggest is shown in Figure 6.7, where the child is seated on the parent's knee, but facing toward the rear. In this position the child is already pressed against the seat back in front. The child's head and body are held to the side of the parent instead of being in front of the parent's shoulder. Another position, recommended by at least one airline, is to hold the infant diagonally across the chest in the traditional "burping" position (see Figure 6.8). In any of these positions I believe it is possible that both the child and the adult could be injured during impact as a result of striking each other. Or the child could be thrown free due to the inability of the

FIGURE 6.7. An infant may also be held on the knee of the parent.

FIGURE 6.8. An infant can be held diagonally across the chest by the parent.

parent to hold it during impact. Because of the difficulty of experimenting
with brace positions using human adults and infants, there has been no
comprehensive experimental research on brace positions for either infants
or adults under realistic crash conditions.

EXIT LOCATIONS

Know where all of the exits are. I make a point of sitting next to an
exit whenever I fly since I am familiar with how exits operate. Moreover
I also know that the chances of getting out of an aircraft decrease as the
distance from the exit increases. On several occasions I have spoken to
passengers seated next to me and found that some of them did not know
they were even near an emergency exit. On one flight I asked a passenger
where the nearest emergency exit was and he told me that it was at the
front of the plane. Not realizing that he was seated next to an escape hatch,
he went on to tell me that he had made the same flight three to five times
each week, on the same type of aircraft, so didn't listen to the flight
attendant give the safety briefings anymore. Nor did he read the safety
information card because he felt he knew all of the safety information he
needed to know. Yet if there were an accident and we had to get out of
the plane quickly, this fellow would most likely have started heading toward
the front door, just as the passengers in the Pago Pago accident had, instead
of opening and getting out of the exit next to him. What's even worse, he

was sitting between the exit and other passengers (one of them being myself), and he would have slowed our escape. By virtue of his sitting where he was, he assumed a certain responsibility, not only to himself but to others. He should have known that he was sitting next to an exit, and being there, that he might be the one required to open it.

But being near an exit is no guarantee that that exit will be usable in an emergency. A number of occurrences may force you to try to find another exit. There could be a fire directly outside your nearest exit. If you were to open it, smoke and fire could enter the cabin, and reduce the time you and other passengers have to escape safely. Or the exit may be underwater following a ditching and so shouldn't be opened. Or the accident could have deformed the fuselage so that you could not open the exit. Or the escape slide may not inflate. Because of these and other possibilities, you should know where all the exits are on the plane before the plane takes off.

In summary, there are five things you should think of, or do, before each takeoff and landing. First, wear a coat made of a material that won't readily burn or melt. Second, plan on keeping your shoes on. Avoid wearing high-heeled shoes, but if you do wear them and you must use an inflatable escape slide, carry them with you when you evacuate the plane. Put them back on once outside. Third, keep your safety belt pulled tightly about your hips for each takeoff and landing. Fourth, know what brace position you would get into if an accident occurred. Be aware of what's going on outside of the plane. If it looks like a crash is imminent, brace yourself; there may be no other warning. Last, know where the exits are located on the plane.

REFERENCES

1. "Aircraft Accident Report, DC-9-31, New Hope, Georgia, April 4, 1977," Human Factors Group Chairman's Factual Report, Docket No. 458, National Transportation Safety Board, Washington, D.C., pp. 29–31.
2. Wesley E. Woodson, *Human Factors Design Handbook* (New York: McGraw-Hill, 1981), p. 715.
3. *"Aircraft Accident Report, DC-9-31, New Hope, Georgia, April 4, 1977,"* Report AAR–78–3, National Transportation Safety Board, Washington, D.C., 1978, p. 22.

4. J. J. Swearingen, *General Aviation Structures Directly Responsible for Trauma in Crash Deceleration*, FAA CAMI, Oklahoma City, Okla., FAA Report AM–71–3, Jan. 1971.

5. *Safety Recommendations* A–79–76 through –78, National Transportation Safety Board, Washington, D.C., issued Oct. 4, 1979.

6. *Air Carrier Operations Bulletin No. 69–16*, FAA, Washington, D.C., Dec. 16, 1969.

7. Richard G. Snyder, "Civil Aircraft Restraint Systems: State-of-the-Art Evaluation of Standards, Experimental Data, and Accident Experience," Society of Automotive Engineers, Warrendale, Penna., Paper no. 770154, 1977.

8. "Kids to Use Same Seats in Car, Plane," *USA Today*, June 22, 1983.

9. Richard F. Chandler and Edwin M. Trout, "Evaluation of Seating and Restraint Systems and Anthropomorphic Dummies Conducted during Fiscal Year 1976," Federal Aviation Administration, Washington, D.C., Report no. FAA–AM–78–6, 1978.

10. Richard F. Chandler, CAMI, Federal Aviation Administration, Oklahoma City, Okla., Personal Communication, Feb. 1982.

Chapter Seven

FIRE

Most people don't realize how little time there is to get out of a burning aircraft. A survey revealed that the average airline passenger thought there would be about five minutes to escape if a fire erupted outside the plane after it was on the ground.[1] An external fire, however, can burn through the skin of the aircraft in less than 1.5–2 minutes, and once inside, the smoke and heat can quickly spread, making escape difficult if not impossible.

Worse yet, in a severe accident fire can enter the cabin immediately if sections of the cabin break apart, as occurred when a B-727 crashed on landing at St. Thomas in the Virgin Islands on April 27, 1976. The aircraft had left JFK International Airport with seventy-eight passengers. There were four flight attendants on board. Two were seated on the jumpseat attached to the rear door, but only one survived the accident. The following, with names deleted, is her account as given to the NTSB:

As we approached the runway the aircraft was swaying from side to side but it was nothing new to us. We seemed to drop down on the runway when we landed. It was a startlingly hard landing. We seemed to float for a moment and then we were moving down the runway fast. I remember thinking—"Are we landing or taking off?" and I may have said this to [the other flight attendant] but I can't be sure. I do think we experienced a normal full reverse of the engines as one is so accustomed to feeling immediately following touchdown. Then the plane accelerated and I knew we were attempting to take off [from] the runway. I said to her, "We're aborting our landing." I felt as though we were moving at an incredible speed down the runway. It was at this time that we knew we were in trouble. We started to yell "Grab Ankles" but I don't remember the words ever coming out of our mouths completely because then came the impact. At this point the noise of our engines was unbelievably deafening as though we were completely surrounded by the sound of them. Out of reflex my eyes shut tightly. She and I had linked our arms together and we held on, waiting. I don't recall many separate impacts—it seemed as though it was just one long one. The impact sounds were of shattering glass and ripping or crunching metal like we were disintegrating. I heard her say "We've got to get a fire extinguisher," but her voice sounded way off as if she was in deep shock and it seemed to come from the left side of me. We must have still been experiencing impact forces or otherwise I would have had my eyes opened, as I did the minute it all stopped. When it was all over and my eyes opened, I couldn't believe I was still alive. I was alone in the tail section. I never felt her leave my side; had I, I would have grabbed her if we were still moving.

Nevertheless, she was gone and I never saw her again. Nothing could have prepared me for what I saw before my eyes. There were piles of debris all around me. Approximately four feet in front of me was a wall of fire between me and the aisle leading into the coach cabin. There was thick, black smoke churning all around me, causing me to choke and fight for each breath of air. I couldn't see a thing even if it was inches in front of me. I turned around toward the aft ventral stairs. The panel to the left of the jumpseat, where the emergency light switch is, was either covered by debris or gone completely. I started groping around with my hands but I never found the switch. I felt for the door handle but whatever I tried to move felt jammed. I don't know if I found the handle or just more debris but I felt that I was losing time fast. The fire was consuming all the oxygen and I was gasping for every breath. I could feel that I was quickly suffocating. I turned back around facing forward. I was able to keep a sense of direction as to aft and forward because during all this time I never actually walked or took any real steps. By now the flames were moving in on me fast from the right. I had no idea how deep the wall of fire went or what lay beyond it.

It now seemed the only way out was to try to run through the flames in hopes of reaching the window exits. I felt very alone and I didn't hear any passengers near where I was. Something told me, maybe instinct or something greater, that if I tried to go through the fire that I was sure to perish and I didn't want to die that way. I started crawling and climbing to my left and in an upward incline with the idea to get myself away from the flames. I assumed that I was going to die and if I had to, I was going to try to do it by smoke inhalation before the flames reached me. It was a very clear thought that I had, but by no means had I given up. I kept moving and pushing debris out of my way, and just when I felt that I had no more breath left in me and with one last push, my arms and head came through what must have been a crack in the fuselage. I just couldn't believe that I was out. My torso and legs were still inside the plane and dangling down. My legs weren't touching anything below and I was having a hard time getting any leverage. I kept boosting myself with my arms and finally I was completely out. I had to jump perhaps 8 to 10 feet to the ground and I landed in part of a tree's branches, glass, and some torn wire fencing. My legs buckled beneath me and when I got up I felt a great pain in my right ankle (later determined to be broken) and my shoes were missing. I was limping badly and fighting hard not to pass out. I managed to limp forward to where the left wing was

almost flush with the ground and got up on it. There were 5 or 6 people [at] the aft
left window exit. . . . I started yelling commands to them, telling them to come out
one at a time. This had absolutely no effect on any of them. I started to grab the
shoulders of a woman who was on the bottom who complained that her legs were
caught and she was in a lot of pain. She grabbed me by my hair and started pulling
me inside, using me for leverage to pull herself out. It was strictly everyone for
themselves. I begged her to let go of me—that I was going to get her out and help
her. I finally got her out and then had to fight to keep her from going back into the
plane for her friend. Finally people started to unwedge themselves and I was able to
pull them out. Each time I got someone out onto the wing they wouldn't let go of
me. They were like drowning people. I had to wrestle a couple of them off of the
wing, all the time telling them to get away from the plane. Each time I would get a
person off of the wing I would turn back to the window exit for another. When this
had happened approximately 5 times, I turned back to the window once again but
this time the entire exit was in flames. . . . The heat became so intense that I knew
it was time for me to get off the wing and away from the plane. I saw a man moving
away from the wreckage with the back of his shirt on fire. With the help of some
other people we got him to the ground and smothered the flames. The survivors were
walking up a hill and I started up with them.[2]

This flight attendant fortunately was able to escape through a break
in the fuselage. Her subsequent rescue of other passengers from the window
exit, even though she had a broken bone in her foot, attests to the courage
that can be found among this group of highly trained people.

The importance of fire and smoke on passenger fatality rates can be
seen in Table 7.1. In the ten-year period 1969–1978, the NTSB reported
that 90 (21 percent) of the 430 U.S. airline accidents involved fire. And
these 90 accidents accounted for 1,917 (81 percent) of the 2,354 fatalities.

TABLE 7.1
United States Air Carrier Accidents: Fire vs. No Fire, 1969–1978

	No fire	With fire	Total
Number of accidents	340	90	430
Number of passengers	24,965	7,017	31,982
Number (%) killed—			
all causes	437 (2%)	1,917 (27%)	2,354 (7%)

Source: Testimony of Elwood T. Driver, from the *Hearings before the Subcommittee on Oversight and Review of the Committee on Public Works and Transportation,* Proceedings of the United States House of Representatives, 96th Cong.
1st sess., April 25–26, 1979, NTSB, p. 61.

But even though fire and smoke occurred in these 90 accidents, fire and smoke did not cause most of the deaths. In testimony before Congress in early 1979, Elwood Driver, then vice-chairman of the NTSB, stated that "Since 1975, there have been 118 air carrier accidents [these do not include aircraft involved in military operations]; 25 of these, or 21 percent, involved fire. Of the 2,950 occupants involved in these 25 accidents, 879, or about 30 percent, died from all causes. At least 177 persons, about 20 percent, died solely from the effects of fire or smoke."[3] The more severe accidents are also those which are more likely to involve fire. Many people are going to be injured or killed as a result of impact in these more severe accidents, and the higher death rate cannot be attributed solely to fire or smoke.

It would be easy to overestimate the danger of fire or smoke. They certainly are deadly, and can act very quickly. But keep in mind that over 70 percent of the people in aircraft accidents which involve fire, live. As Driver reported, of the 2,950 people who were in the accidents where fire occurred, only 177 (4 percent) died of the fire or smoke. The purpose of this chapter is to give you a realistic idea of the smoke and fire problem, and some methods on how to cope with it.

TYPES OF AIRCRAFT FIRE

Fuel Fires

The most common source of fire is the kerosene-base fuel used by jet aircraft. The fuel tanks are located in the wings. And fuel lines connect the fuel tanks in one wing with those in the other wing, so the fuel lines must run through the fuselage. Also, many planes have one or all of their engines in the rear of the plane, so fuel lines run from the wing tanks through the fuselage to the tail of the plane. Breakup of the plane in a crash can spill the fuel from the tanks and fuel lines, and this spilled fuel becomes a potential source of fire.

Inflight Fires

Faults in the electrical system can also cause fire. Electrical fires have been known to break out in various locations throughout the plane, and can occur in flight. Fires can also start in the baggage area of the plane.

This probably caused the fire aboard an L-1011 aircraft after it had taken off from Riyadh, Saudi Arabia, on August 19, 1980, with 301 passengers and crew on board.[4] After flying about fifty miles the captain reported to air traffic control that he had a fire and was turning back. Another aircraft flying nearby saw fire coming through the skin of the aircraft at, or possibly below, floor level. The L-1011 made a safe landing, went to the end of the runway, turned onto a taxiway, and stopped. That seems to be the last thing anyone aboard the plane did. No one inside the plane opened any of the doors. When the rescue crew was finally able to open a door from the outside, the cabin was filled with smoke. Everyone on board was apparently dead, probably from the toxic fumes. As the air from the open door entered the cabin, flames erupted and spread throughout the plane.

Fires can also be set accidentally. Some passengers carelessly put their cigarettes out in the paper towel receptacles in the restrooms. This is the probable cause of one accident involving a Boeing 707 which crashed as it approached Orly Airport in Paris on July 11, 1973. Reportedly 120 people died from smoke inhalation before the plane crashed.[5] The pilots, the only survivors, wore smoke-protective masks.

The potential for disaster from a lavatory fire is especially great for a number of reasons: a lavatory with the door closed is a secluded area, and so if a fire did erupt inside it might not be observed (the cabin crew, unable to monitor passengers in the lavatory, cannot tell if someone is smoking inside, or if a child is playing with matches). And if a fire does break out in the lavatory, the air ventilation system, designed to provide fresh air to the lavatory and to ensure that expelled air does not enter the cabin (for odor control), could allow a fire to burn without having smoke enter the cabin and alert the cabin crew.

Waste receptacles must now be lined with fire-resistant material and must be able to contain such a fire. If one were to start inside, it should extinguish itself after the oxygen was consumed. Practically speaking, however, passengers could fill the container to overflowing with paper towels, leaving the container door unable to close. So if a fire started inside of one of these overflowing containers from a carelessly tossed cigarette, it could be fed with oxygen. Even though some aircraft have fire extinguishers installed in the area of the waste receptacle, not all do, so the hazard of a lavatory fire still exists. It is because of this that special warnings not to smoke in the lavatory are made during each flight. Ashtrays are placed outside each lavatory to encourage passengers to put out cigarettes before entering. Even so, I have been told that when the trash containers are emptied it is not unusual to find cigarette butts inside, indicating that not all passengers heed the warnings, thereby risking disaster not only for themselves but for everyone else on board.

Fire/Smoke Detection

In 1979 the FAA established a group of experts to study the problem of inflight fires. Called the Special Aviation Smoke and Explosion Reduction (SAFER) Committee, it issued a number of recommendations including the installation of smoke and fire detectors in critical areas of the plane. These areas included the lavatories and the galleys located below the cabin floor of some wide-body aircraft—these "lower-lobe" galleys, as they're called, are not manned during some phases of the flight, and so if a fire were to erupt it could go unchecked, possibly developing into an uncontrollable fire. On June 2, 1983, a DC-9 was en route from Texas to Toronto when smoke started issuing from one of the rear lavatories. The plane landed quickly, but even so, half the forty-six occupants died, apparently from smoke inhalation.[6] While an accident report has not been issued at this writing, there is the possibility that the fire either started in the lavatory—from an electrical short or a carelessly thrown cigarette—or in the cargo area below the lavatory.

Fire Extinguishers

In addition to smoke and fire detectors, the SAFER Committee recommended that fire extinguishers be strategically placed throughout the cabin. At least some of these fire extinguishers should be of the halogenated hydrocarbons type, such as Halon 1211. Initially Halon 1211 fire extinguishers were used in Europe and other parts of the world, but they were not available in the United States until about 1973 when the U.S. Air Force started using them on airfield ramp patrol trucks. Based on tests conducted at the FAA Technical Center in Atlantic City, New Jersey, in 1980, the FAA encouraged airlines to replace some of their existing fire extinguishers with Halon 1211 extinguishers, or to add at least two of the new extinguishers to their existing complement.

Halon 1211, which is now available in retail stores, has a number of advantages over conventional CO_2, water, and dry-chemical extinguishers.[7] Whereas dry chemical can corrode metal and can affect electrical circuitry—thus limiting the areas in which it should be used—both CO_2 and Halon 1211 leave no residue. But Halon 1211 is three times as effective as an equal weight of CO_2. Halon 1211 is a liquefied gas which leaves the nozzle in a stream with a range of nine to fifteen feet, greater than the range for CO_2. Also, Halon 1211 does not degrade visual acuity as CO_2 does, and Halon 1211 can be stored at a lower pressure and for a longer time. In addition, it is effective on three classes of fires (A, B, and C) whereas water is only good for class A (ordinary combustibles, such as paper), and CO_2 is only good for classes B (flammable liquids, such as oil) and C (electrical) fires.

SAFETY PROBLEMS FACING PASSENGERS

Fire and Smoke

It is very difficult to increase passenger safety by making the cabin interiors out of a material that will neither burn readily nor give off toxic fumes or thick smoke. Since fire causes death, a material that burns readily is obviously unacceptable. Sadly enough, many additives that can be applied to a material to decrease the rate of burning actually increase the amount of smoke and toxic fumes given off.

The problem is that for an aircraft to fly, or at least to fly economically, the material it is made of must be light, strong, and cheap. Plastic meets these three criteria, but unfortunately plastic also burns readily and gives off toxic fumes. Plastic foams, from which seat cushions are made, are highly flammable.[8] However, it appears that a partial solution to the problem may be at hand. The FAA indicates that a seatcover that would fit over the plastic foam cushion could keep the cushion from burning or giving off high levels of smoke. But while these "fire-blocker" seatcovers may stop the seats from burning, carpets and the plastic aircraft panels might not be so easily protected.[9]

When plastic burns in a confined space, such as an aircraft cabin, there are a number of threats to life: smoke, toxic fumes, high temperature, and depletion of oxygen. The smoke produced from a plastic fire is normally very hot and dense. In tests at the Smoke Research Station in Great Britain, eighty-eight pounds of plastic foam were ignited; within two minutes the visibility had fallen to about three feet, and within the next few seconds the visibility was completely obscured.[10] At the same time the temperature of the smoke had reached 1,650°F, so hot that it would be almost instantaneously fatal. Even if the smoke were only a thin layer near the ceiling, the heat radiating downward would probably set fire to the clothing of anyone underneath it.

While the amount of oxygen depletion in an actual aircraft fire is difficult to predict because so many variables affect it, measurements made during plastic foam fires show that the oxygen concentration can fall from the normal 21 percent to the fatal level of 1 percent within two minutes.[11] But a more serious toxicity problem involves the production of carbon monoxide, a by-product of any fire in which organic material is burned. Breathing a concentration of 1 percent carbon monoxide (CO) for just one minute will kill a human. Lower concentrations can incapacitate a person, who could then succumb to other hazards.

Aside from CO there are numerous other toxic gases given off by plastics and fuel fires. These include hydrogen cyanide, hydrogen chloride, oxides of nitrogen, and ammonia. These other gases can reach lethal levels, "but almost always the level of heat, the CO level and the lack of oxygen have already proved fatal."[12]

In addition to the toxicity of the fumes, a major hazard of smoke is that it obscures visibility. One reason is that the fumes are extremely irritating, causing tears in the eyes. Another reason is that the smoke from fuel and plastics is black, allowing very little light to pass.

The FAA conducted a research program on smoke from fuel fires at one of its research facilities, the National Aviation Facilities Experimental Center (NAFEC) in Atlantic City, New Jersey. A surplus military C-133 aircraft was converted to resemble a wide-body aircraft.[13] This test aircraft had no plastic seating or side panels that passenger-carrying aircraft have because the test was conducted to study just the fuel-fire smoke after it entered the aircraft through an open door. The source of the fire was a pan of jet fuel on the ground outside the plane. Inside the cabin the researchers had installed a number of smoke-measuring instruments, as well as various standard and experimental lighting systems.

The most important factor affecting the amount of smoke that entered the cabin was, not surprisingly, the force and direction of the wind. If it blew the smoke toward the open door, the cabin filled with smoke. In this series of tests, the smoke would usually stratify; that is, it would be thicker at certain heights above the floor than at other heights. Normally, it is thicker near the ceiling. In one test (Test 31) a moderate amount of smoke entered the cabin and a dense layer of smoke formed in the two to three feet just below the ceiling. While a person standing upright would not be subjected to a significant amount of heat from hot smoke under these conditions, his vision would be affected by the obscured lighting of the ceiling fixtures. However, in the very next test (Test 32), the temperature at head level for a person standing exceeded 300°F after only two minutes. But even a minute earlier, after only sixty seconds from the start of the test, light was totally obscured within the top three feet of the cabin (sixty inches from the floor and above). This means, of course, that a person would not have been able to see a thing if he were standing upright. (See Figure 7.1.) But below that level (forty-eight inches) a person could still see with relative ease. Near floor level (twenty-four inches), however, another layer of smoke had formed, causing total obscuration within two minutes.

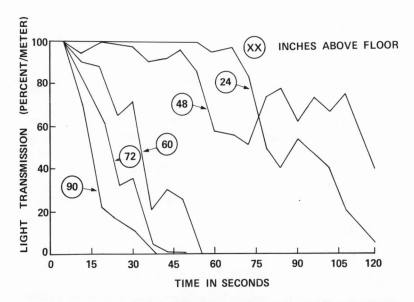

FIGURE 7.1. Amount of light transmitted at various heights above the floor during a test of interior emergency lighting of a cabin during a simulated postcrash fire. Notice that there is less smoke closer to the floor (28 and 48 inches) than at higher levels.

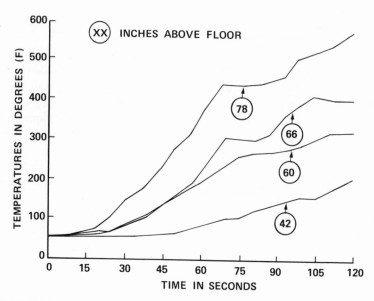

FIGURE 7.2. Temperature increases at various heights above floor level during the same test described in Figure 7.1.

Figure 7.2 shows some of the temperatures measured at various times and levels during the test. Obviously, the higher the level above the floor, the higher the temperature.

It is apparent that when smoke enters a cabin, the person who stands up straight has less chance of getting out of the plane than someone bent over or someone crawling on hands and knees. If the conditions were the same as those in this test, then the temperature of the air at head level would prove fatal. Not only that, but toxic fumes in the smoke could be just as fatal as the high temperature. To make matters worse, the person standing upright would not be able to see exit signs, or anything else that might aid him in finding the emergency exit.

Seeing Exit Signs

Regrettably, it is a common practice aboard aircraft (and in many public buildings, as far as that goes) to place exit signs near the ceiling. The reason, of course, is to allow people who are standing to see the sign over the heads of those in front. But the problem with a sign located near the ceiling is that hot smoke rises and it takes very little of the thick, black smoke emitted from burning fuel and plastics to obscure an exit sign—which may be the only indication of an escape route.

The NAFEC study also examined the legibility of exit signs, as well as other exit indicators, during their smoke tests. It was concluded that increasing the light intensity of the emergency exit signs would not substantially increase the time they would remain visible. A separate study showed that increasing the size and illumination could increase visibility of the signs, but only slightly. [14] The changes in size and light intensity would be inefficient methods because the black smoke quickly blocks out the light. The NAFEC researchers, however, did find that moving the exit signs to about five feet, or lower, could significantly increase their effectiveness. In addition, out of all the experimental lighting systems tested, they found that a string of flashing lights, moving in sequence toward an exit, was perhaps most effective.

These lights had been designed specifically to direct passengers to exits under smoke conditions. In one accident, passengers apparently had such a problem after a DC-9 and a Convair 580 (CV-580) collided on the ground at O'Hare International Airport on December 20, 1972. Whereas there were no deaths on the CV-580, ten of the forty-one passengers and four crew on the DC-9 died. When the DC-9 came to a stop after the collision, fire broke out near the rear of the plane. Two passengers had left their seats and headed forward, but they bypassed the two front exits and continued forward into the cockpit, where their bodies were found. Two other passengers headed toward the tail, but for some reason they failed to find and open an exit there, and they died. [15]

Prior to the NAFEC studies, I conducted tests on the effectiveness of sequentially flashing lights (SFL) to direct passengers to exits under simulated smoke conditions. [16] The idea that SFL could be useful in helping passengers find an exit is based on the fact that if one light in a string of lights goes on then off, followed by the next light in the string's going on and then off, a viewer sees the lights as "moving," or indicating a specific direction. In testing the SFL we found that people had no trouble seeing the indicated directions in various horizontal planes (even under impaired lighting conditions), toward or away from the viewer, left to right, or on a curved path. Not only that, but people could easily see the direction indicated by the lights whether they were standing or on hands and knees, as they might be in a smoky environment. The subjects in the test wore goggles which filtered out over 95 percent of the light, thereby simulating, to some extent, a smoke-filled environment. Since there is no adequate way to expose a person to the smoke given off by burning plastics and fuel without injuring the person, subjects did not experience the eye irritation caused by smoke. Given this limitation, it was found that subjects could detect directional movement with as few as two lights, something that could be beneficial in an aircraft if visibility were limited by smoke.

One problem with using a SFL indicator is that many people will not follow it unless they know its purpose. There appears to be a strong "boarding door attraction" among passengers during an unexpected emergency evacuation of an aircraft. If an accident occurs without warning, passengers would have no time to think about which exit they should use; thus many head toward the door through which they boarded the aircraft. We wanted to find out if instructions to follow the SFL would be necessary to decrease this boarding-door attraction, and we found that they were necessary. When people were not aware of the purpose of the light sequence (that led to an exit), most of them (62 percent) would not follow the SFL but would instead head in the direction of the door by which they had entered. On the other hand when they were instructed to follow the SFL to find the closest exit, nearly everyone (93 percent) followed the directional lights.

Now, suppose a passenger follows the SFL to an exit, and for some reason cannot open that exit. Will he remain there or try to find another exit? We found that six out of the seven subjects who were instructed to follow the SFL to the exit, and who found it inoperable, stayed there even though they had been told to consider the situation as an emergency and try to escape. They were extremely frustrated at not being able to open the exit after following the SFL to it. Several of them said "I give up" and refused to try to get out of their predicament. They expressed extreme frustration, and my belief is that if they were in an actual emergency they would not have tried to find another exit. They did not seem to consider the possibility that another exit might exist. Another group of seven subjects had been instructed to follow the SFL to the exit. But this group was told beforehand that if the exit could not be opened, to try to find another. After spending a brief period trying to open the locked exit, every one of the seven subjects in this group attempted to locate another exit. The differences between the groups in the time spent at the inoperable door were statistically significant: seventy-three seconds for the group without the special instructions versus thirty-two seconds for those told to find alternative exits. Also, the number of people trying to locate an alternative exit was statistically significant.

Further tests were conducted aboard a B-720, in which the results were clearly in favor of the SFL.[17] While special instructions were needed to help passengers use the SFL to find an exit, the SFL greatly reduced the number of errors (the number of wrong turns made before turning into the row leading to an exit), and it also decreased the time it took for them to reach the exit by over 50 percent.

There are potential problems with any automatic system such as the SFL which would direct passengers to an exit. One problem is how and when the system is to be activated. If it doesn't start to operate until the exit is opened, then it would not be useful in getting the first person to it. Another problem is that the system should not direct passengers to an exit that cannot be safely used. An exit with a fire directly outside, or where an emergency escape slide is unusable, should not be one to which passengers are directed. But overall, it appears that the SFL is a potentially useful device for assisting passengers in finding exits in aircraft when the normal exit signs are obscured by smoke.

SURVIVING AN AIRCRAFT FIRE

Don't Cause It

If you inadvertently find yourself in a lavatory with a lit cigarette, make sure you don't put it in the paper towel waste container. Flush it or stub it out in the ashtray outside the door. If you open a lavatory door and see fire or smell smoke, quickly close the door in order to contain the fire and immediately inform a cabin attendant.

Cover Your Skin

If you have time to prepare for an emergency landing, then protect yourself from fire by covering as much of your skin as possible. If you have brought aboard a coat and hat, put them on. But women should remove nylon stockings since these can cause severe skin burns if they melt. Also, the blankets found on most planes can be useful. They are usually made of wool, one of the less flammable materials, and covering your head, shoulders, and hands with one would give added protection.

Know Where the Nearest Exits Are

The hypothetical story of a man in a burning plane who had moved toward an exit was related in Chapter Two. As he got closer, he noticed the flames approaching, and because of fear and the choking smoke, he started pushing against those in front. This slowed the escape of those ahead of him, thereby reducing his own chances of getting out. Overpowered by a feeling of hopelessness, he gave up and sat down.

There are a number of things that you can do so as not to find yourself in this situation. Sit near an exit, if possible, because the time to get out from a burning aircraft can be very short. (You can ask at the ticket desk for a seat near an emergency exit—many times they are available.) Also, know where alternative exits are. The first exit you come to may not be usable and you will need to know where to go after that. Since I know of no plans to install an SFL system aboard airliners, you will have to rely on your memory to find the closest exit if smoke enters the cabin and obscures the exit signs.

Move Quickly

It is a general rule that if there is an accident, you should *not* stay seated once your plane comes to a stop. This is especially true if there is any indication of fire, either inside or outside the plane, or if the plane has landed in water. Move quickly to an exit.

Don't Breathe the Smoke

Breathe as little of the smoke as possible. Smoke usually stratifies, concentrating at the higher levels. Bend over, or even crawl on your hands and knees if you must, to keep your head out of the smoke. There may be some fumes very close to the floor, so find a level where you can keep your eyes open.

Go to Alternative Exits

If you are in a line in which everyone else is pushing and it doesn't seem to be moving, head toward a different exit. If an aisle is blocked by debris, then climb over the seats. Many planes, though not all, have seats with a "breakover feature" where, by exerting about a thirty-pound force, the seat backs can be pushed forward so that they lie almost flat. This could greatly increase your speed in moving toward a different exit if the aisle is blocked. Head toward an exit where people seem to be getting out.

Even if you don't see another exit, you may be able to hear the flight attendant's commands to passengers who are escaping the plane. Flight attendants are trained to yell such phrases as: "Jump!" "Form double lines!" "Help at the bottom of the slide!" and "Hurry!" Head toward that exit.

Check Outside Before Opening an Exit

If you arrive at an unopened exit, pause before opening it. A fire outside the plane does not always indicate a need to evacuate. Small fires, such as from a burning tire that had overheated on landing, can be put out by the airport fire department. Passengers should not start opening exits and evacuating the aircraft in this situation because it is not uncommon for injuries to occur during an evacuation itself (why this is so is covered in Chapter Eight). Just remember, if the situation does not appear too serious, don't open any of the exits unless you hear or see flight attendants doing so. Then follow their directions.

But if there is an extensive fire outside, or fire or thick smoke inside, then go as quickly as you can to your closest exit and be prepared to open it if no one else is there. But first, it is extremely important to look out through the window in the door—if you see fire or smoke directly outside, do not open it. The NAFEC studies found that a deadly amount of toxic fumes and smoke of extremely high temperatures could rapidly enter a cabin through an open door. And doors on some aircraft cannot easily be closed once opened. Should it be at night, you might inadvertently open the door and allow smoke to enter. But given a very critical situation inside the plane, it would probably be better to take a chance and open the door, since rapid escape in such a circumstance is imperative.

On most planes there are exits at each end of the cabin, but you would not find them if you stayed in the main aisle. Most emergency exits are on the side of the fuselage, so if you stayed in the main aisle and went forward, you could end up in the cockpit, as did two of the passengers in the DC-9 accident at O'Hare.[18] And if you went aft, you would only find emergency exits in the tail section of *some* planes, such as the DC-9, the B-727, and some BAC 1-11 aircraft.

In most planes you will have to turn left or right off the main aisle to get to an exit. Make sure you know how far you have to go before turning. A good habit before takeoff is to count the number of seat rows, either forward or backward, you would need to pass before turning. Then if you have trouble seeing you could still reach an exit using your sense of touch.

Do not run through a wall of fire unless there is absolutely no other escape route. The flight attendant in the accident recounted at the beginning of this chapter apparently did just this in her search of a fire extinguisher, and she didn't survive. Don't assume that a wall of flame is thin, or that there is even a floor on the other side.

In summary, there is certainly a danger from fire and smoke if you are in a plane accident. But don't give up all hope, even if the fire is large and the smoke is filling the cabin. There are a variety of ways out of the plane. Prepare yourself in advance, even if there is no indication of an accident. Keep your coat on during landing and takeoff. Sit near an exit, if possible, and prepare yourself mentally by having some idea of where the closest exits are in front of you and behind you. Then don't sit and wait for help from rescue crews. They usually take several minutes to reach the scene, but that may be several minutes too long. Get out of your seat and go to an exit. The faster you get there the better. Don't stay in a line that isn't moving, and if it is moving, resist the urge to push forward because this will only slow the evacuation. If smoke makes it hard to see or breathe, bend down or crawl toward the exits, but move quickly. When you get to the exit, look outside for fire or smoke before opening it, and don't open it if you see that the flight attendants are not opening theirs. If you decide it must be opened, do it quickly and get out of the plane. Once outside, help other evacuees to move quickly away, and don't stay near the plane. Needless to say, because of the flammability of spilled fuel, resist the urge to light a cigarette.

REFERENCES

1. Daniel A. Johnson, "An Investigation of Factors Affecting Aircraft Passenger Attention to Safety Information Presentations," report prepared for Operations Section A, FAA, Washington, D.C., Aug. 1979.
2. "Survivors' Statements, B-727 Accident, April 27, 1976, St. Thomas, Virgin Islands," Docket No. SA-435, Exhibit No. 6-B, National Transportation Safety Board, Washington, D.C.
3. Elwood T. Driver, in *Hearings before the Subcommittee on Oversight and Review of the Committee on Public Works and Transportation,* Proceedings of the United States House of Representatives, 96th Cong., 1st sess., April 25–26, 1979, p. 5.
4. "Cargo Hold Fire Cited in Saudi Accident," *Aviation Week and Space Technology,* July 12, 1982, p. 39.
5. R. G. Snyder, *Advanced Techniques in Crash Impact Protection and Emergency Egress from Air Transport Aircraft,* NATO, AGARDograph no. 221, June 1976.
6. "23 Killed When DC-9 Bursts into Flames over Cincinnati," *Seattle Post-Intelligencer,* June 3, 1983.
7. "Inflight Cabin Fire," *Flight Safety Digest* (Flight Safety Foundation, Washington, D.C.), Nov. 1982, p. 1.
8. John Horsfall, "Reducing the Fire Hazards in Modern Aircraft Cabins," *Fire,* Nov. 1980, pp. 299–300.
9. "FAA Drafts Changes in Fire Rule," *Aviation Week and Space Technology,* July 4, 1983, p. 28.
10. Horsfall, "Reducing the Fire Hazards."
11. Ibid.
12. Ibid.
13. James E. Demaree, *A Preliminary Examination of Interior Aircraft Emergency Lighting under Simulated Postcrash Fire and Smoke Conditions,* Report no. NA-79-46-LR, NAFEC, FAA, Atlantic City, N.J., 1979.
14. P. G. Rasmussen, B. P. Chesterfield, and D. L. Lowrey, "Legibility of Smoke-Obscured Emergency Exit Signs," *Proceedings of the Human Factors Society, 1980,* Human Factors Society, Santa Monica, Calif.
15. *Aircraft Accident Report, McDonnell-Douglas DC-9-31 and Convair CV-580, O'Hare International Airport, Chicago, Ill., Dec. 20, 1972,* Report no. NTSB-AAR-73-15, National Transportation Safety Board, Washington, D.C., 1973.
16. Daniel A. Johnson, Jeffery Erickson, and David M. Zamarin, "The Effectiveness of Sequential Flashing Lights to Direct Passengers to Emergency Exits," *SAFE Journal* 8, no. 4, 1978, 24–31.
17. Ibid.
18. *Aircraft Accident Report, McDonnell-Douglas DC-9-31 and Convair CV-580, O'Hare International Airport, Chicago, Ill., Dec. 20, 1972.*

Chapter Eight

EMERGENCY ESCAPE AFTER AN ACCIDENT ON LAND

If you must ever escape from an airplane, you will have no chance to practice and little time to give it much consideration. Yet mistakes are possible, mistakes that can affect the safety of everyone aboard. This chapter is devoted to helping you avoid these mistakes.

When you leave your seat, *don't* take any of the baggage you carried with you aboard the plane, including attaché cases, duty-free liquor, or heavy purses. There are several reasons for this. Probably the most important is that many objects brought aboard the plane have points or corners sharp enough to deflate an escape slide. Even many briefcases have corners that could deflate a slide were they held by a passenger moving down the slide. If you were to deflate a slide, it could not be used by others, and this could directly lead to injury and possibly the deaths of passengers waiting to escape.

A second reason not to have carry-on baggage with you is that it can only slow your escape through the exit. When you get to the door on a wide-body aircraft such as the DC-10, you will find that the floor of the plane is about sixteen feet above the ground, equivalent to the height of a two-story building. Many people hesitate at the doorway before jumping into the escape slide when they have nothing to carry. But when carrying something, most people will hesitate even longer trying to figure out the best method for getting out of the plane. The same holds for other types of exits. If you have ever tried to go down stairs quickly with a suitcase or bag in your hand, you know that you are more cautious, and therefore proceed more slowly, than if you were carrying nothing. Also, getting out of overwing window exits, the small exits which lead out onto the wing, are difficult enough when your hands are free. Baggage can only slow your escape.

A third reason not to carry baggage is that it is potentially dangerous. If you are carrying something as you jump into the slide, you are more likely to injure someone, even yourself. During the evacuation of 238 passengers from a DC-8 after a hard landing on December 29, 1980, one passenger was seriously injured when he went down an escape slide with two overcoats in his arms. About halfway down, his legs became entangled and he fell off the slide, fracturing his jaw and wrist on the pavement.[1] If you must jump into an escape slide or slide off a wing's surface (which can be over six feet above the ground) you will be moving relatively fast, and anything in your hands can be dangerous, not only to yourself but to anyone unlucky enough to be near you.

And if these were not enough reasons, then a final reason is that when you get to the door, the flight attendant is likely to take from you whatever you are carrying before you leave the plane. So if you have something valuable in your briefcase or purse, put it in your coat, if it fits, and wear your coat. If it doesn't fit, leave it in the plane.

The problem with passengers' taking carry-on baggage during an emergency evacuation is seen in the aftermath of an accident which occurred at Los Angeles International Airport on March 1, 1978, as a DC-10 aborted a takeoff because of a series of flat tires. The plane was loaded with fuel and carried 186 passengers whose average age was sixty, en route to Hawaii.

According to the NTSB report, the runway at Los Angeles was wet from a light rain but the temperature was a warm 59°F. After receiving clearance to take off, the large plane accelerated normally to about 152 knots when the captain heard a loud "metallic bang" followed by a "quivering of the plane." The left wing dropped slightly. The captain immediately applied full pressure to the brakes, cut power by bringing the engine thrust levers back to idle, and actuated the reverse thrust to further slow the aircraft. When only 2,000 feet of runway remained, the crew in the cockpit realized that the plane would not be able to stop on the runway surface. The captain kept applying full brake-pedal force as well as full reverse thrust as he steered the plane to the right in order to miss the runway lights at the end of the runway. About 100 feet beyond the runway, the left main landing gear of the heavy plane broke through the surface of the pavement, which was not designed to carry such a heavy load. As a result, the left wing tip dropped and the left engine was torn off, resulting in a fire on that side of the plane.

Luckily, the fire department at LAX was alert and saw the problem as it developed. Firetrucks were racing toward the plane even before it stopped, a fact which undoubtedly saved a number of lives.[2]

Below is the testimony of a flight attendant, whom we will refer to as Judy Hill,* who was stationed at door One-R, the front door on the right side of the plane. As the pool of burning fuel spread from the damaged left wing of the plane, heat from the fire caused the escape slides to start bursting. Miss Hill, who was at the last door through which passengers could escape, gave this report to a hearing officer of the NTSB:

> After I had taken my seat, the aisle side of the front row, by One-R, and fastened my seatbelt, and Joan Kilpatrick was to my left, I was just sitting there as we were starting to taxi, and we were gaining speed.
>
> I was just thinking about personal things, and I heard a pop. I can't really call it an explosion. It felt like we blew a tire. I have experienced this before, and it felt the same way, and Joan and I held hands, and we just kind of looked at each other and were very calm and just sat there.
>
> The aircraft was shimmying a little bit, shaking a little bit, and we heard another pop, and with that, the aircraft shook a great deal.
>
> Magazines fell down, were hitting us on the heads, and I noticed the movie screen itself came out of the ceiling. There were objects flying around the cabin, and with that, I gave the command to keep your heads down, to grab your ankles and keep your heads down, and repeated those commands until the aircraft came to a complete stop.
>
> The passengers obeyed this command, and after we came to a complete stop, which I thought was an interminably long time, we seemed to be going very fast, and not slowing down like any other aborted takeoff I had experienced.
>
> I got out of my seat, and could see flames that would intermittently pop up as I looked out the left side of the aircraft.
>
> I had good visibility from this point, and [on] the right side, I could not see any flames, but I could see a great deal of very black smoke. With the flames that I saw, I knew Joan was at the door, and I stepped into the cockpit, and told the Captain that there were flames on the left, and he said "Evacuate," and I stepped out of the cockpit.
>
> Joan, I knew, was waiting for me to give some kind of command. I told her to hit the door, and she said, "I am," and I turned to the passengers, or stepped in front of the jump seats to protect her, and told the passengers to stay where they were for

---

* Although the parties referred to in this incident are actual people, the names used in the account are fictitious.

a minute, and I turned around, the door was not open. I said, "Joan, open the door," and she said, "I am trying," and the door came open, and the slide fell inside the aircraft.

It just—it dropped down, and toppled inside, and I said, "Kick it out, Joan, kick it out," and we both got behind the slide and pushed it outside, and then I told everybody to come this way, and to get out, to leave everything and get out.

We immediately started our evacuation. The two passengers in 2-K and -L . . . followed directions very well, but I was looking for able-bodied passengers, and I did not feel they were able-bodied, and told them to go ahead and get out. [During emergencies flight attendants may ask able-bodied passengers to help—in this case, she would ask some passengers to help others get off the slide at the bottom, and in this way, speed up the evacuation of the plane.]

I was grabbing luggage with one hand and throwing it over the seats. The passengers had moved into the aisles, and I was throwing it back over the seat, because I was afraid that it would rip the slides. I don't know if it was a valid fear or not, but I didn't want that luggage going out, and a lot of people were bringing a lot of carry-on luggage with them. It was a great problem for us—for me.

And we kept people moving as fast as possible. I showed a lady how to hold her baby to do down the slide. I told her to put it in her left arm and hold it against her chest as tightly as she could, and to go, and I saw some tennis rackets coming up, grabbed them with one hand and threw them, and pushed her out with the other hand, assisted her, and kept them moving as fast as possible.

They just kept coming, and we just kept working. . . . I would keep watching, and I wanted to keep an eye on the fire, where it was, and if our exit was considered usable at that point.

I was aware of certain conversations around me, and I soon became aware that we had probably the only usable exit on board. Passengers were hesitating to go down the [slide]. It was very steep at that point, and the people were old, and at one point I saw a pair of plaid pants standing at the door, and I told him to go, and had my hand on his back, and I was getting more people up to go, and I turned around and he was still there, and I said, "I said go, god damn, I mean go, the plane is on fire, and I want you to go," and pushed him out, and got more people in [the slide].

And I was just getting them out as fast as I could—at different points, when I could see an able-bodied passenger come by, would tell them to get down that slide, and get those people off that slide, and get them away from the airplane as quickly as possible, to get them away from there and get them up off the slides.

I was afraid that people were going to be jumping on each other, but I still felt it was my responsibility to get them out at that point, and we had a lot of physical work to do. . . . I looked back to the aisle to see how many more people were coming.

I saw a lot of smoke rolling up the aisles. It was up to the First Class galley, and there was some dark red flame under some of the smoke on the left side, and I hoped that there weren't many more people, and I saw [another flight attendant] come up the aisle, and he said, "Everybody is off of the back. We can get off," and a few more people went down the slide.

I was aware of a man holding a little boy, to my right, and I wanted him to go

down with the little boy, and some other people went. I am not upset. I just have a hard time—
[Hearing Officer: "It's okay."]
—remembering. I don't want to go too fast. —Anyway, I felt it was about my turn to go, and that I had done all I could on board, and I looked out the door, and I couldn't find the slide. There was liquid flame under the door area itself. It was rolling toward the front of the airplane, and I thought I could go, maybe hand over hand down the slide, but it had gone back under the fuselage, and I couldn't get hold of it. It was a long way down.

And I remembered—I thought, "I may have waited too long here," and I remembered the cockpit. Another flight attendant came up behind me and said, "We're not going to make it. I know we're not going to make it," and I said, "Oh, yes we are," and grabbed her hand and threw her in the cockpit, and I thought about closing the door, and I thought it would waste precious seconds.

And the man with the little boy was going out the window. I realized that some of the people were hurting themselves going down the rope, and I have three great strong brothers, and I was raised in Wyoming and Colorado, and I knew how to go down a rope, and I took one moment to wrap it around my foot, and go down it so I wouldn't hurt myself—because I remembered I still had some work to do out there, outside, and I didn't want to be injured.

And so I was the next-to-last person off the aircraft.[3]

Luckily, the man was able to slide down the rope, holding the little boy, without either being injured. Unfortunately, however, two passengers died at the scene of this accident as they tried to escape from the aircraft using the overwing escape slide. Apparently they were overcome by the smoke before they could get away from the plane. Also, two other passengers died three months later as a result of their injuries.[4] But the potential for more deaths was great. And there would have been more deaths if it were not for the actions of Miss Hill and other crewmembers on board the aircraft with her. But her job would have been easier if she hadn't been obliged to keep taking the carry-on baggage away from passengers. If the baggage carried by one of those passengers had ripped and deflated the slide, many passengers might not have gotten out of the plane.

The rope used by Miss Hill, along with twelve other people, is located in the cockpit. Designed to be used primarily by pilots, it requires a certain skill and hand strength to descend safely. It was not designed for use by the type of untrained elderly people who were on this plane. If fewer passengers had carried baggage to the door, the evacuation could have gone faster and perhaps all the people could have gotten out by the relatively safe inflatable slides, and none would have had to use the escape rope.

TABLE 8.1
Passenger Emergency Exits

Type	Minimum height (inches)	Minimum width (inches)	Floor level or hatch	Passenger seats per pair of exits
A	72	42	Floor	110
I	48	24	Floor	45
II	44	20	Floor	40
III	36	20	Hatch	35
IV	26	19	Hatch	30

TYPES OF EXITS

Exits are categorized both by their size and by whether or not they are "floor-level" exits. A floor-level exit is one in which the bottom sill of the exit is level with the floor. Some exits, such as overwing window exits, have sills above floor level. Both of these factors, size and sill height, affect the speed with which people can get out of an exit. The height and width of the opening of the exit are major determinants of its size, but the radius of the corner is also important. Two openings of the same height and width may look quite different; one could be rectangular and the other like a slit, wide in the center but narrow at the ends. So the corner radii are not allowed to be any greater than one-third the width of the exit for narrow exits, and one-sixth the width of wider exits; this ensures that the exits are primarily rectangular, thereby providing an opening easily used during escape.

Table 8.1 lists most of the types of exits you will find on aircraft. Type II and Type IV exits are less common than Types A, I, and III.

HOW TO OPEN EXITS

There is no standard way to open emergency exits on airplanes. Various aircraft manufacturers have developed different handle mechanisms over the years, and have apparently been reluctant to change their design simply to be similar to that of another manufacturer. Besides, there has been no consensus among designers on the most desired characteristics for door handles, such as size and location of the handle, forces required to operate it, direction of movement, and whether the handle used in an emergency should be the same as the handle for opening the door in the nonemergency situation. Nevertheless, standardization would be desirable for at least two reasons. First, if there were only two or three different ways in which exits could be opened, passengers might be better able to open an exit if a flight attendant is not available. Second, it would reduce the number of hours needed for crew training.

There is hope for standardization in the future. The International Air Transport Association (IATA), an association comprised of many of the world's airlines, initiated an effort in the early 1980s to come up with common standards for door operation. Even though manufacturers do not have to follow IATA recommendations, there will probably be a trend toward adopting the standards they set. This would affect only those aircraft designed in the future, however.

In the meantime there will continue to be a variety of methods for operating emergency exits. In the event of an emergency, you should have an idea of what to do and what not to do if you are the first to reach an unopened exit after an accident.

Type III Exits

Passengers are many times the only ones available to open Type III exits. Virtually every narrow-body aircraft has either one or two pair of these exits near the center of the plane, over the wings. An exception is the B-757, a narrow-body plane most models of which have Type I and Type A exits; there is still the possibility that some models will have Type III exits, however. On the other hand most wide-body aircraft have a combination of Type I and Type A exits, and except for the B-767, have no Type III exits.

Flight attendants are usually stationed near doors (Type I or Type A exits) and seldom near Type III exits. Doors are almost always located at each end of the cabin in narrow-body aircraft. On some aircraft a flight attendant may also be stationed near the overwing window exits, but in these unusual cases a passenger should still know how to open the exit because there are usually two, and many times four, Type III exits on the plane. A flight attendant can only open one at a time, a procedure taking ten to fifteen seconds. To open four would take forty to sixty seconds, much too long in many emergencies.

A Type III exit has a removable hatch. This hatch has a window in the center of it, and a handle for opening the hatch is located above the window. This handle may have a decorative cover over it which must be pulled off. To remove the hatch, pull the handle down. When this is done, the hatch will usually remain in the opening until it is lifted out. These exits, as well as virtually all of the other exits on aircraft, are "plug-type" openings, meaning that the edges are beveled so that the inside of the hatch is larger than the outside. This is a safety measure. When the air pressure inside the cabin increases relative to the outside pressure as the plane ascends, the greater air pressure pushes the hatch outward. Without the beveled edges, a hatch could be pushed through the opening. But in the case of plug-type exits, the outside opening is smaller than the inside edge of the hatch so when air pressure pushes the hatch against the frame of the opening, it seals the opening even tighter at higher altitudes. (See Figure 8.1.)

One consequence of this design is that the hatch does not open out-

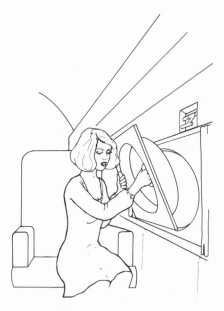

FIGURE 8.1. Plug-type exits are common on jet aircraft. The outside opening is smaller than the inside so increased pressure will not force the hatch through the opening.

ward—it must be lifted into the cabin. In addition, most hatches have one or two "pins," usually on the bottom, which fit into openings in the window sill. Therefore the window cannot be pulled straight into the cabin, but must be lifted upward and then inward. A hand-hold at the bottom of the hatch makes lifting up the window relatively easy. The hatch can be lifted inward by someone either seated or standing. (See Figures 8.2 and 8.3.)

FIGURE 8.2. To open most window exits, a handle must be pulled; then the hatch must be lifted up and inward.

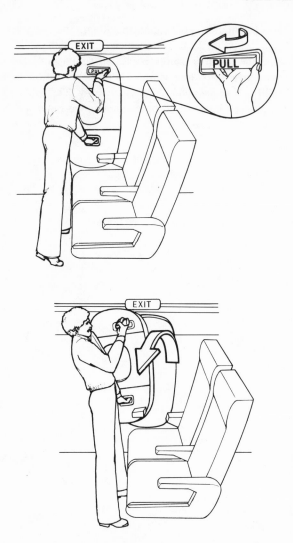

FIGURE 8.3. Hatches may also be removed while standing.

Although this is a somewhat complicated explanation of how to open a Type III exit, in reality the hatch can be removed rather quickly.

The next question is what to do with the hatch: Should you throw it outside or keep it in? If kept inside, it might hinder escape. Some airlines suggest putting it on the armrests. (See Figure 8.4.) This will keep it off the floor, thereby allowing access to the exit. Other airlines suggest putting it in the row of seats ahead or behind the row leading to the exit. (See Figure 8.5.) One problem with either of these methods is that passengers might occupy these seats.

An alternative method, and one that I think is preferable, is to push the exit through the opening and let it drop outside. A possible problem with this alternative is that, once outside, passengers could trip over the hatch. The question is whether one or two hatches lying on each wing would pose a significant risk to passengers trying to escape, especially in the dark.

In August 1975 the DC-9 Series 50 was being certified for flight by the FAA. Part of the certification process requires that a full load of

FIGURE 8.4. Some airlines suggest putting the hatch on the seats.

FIGURE 8.5. Other airlines suggest that the hatch be put on the seats in front of the exit.

passengers be seated aboard the plane, and at a signal, evacuate the plane within ninety seconds, using just half of the exits. The evacuation must be conducted at night or under darkened conditions. The only light may be that from the aircraft's emergency lighting. Passengers must not have been in an emergency evacuation in the preceding six months, and they must represent the population of passengers on a "typical" flight: 5 percent over the age of sixty, between 5 and 10 percent under the age of twelve, and 30 percent in each age range must be women. The crewmembers must be actual flight attendants and pilots from an airline. And no one aboard the plane must know which exits will be usable and which are blocked and cannot be opened. Just before the start of the evacuation demonstration, hand luggage and blankets are strewn about the floor to simulate the conditions following a rough stop after an aborted takeoff.

In the DC-9 Series 50 evacuation demonstration, the passengers received safety briefing cards with all the required information, including instructions on how to open the overwing exits. But the briefing card did not tell them what to do with the hatch once it was taken out of the window opening. An analysis of the videotape taken from an inside camera showed that the passengers seated next to the overwing exits apparently did not know what to do with the hatches. Each opened an exit but held it in their laps, thereby blocking access to the opening, until a flight attendant arrived. She told them to throw the hatches onto the wing, where they remained during the entire evacuation.

External videotape cameras recorded the movement of passengers as they exited through the Type III exits and ran toward the rear of the wing. Sixty-six people went through the two exits and got off the wing in less than eighty seconds from the start of the test. None of them tripped on the two hatches lying just outside the exit opening. Apparently, the emergency lighting on the plane was sufficient to allow the passengers to avoid the hatches.

Incidentally, in an evacuation demonstration of a later model of this plane, the DC-9 Series 80, the briefing card instructed passengers to throw the hatches outside. After the start of this evacuation the passengers next to these exits quickly opened them and threw the hatches outside, demonstrating the importance of complete instructions. In this evacuation demonstration, however, the FAA allowed the hatches to be removed from the wing to preclude the possibility of injury to those evacuating the plane.

In summary, a person might trip on the hatch if it were lying on the wing outside an exit, which could cause injury, though probably of a minor nature. But a person could also trip over it if it were left inside. Worse yet, it could hamper those trying to get out. You should read the instructions on the safety information card regarding placement of the hatch; if the instructions are to throw it outside, then by all means, do so. If the instructions are to place the hatch in a seat near the exit, put it there if the seat is unoccupied. If the seats are filled, you may have no alternative but to throw the hatch outside. Get rid of it as quickly as possible, because leaving through a Type III exit is not as easy as through a door exit.

The sill of the Type III exit is above floor level, so you must step over it to get onto the wing. The distance from the sill down to the wing can be as much as twenty-seven inches. The best way of going out a Type III exit is to put one leg out followed by your head and shoulders, then your other leg. Referred to as the "leg-body-leg" method, this is probably the fastest and safest way to get out. (See Figure 8.6.)

Once on the wing, you must decide how to get off. Ideally, the pilot will have put the flaps, which are movable sections of the rear edge of the wing, in the down position. These provide a rounded sliding surface. It is possible, however, that you could be in an accident in which the flaps are damaged, or there is fire behind the wing. If so, you will need to find an undamaged area of the wing as close to the ground as possible, and away from fire.

If you are on the wing, be careful that you don't fall or slide on rows of small sharp pieces of metal sticking up out of the wings of many aircraft (see Figure 8.7). These are called vortex generators, which are on the wing to modify the flow of air over the wing's surface to provide improved lift. As you leave the exit opening you will see a pathway with arrows, usually leading toward the rear. Following this pathway will keep you from inadvertently stepping on the vortex generators.

If you do slide down the flaps, be prepared for a jolt as you hit the ground because you could be sliding from a height of six to eight feet. Injuries can occur here,[5] and so it is a good practice for one or two passengers on the ground to help others as they slide off the wing.

Because of the potential for injury, airlines don't want passengers to use the overwing exits unless the fastest evacuation possible is required. In what is called a "precautionary evacuation" the captain may decide that

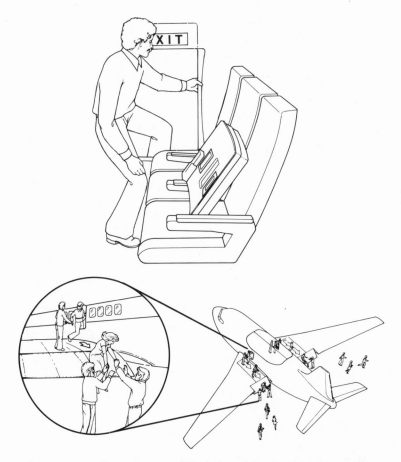

FIGURE 8.6. It is recommended that you put one leg out, followed by your head and body, and then your other leg. You should then go to the rear of the wing and slide off the lowered flaps.

the passengers must get off the plane quickly, but that in his opinion the potential for injury inherent in the use of the Type III exits is not justified. There may be a bomb threat and the captain may determine that all the passengers should quickly get out of the plane using just the evacuation slides at the doors. If you hear an evacuation command from a flight

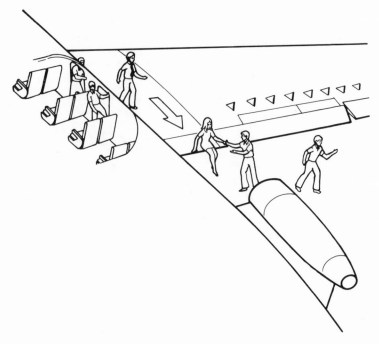

FIGURE 8.7. Following a pathway next to the fuselage will keep you from inadvertently stepping on vortex generators found on the upper surface of some wings.

attendant or the cockpit crew, listen carefully before deciding whether to use a Type III exit.

Some aircraft have Type III exits which are not located at the overwing area. Some Convair aircraft, such as the CV-580, have Type III exits both at the overwing areas and at locations behind the wings (see Figure 8.8). When you open one of these exits, you'll find the end of a rope, made of fire-resistant material, in the frame of the opening. Pull it until the rope is completely extended—it should be long enough to allow you to reach the ground. But it may not have any knots in it, and an unknotted rope is difficult to use without practice. Many people weigh more than the strength in their hands will be able to hold, and so, just as Miss Hill described in her descent from the DC-10 cockpit, you should wrap the rope around one foot to slow your descent.

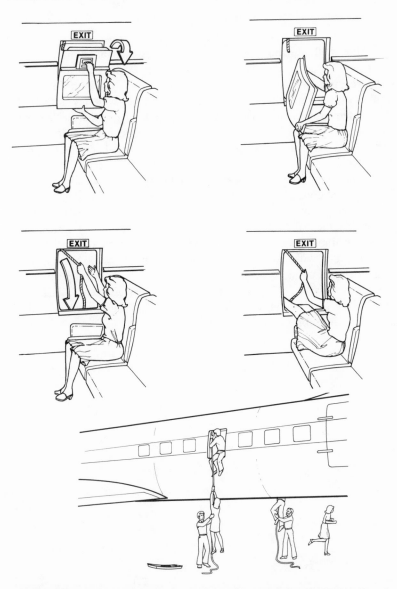

FIGURE 8.8. Though not common, some planes have Type III exits behind the wings. An escape rope must be pulled from the window sill. When it is fully extended, the person can then climb down the rope.

Type I Exits

Almost all airplanes, narrow-body and wide-body alike, have at least one pair of Type I exits. The B-767, a wide-body plane, is possibly the only exception, having Type A and Type III exits. Type I exits are floor-level exits, and must be at least twenty-four inches wide and forty-eight inches high. But many are larger; the boarding doors on most narrow-body aircraft are Type I exits, yet most are seventy-two inches high. Nearly all Type I exits have inflatable escape slides attached to them, though some have stairs.

Type I exits on most narrow-body aircraft operate in a similar manner. Typically the door handle is in the center of the door and consists of a bar which must be rotated, perhaps as much as 180 degrees (see Figure 8.9). Commonly the handles on one side of the plane are to be turned in a clockwise direction and those on the other side in a counterclockwise direction. You will know which direction to turn the handle because there is an arrow on the door pointing from the closed to the open position.

Certain Type I doors operate in a somewhat different manner; the door handle of the right rear door on some B-727 planes must be rotated from bottom to top (see Figure 8.10).

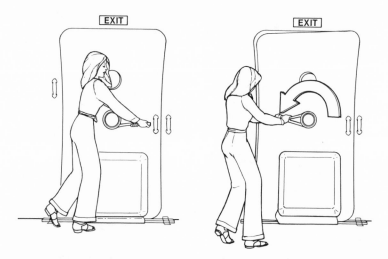

FIGURE 8.9. Door-opening methods common on many Type I exits on narrow-bodied planes.

FIGURE 8.10. On Some Type I exits the handle must be pulled inward, then rotated upward.

Tail Exits

Tail exits, though technically not classified as Type I exits, nevertheless are similar to Type I exits in width. Tail exits are found on two very common airplanes, the B-727 and the DC-9, as well as on the less common British-made BAC 1-11. A tail exit can be either a set of stairs which lead down to the ground through the bottom of the plane's fuselage (technically called a ventral exit) or an escape slide that leads directly out of the tail of the airplane (called a tail-cone exit). The B-727 and the BAC 1-11 have ventral stairs, while the DC-9 has a tail-cone exit.

Methods of opening the tail exits vary from one model to the next. On the B-727 you must first open the door in the rear of the passenger cabin. A step or two behind the door you will find a panel to your left, inside of which is a lever that must be pushed outboard, away from you. This should lower the stairs. On early models of the B-727 (Series 100), moving this handle might not always result in lowering the stairs; in later models it will. If you are on the earlier model and the stairs don't lower after the handle is pushed, close the panel door. Just aft of the panel you'll find a smaller panel; remove the cover and break a second cover, and inside you'll find a handle or wire loop—pull it. This will cause the tail to fall to the ground. (See Figure 8.11.)

Some, but not all, BAC 1-11s have ventral stairs, and these are operated quite differently from those on the B-727. After the cabin door is opened, on your right as you are looking toward the rear is a handle which must be pulled toward you and then pushed toward the rear of the plane (see Figure 8.12).

These ventral stairs would probably not be usable in case of an accident in which the plane ended up lying on its belly (e.g., a "wheels-up" landing). If this happened, the stairs might not fall far enough to allow you to escape. C. H. LeRoy reported on a B-727 accident which occurred in November 1965.[6] The plane, with ninety-one passengers and crew, landed hard several hundred feet short of the runway at Salt Lake City. Both main landing gears were sheared off on impact and the right one punctured the fuselage near the fuel lines that supply the rear engines. Fire, "like a flame thrower," broke out immediately inside the cabin as the plane slid along the runway. Passengers had started opening some of the exits even before the plane came to rest.

The fire and smoke were intense near the rear of the plane, and the flight attendant stationed at the tail exit and two men passengers attempted to use the ventral stairs in the tail. But the stairs lowered only about six inches. The flight attendant went to the top of the stairs in an effort to get to another exit but was turned back by the smoke and fire. Fortunately, as the plane was sliding on the runway it turned so that the tail was pointing into the wind. The wind blowing into the small opening around the lowered stairs kept smoke from building up inside where the three were trapped. The two men and flight attendant yelled and pounded to attract attention, but none of the firefighters heard. Finally, the flight attendant had the men move back so she could get closer to the opening, and stuck her hand out to attract attention. This worked. A fireman pushed the nozzle of a hoze through the crack, one of the men took it, went to the top of the stairs, and sprayed through the doorway to keep the fire out and the temperature down until they could be rescued.

Outside, an all-out effort was started to rescue the survivors. Attempts were made to chop through the tail fuselage with an ax, to cut through it, to lift the rear of the plane so the tail would drop further, and to get the fire down so rescue could be made through a hole in the cabin. This last method was the first to succeed; firemen entered the cabin and rescued the three about thirty minutes after the accident. Even though the exit wasn't usable, it did provide a safe refuge for these three people who were luckier than a number of others who didn't survive.

The tail-cone exit, found only on the DC-9, does not have the disadvantage of being inoperable if the landing gear is sheared off and the aircraft ends up lying flat on the ground. To operate the tail-cone exit you must open the door at the rear of the cabin. This is usually a floor-level door, though some models have a hatch which must be lifted out (see Figure 8.13).

Opening this door on the DC-9 Series 80 model causes the tail cone to drop off and the slide to inflate. On earlier models (Series 10–50) you will have to walk on a relatively dark ramp toward the tail of the plane, making sure you bend down to avoid hitting overhead structures. Find a red handle (this should be illuminated by emergency battery-operated lighting) that will be on your right as you are facing aft, and pull it to release the tail cone. As the cone falls away, it will pull the slide out, causing it to inflate. (See Figure 8.14.)

To lower stairs on all planes you must...

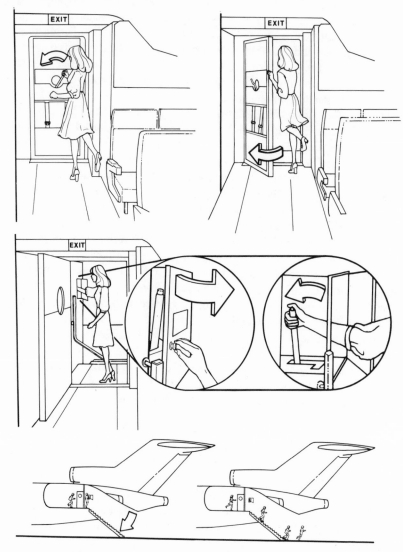

FIGURE 8.11. Operating the rear stairway exit on the B-727.

On some planes if stairs are jammed you must also...

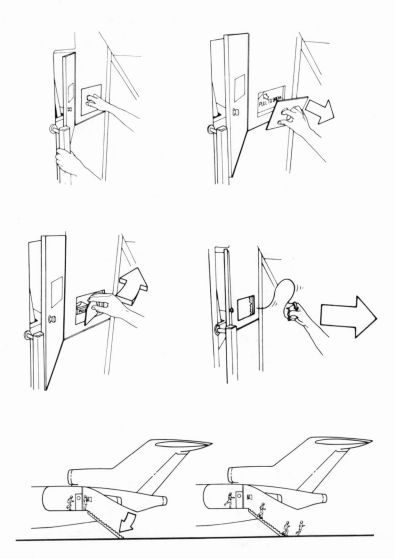

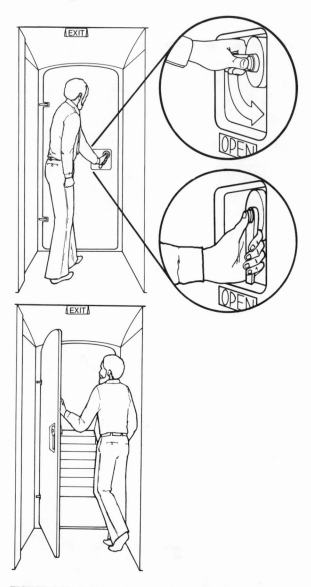

FIGURE 8.12. Operating the rear stairway exit on the BAC 1-11.

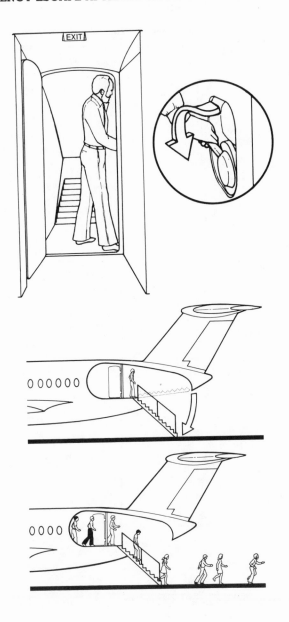

Some airplanes have doors ... Others have hatches

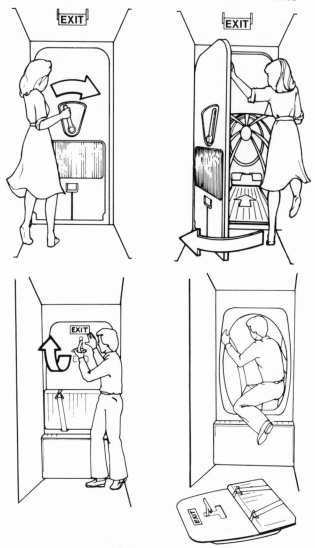

FIGURE 8.13. Opening into the tail cone of the DC-9. Most planes have a door (*top*) but some have a hatch which must be removed (*bottom*).

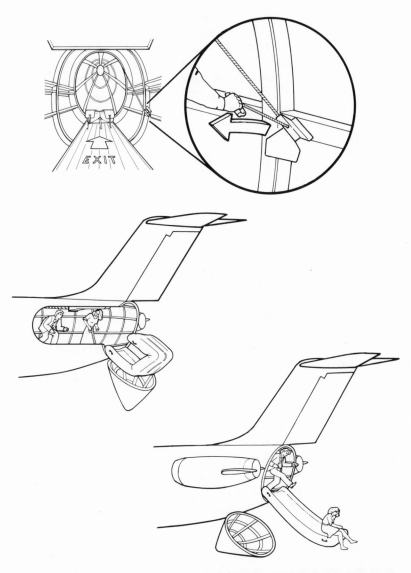

FIGURE 8.14. After the hatch or door is opened leading to the DC-9 tail cone, then a handle must be pulled to release the cone from the plane, thereby causing the slide to inflate. On the DC-9 Super 80 these steps occur automatically when the door is opened, as shown in Figure 8.13.

Stairs

Many B-737s have escape slides at all four of the floor-level exits. Some models, however, have stairs rather than an escape slide at the left rear door, which are usable during emergencies. That is, even if the emergency power is cut off, the door can still be opened and the stairs deployed. To open this door, a lever must be pulled toward you and the stairs pushed out (see Figure 8.15).

On some wide-body aircraft the Type I doors operate in a quite different manner from those on narrow-body planes. The two front doors on the DC-10 are Type I exits, and each has a handle, located on the partition forward of the exit, which must be lifted upward (see Figure 8.16). Then, because it is a plug door, it will move in a couple of inches before moving up into the ceiling. The slide should then drop out and automatically inflate.

Similarly, the L-1011 also has just one pair of Type I doors, but they are located in the rear of the plane. To open one of these doors, a plastic cover must be removed and a handle pulled down (see Figure 8.17). As with the DC-10, the door moves inward before moving up into the ceiling, and the slide should also drop out and inflate automatically.

Probably the most significant feature of the Type I door, a feature which sets it apart from other exits, is its width. It is wide enough to allow one person to pass through it in a standing or crouched position. Type III exits allow only one person to pass, but that person must step through the opening in the leg-body-leg method, a rather slow process. Type A doors, on the other hand, are wider than Type I exits, and allow two people to go through side by side.

Door width plus escape slide width are the main factors affecting evacuation speed at floor-level exits. During an emergency evacuation a bottleneck may occur at the door. (This assumes that the accident didn't cause excessive damage to the interior of the plane which prohibited passengers from getting to the doors in the first place.) Inside the cabin people usually move toward an exit faster than they can move through the exit; also, once outside, people can get off the escape slide and move away from the plane faster than they can move through the exits. Thus if a bottleneck occurs, it will probably be at the exit.

People can get out a Type I exit at a rate of about one passenger per second. On most planes a door can be opened and ready for use in about

FIGURE 8.15. Some B-737 have stairs at the left rear door.

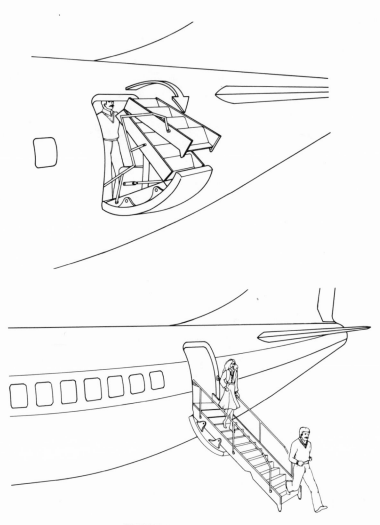

FIGURE 8.15 (*Continued*).

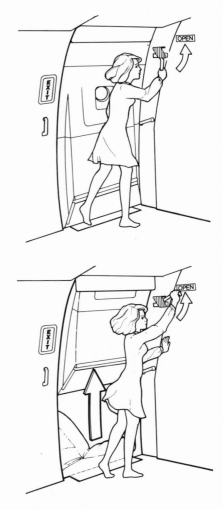

FIGURE 8.16. Opening the DC-10 front door, a Type I exit, causes the slide to inflate in an emergency.

ten seconds. In ninety seconds about eighty passengers should be able to move through a Type I exit. The FAA requires that for each forty-five passenger seats on a plane there must be at least one pair of Type I exits.[7] While allowing only forty-five passengers per pair of Type I exits may seem overly conservative when considering that eighty people can get out, it is not. Keep in mind that eighty passengers *on the average* are able to

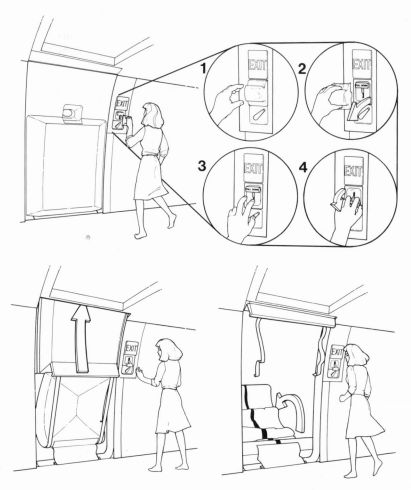

FIGURE 8.17. Procedure for opening a door on the L-1011. This same method will open both Type I and Type A exits. The slide automatically inflates in emergencies.

get out of an exit in ninety seconds. In some evacuation tests more than eighty people will be able to get out, but in other tests fewer than eighty will get out in the same period. Also, these figures were obtained under the relatively ideal circumstances surrounding an evacuation demonstration. Injuries, damage to the aircraft, smoke, and passenger unpreparedness are just some of the factors which could decrease this evacuation rate. Also, there is no guarantee that the cabin environment will remain habitable for ninety seconds, or that at least half of the exits will be usable. When all is considered, the FAA requirement of two Type I exits for each forty-five passenger seats seems reasonable.

Type A Exits

When the wide-body aircraft were developed, the decision was made to use wider doors rather than more doors to accommodate the greater number of passengers. A section of fuselage containing a door is heavier than a section without a door; more doors mean a heavier aircraft, one that costs more to operate.

The FAA allows 110 passenger seats for each pair of Type A doors compared to the 45 passenger seats for each pair of Type I doors. This means that five pair of Type I doors would be needed for 225 passengers, but only two pair of Type A doors could accommodate 220 passengers.

Type A exits must be at least 72 inches high and 42 inches wide. Because a Type A exit is heavier than a Type I, and more difficult to open, it is power-assisted: once the handle is moved past a certain point, or the door is moved a short distance, the door will open automatically. Some Type A exits, such as those on the B-747 and A-300, have hinges on the side so the door swings open, coming to rest along the side of the fuselage. Other Type A exits, such as those on the B-767, the L-1011, and the DC-10, have doors which slide up into the ceiling.

Most wide-body aircraft have a combination of Type I and Type A exits. The A-300, L-1011, and the DC-10 each have several pair of Type A exits and one pair of Type I exits. The B-747 has either four or five pair of Type A doors, depending on the model, in the main cabin and either one or two Type I doors in the upper lounge area.

The Type A exits found on these five different kinds of aircraft (B-747, B-767, DC-10, L-1011, and A-300) are operated in different manners. On the DC-10 and the B-767 the handle may be either to the left or the right of the door. Lifting the handle causes the door to move first inward, then up into the ceiling (see Figures 8.18 and 8.19).

The B-747 door, though larger, appears similar to doors on earlier models of Boeing aircraft, ranging from the B-707 to the B-737. The

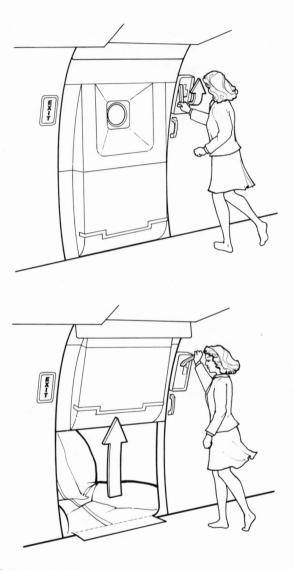

FIGURE 8.18. Opening a Type A door on the DC-10 causes slide inflation in an emergency.

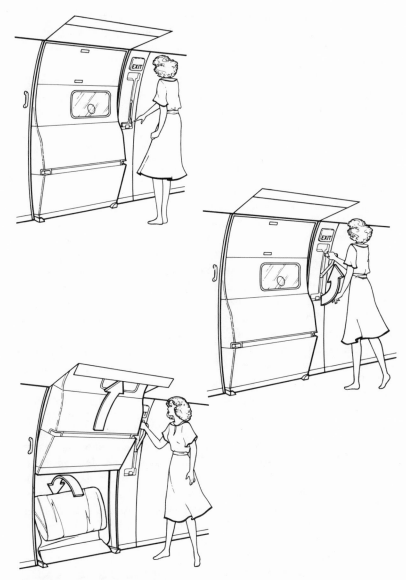

FIGURE 8.19. On the Boeing 767, the Type A exit is operated in this manner.

handle is on the door and must be rotated clockwise on the left side of the plane or counterclockwise on the right side. When the door is pulled slightly inward, the power-assist feature will take over and open the door automatically (see Figure 8.20).

The A-300 is a combination of the above two handle operations. The handle is on the door, as on the B-747, but must be lifted upward, as on the DC-10. When this is done, the door automatically opens outward and slides along the fuselage (see Figure 8.21).

ESCAPE SLIDES

In early days of aviation you might have traveled on airplanes such as the DC-3, which made its appearance in the mid-1930s. A few are still flying but are not used by major airlines. To escape from the DC-3 the 26 passengers had only to step out onto the ground. Later aircraft, such as the 95-passenger DC-7 which started flying in the mid-1950s, had door sills high enough above the ground so that escape devices, such as hand-held canvas chutes, had to be used (see Figure 8.22). The first two or three passengers used a rope to descend to the ground, and then held the ends of the chute while other passengers slid down. The early 1950s also saw the advent of the Comet, the first passenger-carrying jet aircraft, which was made by Hawker Siddeley, a British firm. This was closely followed by the B-707 and the DC-8. Jet planes, more efficient than propeller-driven planes, can carry more passengers. But because of the planes' larger size, the floors are higher off the ground: B-707s, which can carry 160 or more passengers, have door sills about 10.5 feet above the ground. Since hand-held chutes or rope ladders are not efficient enough to allow many passengers out in a short time, inflatable escape slides were developed. The first wide-body aircraft, the B-747, arrived on the scene in the late 1960s. Its huge size allows some models to carry over 500 people. Nevertheless the door sills on the main deck are sixteen feet above the ground. In the upper deck lounge, which has either one or two Type I exits, the door sills are about twenty-six feet above the ground.

The inflatable escape slide used on Type I exits, the door exits on narrow-body jet planes, is a single-lane slide. It's designed for one person to jump into at a time, although several people can be on it simultaneously

FIGURE 8.20. Procedure for opening the Boeing 747 Type A exits.

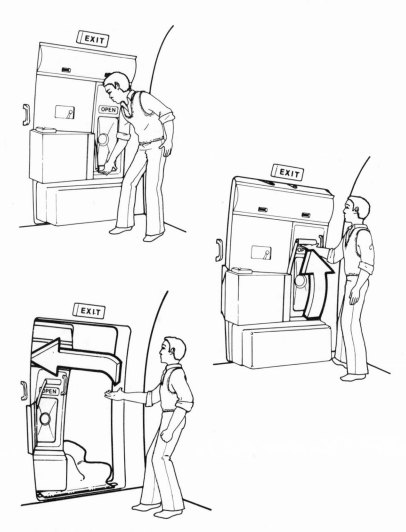

FIGURE 8.21. On the A-300 Type A door, simply lift the handle; the door will automatically open and the slide inflate.

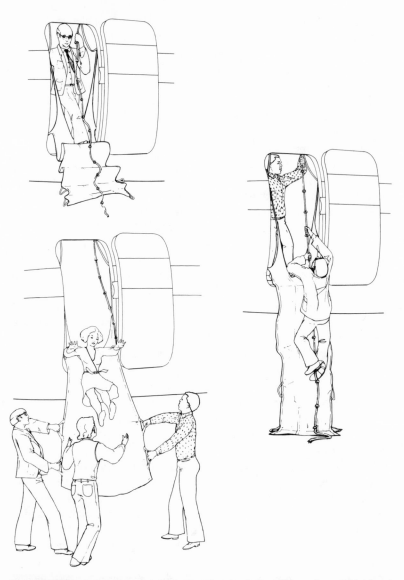

FIGURE 8.22. Hand-held canvas chutes were common in the 1950s, and can still be found on some aircraft around the world. They are no longer allowed on passenger-carrying aircraft in the U.S.

(see Figure 8.23). Type A doors are equipped with double-lane slides, which allow two people to leave the plane side-by-side.

An escape slide is comprised basically of large inflatable tubes, a sliding surface, and a tank of compressed gas underneath the slide. Most slides are yellow-orange in color, but this may be changing. In some accidents, such as the one Miss Hill was in, just the heat from the fire can deflate the common yellow-orange slides. As a result some slides are now being manufactured which have a highly reflective surface which will extend the time they can be near a fire without bursting.

The slide and the compressed-gas cylinder are stored in a container on the lower section of the door. Just before takeoff, the flight attendant "arms" the slide by attaching an end of the slide to the floor of the plane. If the door is opened when the slide is armed, the slide will be pulled out of its container and fall outside but will remain attached to the floor. Or so it is designed. But as Miss Hill reported, it may not necessarily fall out. A variety of reasons may account for this, such as damage caused by the accident itself. Thus if the slide doesn't fall out, it must be pushed out. Some slides automatically inflate once they drop below the level of the door sill, but others inflate only after a handle, located at the top of the slide, is pulled. Moreover, even automatically inflating slides can have a malfunction and not inflate. If this happens, you will need to pull the backup inflation handle at the top of the slide (see Figure 8.24).

When the plane reaches the terminal gate after landing, flight attendants "disarm" the slides so the doors can be opened without inflating the slides. Mechanical and human errors do occur, however, and slides are occasionally inflated by mistake. This is an expensive error since the slide must be repackaged prior to takeoff, a process requiring certified personnel who are not available at all airports.

The opposite error, much more serious as far as safety is concerned, can occur in an emergency: someone may disarm the slide before opening the door, resulting in an emergency exit with no escape slide. To keep from doing this you should know how to open the door without disarming the slide.

Figure 8.25 is a closeup of the L-1011 door-opening controls. After the aircraft has left the terminal, the flight attendant will arm the slide by turning the lever from the "Detach" to the "Engage" position. In the "Engage" position the slide is armed. The lever should remain in this

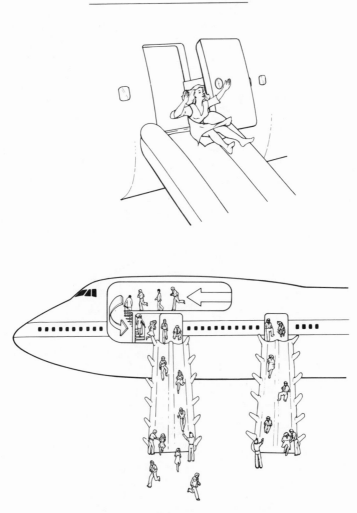

FIGURE 8.23. People jumping into a single-lane slide (*top*) and double-lane slides (*bottom*).

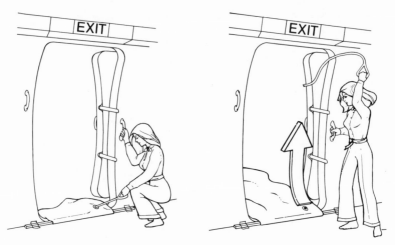

FIGURE 8.24. Pulling a slide-inflation handle.

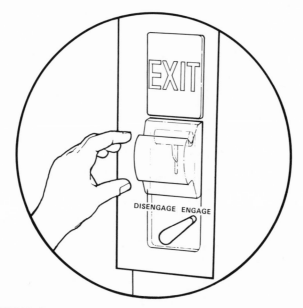

FIGURE 8.25. Detailed view of the L-1011 slide-arming lever. The small lever at the bottom will point toward either "Engage," or "Disengage." When pointed to "Engage," the slide will inflate when the door is opened.

position until the flight attendant switches it back again after the flight, and the plane is once again at the terminal gate.

To open the door in an emergency, the plastic cover must be removed and the red handle pulled down, as shown in Figure 8.17. This will cause the door to move up into the ceiling. Do not touch the disarm lever if it is in the "Engage" position. If you accidentally did turn it to the "Detach" position and opened the door, you would not have an escape slide at that exit.

Figures 8.26 and 8.27 are detailed views of the DC-10 handles. The slide-arming handle is the small handle next to the emergency door-opening handle. Lifting the small handle disarms the slide. To open the door and have the slide inflate in an emergency, just lift the large handle, which will be colored red (Figures 8.16 and 8.18). Some people may be inclined to lift both handles simultaneously, or the small one first, which will disarm the slide. If this is done, then the door will go up into the ceiling with the slide still attached. And if there was no electrical power aboard the plane (and there probably wouldn't be, since the pilots will most likely have shut down the engines which generate the electricity) it would be almost

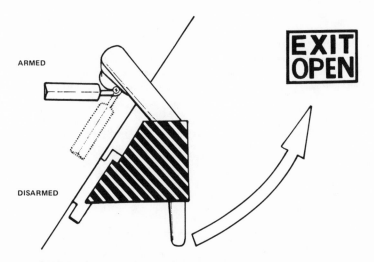

FIGURE 8.26. The front left door of the DC-10. The small handle on the left must be in the "Armed" position if the slide is to be inflated when the large handle (which is red) is lifted. The right front door is a mirror image of this arrangement.

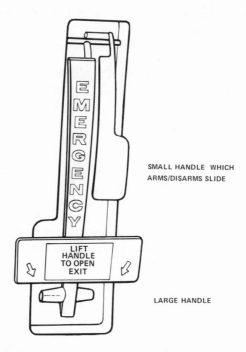

SMALL HANDLE WHICH
ARMS/DISARMS SLIDE

LARGE HANDLE

FIGURE 8.27. The handles that operate the six Type A doors of the DC-10. The small handle must be flush with the wall to arm the slide. Lifting the large handle, which will be red, will open the door and inflate the slide. The cover over the large handle, there to prevent inadvertent operation of the emergency handle, will fall away when the handle is lifted.

TABLE 8.2
Evacuation Rates at Various Types of Exits[a]

	Hand-held chutes	Type III	Type I	Type A
Passengers per second	.19	.5	1.0	1.74
Passengers out in 1 minute	11	30	60	104

[a] The figures in the hand-held chutes category are reported by Barry King.[8] The remaining figures are averages based on records of evacuations collected by the author. Evacuation rates vary considerably from one evacuation to another, and depend on many factors, including passenger preparedness, flight attendant leadership, damage to the aircraft, and injuries. The times do not include exit-opening or slide-preparation times.

impossible for a passenger to get the door or slide back down again. Pulling the handle down will not lower the door when the electrical power is off.

A simple rule in operating these doors is this: *Do the obvious*—if there is a placard on a handle with a phrase such as "Pull to Open," pull it. Don't try to outguess the design engineers; they have tried to make the system as simple as possible.

Passenger Behavior When Using Escape Slides

How quickly passengers move through the bottleneck at the door sill affects how quickly the plane can be evacuated. In the 1950s, when hand-held canvas chutes were common, most passengers sat down on the door sill and scooted off into the chute. Barry King, who was with the Civil Aeronautics Administration in 1951, reported escape times which, if compared with those obtained on current airplanes today, were indeed very slow.[8] On the average, a group of passengers took over five seconds each (0.19 passengers per second) to get from the doorway into the slide. What consumed the most time for these passengers was getting into a sitting position. In another test, trained flight attendants took an average of 2.54 seconds (0.39 passengers per second) to get out of the plane. While faster, this rate was considerably slower than the current rate of about 1 passenger per second at a Type I door, or 1.74 passengers per second at the wider Type A door. (See Table 8.2.)

Several reasons account for the increase in speed. When hand-held chutes were common, passengers were allowed, even encouraged, to sit. Now flight attendants are trained to make sure that passengers *don't* sit down at the door sill. This is not always an easy matter, considering the height of the door above the ground and the sharp angle (about 45°) of the slide to the ground. In evacuation demonstrations of the DC-10 we found that a person who sat at the door sill was significantly slower than one who jumped into the slide.[9] The transition time from door sill to escape slide was 1.208 seconds for a "sitter" and 0.875 seconds for a "jumper." While this one-third of a second may seem inconsequential, the fact is that 100 sitters would take about 33 seconds longer to get out of the plane than 100 jumpers. This 33 seconds could be of considerable importance to those at the end of the line if there was fire.

I was interested in the differences between people who jumped into the slide and those who sat down. The videotapes of 1,048 passengers who participated in four separate evacuations from the DC-10 were examined in detail.[10] Each of the passengers was identified by a numbered vest, later used in ascertaining that person's age and sex. These numbers could be seen on the video even though the tests were conducted in the dark by using low-light-level cameras and cameras sensitive to infrared light (a light not visible to the naked eye).

When the passengers got to the doorway it appeared to be completely dark outside except for the emergency lighting on the escape slide. In one evacuation test none of the passengers received any special instructions about how to get into the escape slide, except that when they got to the doorway a flight attendant told them to jump into the slide. Of the 217 passengers in this test, 130 (59.9 percent) jumped into the slide. The others sat at the door sill and scooted off. In other tests some passengers received a briefing card which instructed them, by means of pictures and words, to jump into the slide (see Figure 8.28). This increased the percentage of jumpers; of 401 passengers who read briefing cards instructing them to "Jump," 272 (67.8 percent) jumped into the slide. The increase in jumpers was statistically significant. While this was certainly a desired increase, it still meant that almost a third of the passengers were sitting at the door sill, which could not only slow down an evacuation but could even cause injury, as is explained below.

Both age and sex were factors affecting how long a person hesitated at the door sill. Men twenty to forty years of age hesitated the least, and

FIGURE 8.28. Pictorial instruction telling passengers to jump into the slide.

women fifty and above, the longest. In between were younger women and men fifty and above. I was interested in how sex and age affected escape behavior. Did the older men, and most women, actually move more slowly than younger men, or were they more likely to sit at the door sill? An analysis revealed that women jumpers were no slower than men jumpers and women sitters were no slower than men sitters. Older women who jumped were just as fast as younger women who jumped, and older women sitters were just as fast as the younger women who sat. The only statistically reliable difference was that twenty-year-old male sitters were slightly faster than men fifty years old and above who sat. But overall, the differences between the old and the young, and between men and women, were that more young people, especially young men, were likely to jump into the escape slide. Others took longer to get out because they were more likely to sit down. The conclusion was that if more people could be induced to jump, then everyone might get out faster. But it wasn't clear why more people didn't jump.

Possibly they misinterpreted the meaning of the instructions. Even though the briefing card showed a passenger jumping into an escape slide, it may have been interpreted by some to mean, simply, to hurry. And when these people got to the top of the slide they may have felt that quickly sitting and scooting off would be quite sufficient considering the height and steepness of the slide. But as we knew, a person cannot sit and scoot as quickly as he can jump. So safety cards were designed which told passengers to jump and *not* to sit. Pictures showing a person jumping, and showing a person sitting with an "X" through it to indicate not to sit, were used (see Figure 8.29). It was hoped that this would leave no doubt in the minds of the passengers: when you arrive at the door you can either jump into the slide or sit, but sitting is not allowed. In subsequent evacuation tests, those who saw this "Jump–Don't Sit" card were more likely to jump than those who saw only the card instructing them to jump. Of the 430 passengers who saw the "Jump–Don't Sit" card, 316 (73.5 percent) jumped, significantly more than those who saw the card instructing them only to "Jump."

However, 26.5 percent of the passengers still didn't jump, and I was interested in finding out what influenced their behavior more than the instructions given on the safety information card or by the flight attendant. One factor was the behavior of the person ahead of each passenger; passengers tended to imitate those in front, at least at some of the doors. The

FIGURE 8.29. Instructions to jump and not to sit.

imitation was quite noticeable. Typically, several people in a row would jump into the slide, then someone, usually a woman, would sit. Passengers who followed her were more likely to sit than if she had jumped. After several sitters, another passenger, usually a man, would jump and several passengers after him would also jump. An analysis of the behavior of 760 passengers in two different evacuation tests aboard the DC-10 revealed that these results were statistically significant. Passengers tended to imitate those in front, and the person who started a string of sitters was more likely to be a woman than a man, whereas the person who started a string of jumpers was more likely to be a man. But imitation was found only at the front and rear doors of the plane, and not found at the two middle doors, though why this should be was not clear.

Another reason why some passengers didn't jump into an escape slide may have been fear of injury. In actuality there may be a greater chance of injury while sitting. In one instance a woman sat at the door sill and right behind her was a tall man who, of course, stopped moving forward as she sat down. Other passengers behind him, however, kept moving forward since they could not see the seated woman. When this happened he was pushed over the top of her, and as he tried to step around her he fell head first off the side of the slide. Luckily, safety nets had been installed and he was not injured. But if this had occurred during an actual emergency evacuation he could have been seriously hurt. While the lady was uninjured, she also could easily have been hurt had he fallen directly on her. I am not aware of any serious injuries which have occurred as a result of jumping onto an undamaged escape slide.

Many of the injuries which occur during actual evacuations are of a minor nature. One of the most common, and least serious, occurs when a person rubs against the surface of the slide. It is a piece of canvas with a rubberized coating, and if you hit it with a bare elbow when sliding down you might easily receive an abrasion. If you ever must use one of these slides, remember not to grab the sides of the slide, or to try to slow yourself by pushing against the sides. The slide itself will act to slow your descent before you reach the end through changes in texture or shape near the end.

Serious injury can occur if you use a slide which shouldn't be used. Don't use a deflated slide, or one that does not reach the ground, unless there is absolutely no other way out of a plane and you must get out immediately. During takeoff from San Fransisco a B-747 with 199 passengers hit the lights at the end of the runway.[11] The structures holding the lights pierced the underside of the aircraft and three sections of metal rammed through the cabin floor. One section severely injured the leg of one passenger and badly lacerated the upper arm of another. A second piece of metal impaled four unoccupied seats, one behind the other, and according to one passenger, stopped four inches from his daughter's chest.[12] A third section passed through several seats and lavatories in the rear of the plane. Incredibly, only two passengers were injured, and luckily there were two physicians aboard. They, along with a flight attendant, who was a nurse, gave medical assistance to the injured passengers. But the aircraft had lost three of its four hydraulic systems and had sustained other damage, a consequence of which was impaired control of the steering during landing.

The aircraft, which was to have flown to Japan, was filled with fuel that had to be dumped before it could safely land again at San Francisco. This process took one hour and 42 minutes, during which time news of the accident spread. When the plane finally landed there were many cameras recording the event. It landed very hard, damaging its landing gear. It veered off to the right onto an unpaved surface and came to a stop about a mile from where it landed.

An emergency evacuation of the plane was ordered. Unfortunately, four of the ten evacuation slides were unusable, some because of damage which occurred during impact with the light standards or the hard landing, and one because the wind was so strong it blew the slide horizontal to the fuselage. As the evacuation proceeded many passengers moved to the rear exits, most of which were usable. This shifting of weight, plus the fact that the landing gear had been damaged, caused the huge airplane to settle back onto its tail. When this happened the forward doors, with their slides attached, lifted upward so that the slides hung straight down. In this position they should not have been used—but they were used and eight serious injuries resulted. More people were injured getting out of the plane than during the accident.

In summary, there are many variations on where doors are located on the plane, how they are opened, and how the slides are inflated or the stairs lowered. This information is provided on the passenger safety information cards, or in some cases shown in passenger briefing movies. Don't open exits if there is fire or smoke directly outside. At night you might not realize beforehand that it's smoky outside until the exit is opened, in which case you should try to close the exit again, something which is not always possible. If there is fire or smoke outside, use another exit. If you open a Type III exit, get rid of the hatch by either throwing it outside or putting it on an empty seat—don't put it in the aisle leading to the exit where it can trip up other passengers. At Type I or Type A exits, use the emergency door-opening handle—don't pull any other levers or handles since you could accidently disarm the escape slide. If the escape slide does not fall out when the door is open, push it out. If it doesn't inflate, pull the inflation handle. Evacuation slides are very effective devices for helping a large number of people get out of a plane in a short time. Keep in mind, however, not to carry any hand baggage with you to avoid deflating the slides and causing injuries. In addition, read the safety information card to see if you should remove your shoes. Once outside, move quickly away from the plane to a distance of about 500 feet, preferably in a direction against the wind. Again, refrain from smoking because the fuel could ignite.

REFERENCES

1. *Special Investigation Report*, National Transportation Safety Board, Washington, D.C., Report no. SIR 81–4, 1981.
2. *Aircraft Accident Report, DC-10, Los Angeles, Calif., March 1, 1978*, National Transportation Safety Board Report no. AAR–79–1, Washington, D.C., 1979.
3. Deposition given before the National Transportation Safety Board in an investigation of an accident involving a DC-10, Registry N68045, at Los Angeles, March 1, 1978, Investigation no. DCA 78–A–A995, vol. 2, pp. 50–77.
4. *Aircraft Accident Report, DC-10, Los Angeles, Calif., March 1, 1978*.
5. *Special Investigation Report*, Report no. SIR 81–4, p. 7.
6. C. Hayden LeRoy, "Survival Study: Modern Commercial Jet Aircraft Landing Accident with Subsequent Interior Fire," paper presented to the Aerospace Medical Associations 38th Annual Scientific Meeting, Washington, D.C., April 11, 1967. LeRoy is an air safety investigator with the NTSB, Washington, D.C.
7. *Federal Aviation Regulations, part 25.807*.
8. Barry King, *Aircraft Emergency Evacuation: A Method for Evaluating Devices, Procedures and Exit Provisions*, Office of Aviation Safety, Civil Aeronautics Administration. U.S. Department of Commerce, April 1951.
9. Daniel Johnson, and H. B. Altman, Jr., "Analyses of Passenger Behavior during Four Full-Scale Emergency Evacuations," Report no. MDC J5423, Douglas Aircraft Company, Long Beach, Calif., 1972.
10. Daniel Johnson and H. B. Altman, Jr., "Effects of Briefing Card Information on Passenger Behavior during Aircraft Evacuation Demonstrations," *Proceedings of the Human Factors Society Convention*, Human Factors Society, Santa Monica, Calif., 1973.
11. *Aircraft Accident Report, Boeing 747, N747PA, Flight 845, San Francisco, Calif., July 30, 1971*, Report no. NTSB–AAR–72–17, National Transportation Safety Board, Washington, D.C., 1972.
12. "Peril in the Escape Chutes," *National Observer*, Aug. 9, 1971.

Chapter Nine

DITCHINGS

There are many potential hazards associated with a ditching—an unexpected water landing in which there was little, if any, preparation time. The plane may have touched down so smoothly that you wouldn't even realize it had stopped on water and not on land. On the other hand it may break apart and quickly sink. You may have already put your life jacket on, or there may not even be any life jackets on your plane. The water outside could be calm and mild, or it may be freezing with waves twelve feet high. You may have ended up so close to the shore that you could walk to it, or you might be thousands of miles from land. There may not be fire, or floating fuel could set the surface of the water ablaze or cause chemical burns. There may or may not be enough life rafts aboard. If there are, you may not end up on one that has a radio transmitter signaling your position. Rescue craft may be there as soon as the plane touches down, or it could take many hours to find and pull you from the sea.

With so many potential hazards it may seem ludicrous to state that flying over water is really quite safe. But it is true because of the very high reliability of jet airplanes. Ditchings used to be relatively common with propeller-driven airplanes, but they are very unusual with jet airplanes. Even so, the probability of having one is not quite zero.

A DC-9 which ran out of fuel was ditched thirty miles from St. Croix, Virgin Islands, on May 2, 1970. There were six crewmembers (the captain and first officer, a navigator, a purser, a steward and stewardess) along with fifty-seven passengers. Of the sixty-three people aboard, forty survived. All crewmembers, except for the stewardess, were rescued. Of the sixteen men and twenty women pulled from the ocean, one of the men was pronounced dead on arrival at the hospital; the remaining thirteen men, six women, and two children were lost at sea. Much of the information given below comes from NTSB reports.[1]

The aircraft departed from JFK in New York and headed for St. Maarten in the West Indies. The entire flight took place during daytime. Nearly all of the passengers had flown before. The preflight briefing included a demonstration on how to use the life jackets, information which was also provided on the safety information card. The card also gave information on emergency brace positions and methods of escape, information that would be vitally important before the flight was over.

The aircraft had more than enough fuel to reach St. Maarten, but when nearing the airport the pilot was told by ATC that the airport was below landing minimums; that is, the weather didn't allow enough visibility for a safe landing. The pilot then requested, and received, routing to San Juan Airport. Later on he was informed that the weather at St. Maarten had improved, and since that's where the passengers had wanted to go in the first place, he headed back. But again the weather at St. Maarten worsened. After several circling approaches in which the crew apparently decided it would be too risky to land, they asked for and received direct routing to the St. Thomas airport. By this time there wasn't enough fuel left to get to St. Thomas.

Approximately ten minutes before the actual ditching, the captain called the purser to the cockpit, telling him to have the passengers put on their life vests as a precautionary measure because they were low on fuel and might have to ditch. Actually the ditching was inevitable, but the purser didn't realize the seriousness of the situation. He went to the rear of the plane and told the passengers over the public address system to start putting on their life preservers. In the front of the plane the steward and stewardess began helping passengers find and don their life vests.

The purser made his way to the forward section, helping passengers with their life vests along the way. Many passengers later reported that they had difficulties in finding and removing the life vests from beneath the seats. A major problem was unsnapping the strap that holds the packet containing the life vest under the seat. Other passengers needed help putting on their vests.

At least five passengers did not refasten their safety belts after donning their vests. Several took pillows from the overhead rack, assuming different forms of brace positions. Some passengers looked out the windows, thinking that the descending plane was making an overwater approach to the runway—but there was no runway ahead of them. The pilots did not make any announcements to the passengers, perhaps because the ditching of an aircraft is an unusual maneuver, requiring great skill. The pilots must slow the plane as much as possible by landing into the wind, the direction of which is sometimes hard to determine from a plane over the ocean. Also, they must strike the water in such a direction that the aircraft does not break apart from hitting a wave on the wrong side of the crest, or at the wrong angle. The pilots may have been so busy with this that further information to the passengers may have seemed of secondary importance.

The navigator, who was positioning one of the life rafts near a forward exit, suddenly sensed that the aircraft was about to hit the water. He shouted to the purser and steward to sit down. While he didn't have time to fasten his safety belt, he was able to hold onto it during the accident.

Several survivors reported that just before impact the lights in the plane went out, probably because the engines, which supply electrical power to all but the emergency lights (which operate on their own batteries), ran out of fuel. Survivors described the deceleration as three extremely violent impacts. The force threw forward all who didn't have safety belts on, including the stewardess who was standing in the aisle helping two passengers put on their vests. At least eleven passengers, eight of whom survived, were thrown from their seats: five because they did not have their safety belts fastened, and six because their safety belts snapped and failed to hold them. One couple reportedly unfastened their belts before impact in order to be able to evacuate faster. Although they survived, this was an extremely dangerous, foolhardy gamble. Many unrestrained passengers, including the stewardess, were thrown to the forward end of the cabin, injuring and killing not only themselves, but those seated there.

The plane immediately started to fill with water, and floated for only about five or six minutes. Fortunately, there was a man aboard who made it a point to sit next to an exit whenever he flew. (The similarity between this man's actions and Horsfall's behavior, described in Chapter One, are striking.) After the plane came to a stop in the water this man, who was mentally prepared for the emergency, opened the overwing exit. This opening became the focal point which attracted immediate attention in the now-dim cabin, and through it three-quarters of the survivors escaped. It was the only emergency exit opened from within the cabin (with the exception of the galley door, which was not visible from the passenger compartment) despite the fact that passengers were seated next to two of the other three overwing exits.

Some of the crew tried to launch a raft at the front of the plane, when it suddenly inflated *inside,* entrapping the first officer who had just come into the cabin. The navigator and the steward couldn't puncture it for lack of anything sharp enough to cut through the tough material. The first officer couldn't remember how he escaped from the plane. The captain, hearing the life raft inflate right behind the cockpit door, climbed out one of the cockpit windows, swam around to the side of the plane, and opened the overwing exits opposite the one opened by the passenger. He helped two passengers out.

Meanwhile, outside the sinking plane the navigator found and inflated an evacuation slide from one of the doors, which served as a rallying point for everyone. The co-pilot climbed on top of the slide and assumed command of the situation, while the captain and the navigator rounded up scattered survivors, bringing them together. It became apparent that there were not enough hand-holds on the side of the slide and only a few people could actually get on top of the slide itself. So the co-pilot had the men remove their ties and belts and tie them to the handles on the side of the escape slide. In this way nearly everyone could obtain some support from the slide. Some passengers, though, many of whom could not swim, relied on their life vests and made no attempt to reach the slide.

A B-727 on its way to San Juan was diverted to the site by ATC to report on the accident scene. It spotted a life raft about fifteen minutes after the ditching. Another aircraft reached the area about thirty-five minutes later and dropped two life rafts. The pilot and navigator swam to the rafts, but were unable to return back to the passengers with them since rafts are not equipped with paddles, motors, or sails. The captain lost sight of everyone, and the navigator, after unsuccessfully attempting to inflate a raft, started towing it back in the general direction of the survivors but exhausted himself.

A Coast Guard helicopter then arrived on the scene, dropping two more life rafts, but one did not inflate and the other was dropped downwind, out of reach of the survivors. Moreover, rescuing the survivors was difficult because of low clouds and rough seas. The first passengers were pulled from the water after a Navy helicopter reached the scene ninety minutes after the ditching. A total of four helicopters, two from the Coast Guard and one from the Marine Corps, in addition to the Navy helicopter, were able to pull the last of the forty-one people (one of whom was dead) from the ocean about three hours after the accident.

Fortunately, this type of accident is rare. It is the only one of its kind to have occurred with a passenger-carrying jet aircraft since the beginning of the jet age in 1955. Survivability of the passengers was undoubtedly improved both because there was a warning period of five to ten minutes, and because the plane settled into the sea in a controlled manner. However, rescue was slow because the accident took place thirty miles from shore.

Because of this ditching, I became interested in the problems associated with overwater flights. On most flights you will fly over some water, so there is a legal requirement that all commercial planes in the U.S. be equipped with seat flotation cushions or life jackets.[2] The seat flotation cushion is easier to use but it doesn't give as much protection as a life jacket. Furthermore, not all seat cushions are flotation cushions. If your plane does not have seat flotation cushions, then you can count on there being life jackets aboard—and some planes have both.

If you are to fly farther than fifty nautical miles (fifty-seven statute miles) from shore, then the FAA requires that your plane not only have a life jacket for each passenger, but that it also carry life rafts, or specially designed inflatable escape slides which also serve as rafts.[3] Some airlines, however, have received waivers from these regulations enabling them to fly farther than fifty nautical miles from shore without having to carry rafts, but they must have life jackets for each passenger—seat flotation cushions alone are not adequate.

SEAT FLOTATION CUSHIONS

Some airplane seat cushions are designed for supporting a person in the water; others are not. But even those not designed as a flotation device are made of polyurethane foam, which will float. But they will not support you for long because, just as with a sponge, when squeezed or held under the surface they absorb water and loose buoyancy. Ernest McFadden, a scientist who was with the FAA's research labs in Oklahoma City, evaluated the buoyancy of a seat cushion not designed for flotation.[4] The test was conducted to see if the cushion would provide enough buoyancy to support a fourteen-pound weight for a period of eight hours. This is one of the requirements under FAA Technical Standard Order TSO-C72b, which, to be approved, all seat flotation cushions must meet. After ten minutes the cushion had lost some buoyancy though it could still support the fourteen-pound weight. It was then taken from the water, the weight removed, and a person took it back into the water for five minutes, also a requirement of TSO-C72b. Although an attempt was made not to squeeze the cushion, it did give off a considerable amount of air bubbles. After five minutes the fourteen-pound weight was again attached to the cushion, which then sank to the bottom, demonstrating that seat cushions not designed for flotation lose buoyancy in the water.

Seat flotation cushions designed to give support in the water have polyurethane foam surrounding a block of closed-cell polyethylene, a substance that does not absorb water. Closed-cell polyethylene remains buoyant even after it has been in the water for many hours. In another study McFadden tested five different flotation cushions, each held by a person in water for a period of eight hours.[5] The buoyancy of each cushion was tested every hour, using a fourteen-pound weight, in a pool of fresh 85°F water. (In colder water, or in salt water, the buoyancy of the cushion would be greater than in warm, fresh water.) Four of the five flotation cushions had greater than fourteen pounds of buoyancy at the end of eight hours, but the buoyancy of one cushion had dropped to twelve pounds, which leads to the question of how much buoyancy is required. Several factors contribute to better flotation:

1. The lower the temperature of the water;
2. The greater the density of the water, e.g., the saltier the water;
3. The lower your body density, e.g., the more fat you have in relation to muscle and bone; and
4. The greater your lung volume.

In another study Ernest McFadden and Hiley Harrison determined the buoyancy of twelve men in warm fresh water. The scientists found that when the men inhaled, eight of them had a positive buoyancy—which allowed them to float—but four did not and would have sunk unless they were able to swim or had additional support such as a life jacket. The buoyancy of these men ranged from 4.59 to −0.96 pounds. After exhaling the buoyancy dropped, ranging from 3.05 to −2.50 pounds. After exhalation, five of the men had negative buoyancy.[6]

But the question of how much buoyancy is needed is not easily answered. From the above study one might erroneously conclude that only

2.5 pounds of buoyancy would be needed to keep even the densest man afloat. But after a ditching, there are other factors to consider. First, you don't simply want to remain floating with your body just at the surface of the water—your head should be above the surface. And since an adult's head can weigh 10 pounds, 12.5 pounds of buoyancy would be needed to keep the head of the least buoyant of the twelve men out of the water. In addition, if the men in the study had been wearing shoes and clothing they might have required more support because these items of clothing have a negative buoyancy of their own. On the other hand if they were in water that was saltier and colder than the water in the above study, water that is more like the lakes and oceans around the U.S., less buoyant support would be needed.

A seat flotation cushion has straps or loops designed for you to hold when in the water, which are located on the reverse side from the one on which you sit (see Figure 9.1). In most cases the flotation cushion is the bottom cushion, but on a few planes it's the back cushion (see Figure 9.2). The safety briefing card should indicate this information.

When in the water, don't hold the cushion tightly against your chest expecting to stay in an upright position with your head out of the water— the cushion's buoyancy will tend to push your chest and head back into the water (see Figure 9.3). Since your scalp is extremely vascular, much heat loss can occur if it is in cold water. Keep your head out of the water

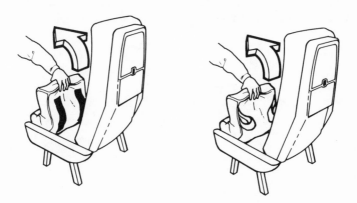

FIGURE 9.1. Some seat flotation cushions are equipped with straps (*left*) and others have loops (*right*) to hold onto when in the water.

FIGURE 9.2. On a few planes, the seat back is the flotation cushion.

to decrease the onset of hypothermia which results from the loss of body heat. Try to ride the cushion, getting as much of your head and shoulders on top as you can (see Figure 9.4).

LIFE JACKETS

The life jackets (also called life preservers and life vests) aboard airplanes are quite different from the ones aboard boats with which you may be more familiar. Those used by boaters are noninflatable while those

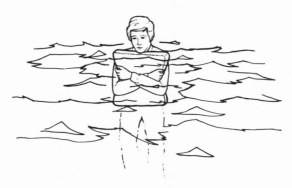

FIGURE 9.3. Trying to hold the flotation cushion in a vertical position in the water will force your head back into the water.

FIGURE 9.4. The correct manner of using the seat flotation cushion is to get as much of your head and shoulders on top of the cushion as possible to avoid hypothermia from the cold water.

on commercial airplanes are inflatable, and are more compact when stowed. One reason inflatable vests are not to be used on boats is because it is difficult to tell if the carbon dioxide cylinders, which inflate the vests, have been expended or not. In one study 500 boaters were given inflatable vests for use on their boats for one year, at the end of which it was found that 20 percent of the vests would not inflate when the inflation tabs were pulled.[7] Many of the unusable vests may have been inflated accidentally during that period and the carbon dioxide cartridges not replaced. In addition, the metal snaps can corrode in the wet environment aboard a boat, so that the straps may not hold the person up in the water. Also, an inflatable vest can easily be punctured aboard boats. But even though these vests are not approved for use on boats, many are stolen each year from planes, probably for use on boats. The boater who thinks this vest will do him any good is mistaken. The U.S. Coast Guard still requires one approved "personal flotation device" for each person on board[8] and no inflatable vest has ever been approved. Hence, a boater with inflatable vests for his passengers could be cited. Worse still, when he needs the vest the boater may find that the snaps won't work or the vest won't inflate. One further problem arises in the event of an emergency when the airplane passenger needs the vest; none might be available if one of the previous passengers has taken it.

On most airplanes life jackets are stowed in a pouch under the seat. There are several exceptions, as in the case when two or three vests are stowed in the back of the seat in front of you, or in front of the person next to you. Another exception is when the vests are stowed in overhead compartments. (See Figures 9.5, 9.6, and 9.7.)

There are several potential problems with vests stowed under the seats. You cannot easily see if the compartment is empty or not. Another problem is that the carry-on baggage of the passenger behind you could be pressed so firmly under your seat that the life vest cannot easily be removed. A third problem is that if your seat is very close to the one in front, you may have some difficulty leaning forward far enough to reach the container. A British Aerospace HS-748 unsuccessfully attempted to take off from Sumburgh Airport in the Shetland Islands on July 31, 1979. It ran off the end of the runway and ended up in the sea about fifty yards from shore. The plane, which was carrying forty-four passengers and a crew of three, immediately started to fill with water. Seventeen of the people did not survive. Of the thirty survivors, six were able to get their life jackets on, though three had problems inflating them. Of the twenty-four who did not use life jackets, six reported that they tried but were unable to remove the vests from the storage containers under the seat. The investigation showed that this problem could have been due to the close proximity of the seats—"the seat in front presented an obstacle to bending forward sufficiently to reach the pouch."[9]

Before an overwater flight you should therefore feel the container to determine if a vest is inside. Try to feel for the snap, which usually has a tag attached to it, which must be pulled down in order to get the container open. You will also be able to tell if the briefcase of the person behind

FIGURE 9.5. The usual storage location for life jackets is in a container under the seat.

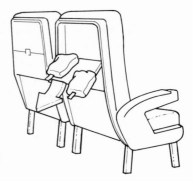

FIGURE 9.6. Some aircraft have vests stowed in one of the seat backs.

you is pushing against the vest. Another problem with vests located under the seat becomes evident following an unexpected water landing when you reach for your life vest but it is underwater.

A B-727 was on approach to Pensacola Regional Airport in Florida about 9:00 P.M. on May 8, 1978, when it landed in Escambia Bay, three miles from the runway, resting in about twelve feet of water. Three of the passengers drowned while forty-nine others, and the crew of six, were

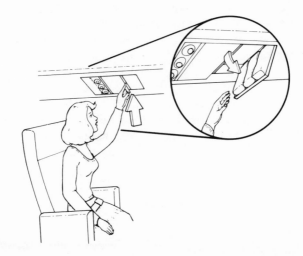

FIGURE 9.7. Some aircraft have vests stowed in an overhead compartment.

rescued.[10] Many of the passengers thought the landing was normal: "I thought we were on land," one passenger said; "it wasn't until the water poured in up to my knees that I realized we were in the bay."[11] Another passenger said, "It was not a bad flight. There was no announcement we were going to crash. Without any warning it went into the water. I thought it was a real bad landing until things started rushing by me. Then I realized we were in the water."

The plane carried life vests under the seats but was not required to have life rafts or seat flotation cushions. Yet twenty-four passengers, and even the crew, believed that the seat cushions could be used for flotation. Fourteen passengers actually tried to use them in the water, but said they came apart, giving no support. Since the plane was on a flight from Mobile to Pensacola, which did not fly over fifty nautical miles from shore, there was no legal requirement for briefing the passengers on how to use the vests. But even those who knew of the vests had trouble removing them from under the seats because of the rising water.[12]

Some of the passengers helped others escape. One man, age sixty-two, helped his invalid wife through an emergency exit out of the plane after getting a life vest on her. But he didn't put one on himself. She got out safely and survived, but he wasn't so lucky. His body was later found floating near the plane.[13]

There are several reasons why there were only three drownings in this accident. Since the water was calm the plane did not break apart on impact. The water was warm so that hypothermia was not a problem. It was only twelve feet deep, so some of the passengers were able to hang onto the plane or stand on the wings until the plane settled deeper into the mud. Most fortunate of all was that a tugboat, pushing a barge, was off course and lost on that foggy night. The 727 came down within 300 feet of the boat. The tug pilot later said, "If we hadn't by chance been there, many people would have died. They couldn't have made it. After they got on the barge, I know it was an hour before the boats found us."[14]

Problems in Donning Life Jackets

One possible cause of some of the problems experienced by passengers trying to put on life vests is difficulty in trying to read the instructions on the vest. Commonly, the instructions are printed on the front of the vest,

FIGURE 9.8. Instructions printed on
some vests appear upside down once
the vest is on.

but when the vest is put over the head the written instructions appear upside
down (see Figure 9.8).

Another method of instructing the passenger, which is surprisingly
common considering how poor the design is, is having the instructions
printed on the back of the vest (see Figure 9.9). The instructions must be

FIGURE 9.9. Some vests have instructions
printed on the back.

read before donning, and then, with the vest on and the instructions out of sight, you must remember how to adjust the straps and inflate it.

I conducted a study to find out how difficult it really was for passengers to put on life vests, and whether videotaped instructions would help them. Specifically, I used an experimental TV demonstration of life vest donning to see if it was any better than the standard demonstration given by the flight attendant, or no demonstration at all. The vest I used had written instructions on the front like the ones aboard the DC-9 that ditched near St. Maarten.[15] The donning method is shown in Figure 9.10.

After removing the vest from its storage container and taking it out of its package, the first step is to put it over your head. You then bring two straps, which hang down the back, around to the front and connect them to a "D" ring. The ends of these straps must be pulled tight to hold the vest around your waist snugly in order to keep it from coming off if you jump into the water. It could come off because the inflated portion of the vest rests on top of your shoulders. If you jumped into the water feet first, the vest would tend to stay on the surface but your momentum would carry you below. Unless the vest straps were pulled tightly around your waist the vest would be pulled off you.

The next step is to pull the inflation tabs. If they don't work, as sometimes happens, then you must blow into "oral-inflation tubes" which are sandwiched between two flaps of the vest. You then pull a tab attached to a battery on the front of the vest; this allows a light, located on your shoulder, to glow once the battery is in the water.

To summarize, a successful donning involves these six steps:

1. Pull the vest over your head.
2. Snap the hooks to the "D" ring.
3. Tighten the straps.
4. Pull the inflation tabs.
5. Blow into the oral-inflation tubes if step 4 did not inflate the vest.
6. Pull the battery tab.

Each of fifty-four subjects were randomly assigned to one of four groups. About half the subjects in each group were men and the other half women. Also, about half the men and half the women in each group were under forty years of age; the others were older. Each subject was tested individually.

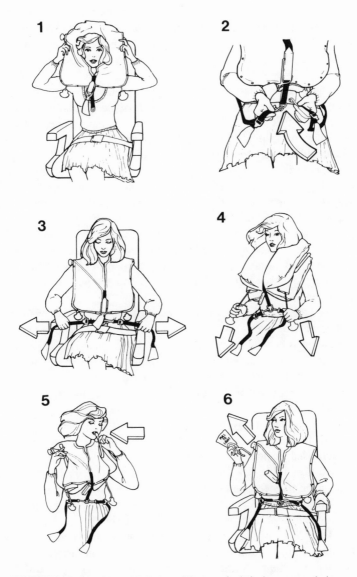

FIGURE 9.10. Donning and inflating a life vest of relatively common design.

Group 1 was the control group, which did not see any special instructions other than the written instructions printed on the front describing how to put on the life vest. Group 1 simulated those passengers who either do not watch, or cannot see, the flight attendant demonstrate how to don a life vest.

Group 2 saw a videotape of a flight attendant demonstrate how to put on the life vest at an apparent distance which would approximate a person standing thirty feet away. This is the distance that a passenger in the rear of cabin may be from a flight attendant giving the demonstration. Group 2 simulated those passengers who pay attention to the safety briefing.

Group 3 saw the same videotape as Group 2, except that immediately after each step in the sequence a closeup view of that same step was presented and appeared as if seen from four feet away. So Group 3 saw each step twice, once in closeup.

Group 4 subjects saw each step only once, but the zoom capability of the lens was used so the subjects saw the flight attendant start each step at the thirty-foot distance. Then the camera zoomed in for detail to the same closeup distance of four feet used in Group 3, and then back out for perspective.

Immediately after viewing the videotape, or in the case of Group 1 right after the subject was told that he would receive no special instructions, each person was handed a life vest which had been folded but unpackaged, and was told to put it on and inflate it as quickly as possible. The carbon dioxide cartridges, already exhausted, would not inflate the vest, so the oral-inflation tubes had to be used. Other than that, the vest was fully functional.

I had expected the performance of Group 1 to be the poorest, and that of Groups 3 and 4 to be the best. And that is what was found. However, I was surprised at how poorly many of the subjects in all four groups performed (see Table 9.1). Two-thirds of those in Group 1 were unable to perform the six steps, and those who did took an average of nearly three minutes. Half the subjects in Group 2 performed these steps, but they took nearly two minutes. The proportion of subjects in Groups 3 and 4 who were able to do all of the six steps was not statistically greater than those in the other groups, but they were able to put them on faster. There was no difference in the performance between subjects in Group 3 and 4.

Since steps 5 and 6 (using the oral-inflation tubes and pulling the battery tab) are of less importance to immediate survival than steps 1

TABLE 9.1

Number of Subjects and Life Jacket Donning Time per
Group for Completing 6 Steps[a]

Group number	Group 1	Group 2	Group 3	Group 4
Number of subjects per group	12	14	13	15
Number to complete donning	4	7	8	7
Average time (sec.) for complete donning	177.25	118.14	97.87	74.86

[a] Based on a set of orthogonal comparisons, Group 1 was significantly slower than Groups 2, 3, and 4 combined, $t = 4.106$, dF $= 22, p < .0005$. Group 1 was also significantly slower than Group 2 alone, $t = 2.63, p < .01$. Group 2 was significantly slower than Groups 3 and 4 combined, $t = 1.93, p < .05$, but Groups 3 and 4 did not differ significantly, $t = 1.24$. There was no significant difference in the number of subjects in each group who completed donning; chi square $= 0.69$.

through 4, performance of the first four steps was analyzed (see Table 9.2). Half of Group 1 was able to perform these necessary steps, taking over a minute and a half to do so; Group 2 took a minute, while Groups 3 and 4 took about forty seconds. But even with the best instructions we could come up with, a third of the subjects simply could not put the vest on correctly or inflate it. Since these subjects were secretaries and engineers of a large aircraft manufacturer, they were probably more sophisticated than the average passenger. Considering that the test was conducted in a well-lighted room as opposed to a crowded airplane filling with water, I believe it's obvious that a problem exists in the design and use of these vests.

In analyzing the errors, I found that no one had a problem putting the vest over the head (see Table 9.3). But without the special videotaped instructions developed for this test, some subjects made the important error of not snapping the straps to the front of the vest, while the most common error was in not tightening the straps once the hooks were snapped. Unless both of these actions are taken, the vest would not give adequate support and could even slip off a person in water. Pulling the inflation tabs was not a problem, but finding the oral-inflation tubes was, especially for those

TABLE 9.2
Number of Subjects and Donning Time for Completing
Steps 1-4[a]

Group number	Group 1	Group 2	Group 3	Group 4
Number of subjects per group	12	14	13	15
Number to complete donning	7	8	11	9
Average time (sec.) for complete donning	97.00	68.75	42.45	39.22

[a] Group 1 was significantly slower than Group 2, $t = 3.44$, $p < .0005$. Group 2 was slower than Groups 3 and 4 combined, $t = 2.45$, $p < .01$, while Groups 3 and 4 did not differ significantly, $t = .1$.

who didn't watch a demonstration. Most subjects pulled the battery tab, but in many cases this was done while the person was trying to inflate the vest; many pulled anything they could grab in an attempt to inflate it. I believe that if the vest had inflated when the inflation tabs were pulled, the battery tab, which hangs down near the waist, probably would not have been pulled.

This test was conducted with one type of vest which, though common, is not the only design available. Other designs have different numbers of straps and some have snaps which connect in a different manner. One design has permanently connected straps. The following conclusions, therefore, are valid only for this type of vest: First, a person who doesn't watch the life-vest demonstration will take longer to put on the vest than one who does watch. Second, showing a closeup view of certain steps in the sequence can decrease the time it takes for passengers to put on the vest. Third, even with the improved instructional videotape developed for this test, many people have great difficulty putting on the vest.

The FAA has determined that passengers should be able to don the vests more quickly, and that vests should have more buoyancy, than previously required. Vests manufactured after January 3, 1985, must meet new criteria, some of which are as follows: The vests must provide the adult with a minimum buoyancy of thirty-five pounds in 70°F fresh water;

TABLE 9.3
Type and Frequency of Errors per Group[a]

Total subjects per group	12	14	13	15
Pulling vest overhead	0	0	0	0
Snapping hooks to "D" ring	3	3	0	0
Tightening straps	3	5	2	6
Pulling inflation tabs	0	0	1	0
Finding oral inflation tubes	8	1	0	2
Pulling plugs to battery	0	1	3	0
Total errors	14	10	6	8

[a] Since each person could have made 6 possible errors, the total number of possible errors for Group 1 was $6 \times 12 = 72$, Group 2, $6 \times 14 = 84$, etc. In Group 1 there were $72 - 14 = 58$ "nonerrors." Analyzing errors vs. nonerrors, significant differences between the groups were found which could be attributed to method of instruction. Using the same orthogonal matrix developed for analyzing time differences, it was found that Group 1 differed significantly from the other groups combined, chi square $= 4.41$, $p < .025$. None of the other comparisons was significant.

donning instructions on the vest must be printed such that a person can read them with the vest on; and it must be shown that an adult, after receiving only the usual flight attendant demonstration, can don the life preserver within fifteen seconds.[16]

Even if these requirements do result in improved life preservers, they will only affect those vests produced after January 3, 1985. Since there is no requirement that vests manufactured before that date be discarded, life vests of current design will continue to be used, and therefore, you should be familiar with how to use them.

All vests used on long overwater flights in the U.S. must have two inflation bladders. (Some other countries allow vests with just one bladder.) These bladders sit one on top of the other, rather than side-by-side: thus if one doesn't inflate, you will still have support which would hold you in the correct position in the water—that is, face up. A requirement for these vests is that they must be able to turn an unconscious person from the face-down to the face-up position within a short period of time. Some vests are able to do this in as little as five seconds. The buoyancy of life vests designed for adults, and used on U.S. aircraft, must be twenty pounds (this will be increased to thirty-five pounds for vests made after January 1985). Although not required to, many airlines have used life vests with thirty-five pound buoyancy for years before January 1985.

Life vests are designed to fit infants, children, and adults. An infant's vest is designed for children weighing less than thirty-five pounds. A child's vest will fit someone weighing between thirty-five and ninety pounds, and an adult's vest is for anyone over ninety pounds. Probably the most common is the adult-child vest, designed to fit anyone weighing thirty-five pounds or more. Since this vest must fit someone as small as thirty-five pounds as well as someone ten times that weight, and not only fit but also provide buoyancy that will keep a person floating face up, it is easy to appreciate why there is not a plethora of different life jacket designs.

Life jackets are basically similar in the manner by which they provide flotation for the wearer. However, there are a number of important differences in how the vests are secured to the body. One common design is the type used in our test; it has three straps, one that hangs down with a "D" ring in front, and two straps with clips on the end that must be brought around to connect to the "D" ring (see Figure 9.11). A similar version has a "D" ring on each of the straps that are brought around to the front, and these "D" rings are connected to two snaps on the front of the vest (see Figure 9.12). Another version has a single strap that must be brought around the waist and connected to a single hook (see Figure 9.13). Yet another version is similar except that it has a safety-belt type of attachment (see Figure 9.14). Some vests have the straps permanently attached so that you must place your arms through loops formed by the straps (see Figure 9.15). A common type found in some countries, though not in the United

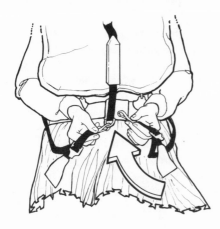

FIGURE 9.11. Attaching two clips to a "D" ring at the front of the vest.

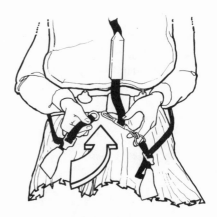

FIGURE 9.12. Attaching two "D" rings
to clips at the front of the vest.

States, has no snaps or buckles, but straps which must be tied together
(see Figure 9.16). In all cases you must adjust the straps to make the vest
fit tightly.

These same vests, though designed for adults and children, may not
fit small children if used in the same way as adults use them. Because the
waist of a thirty-five pound child is relatively small, the strap may be
pulled to its limit and still not fit tightly around the waist, hence when the

FIGURE 9.13. An unusual design
wherein the strap, which is attached to
one side of the vest, is brought around
and connected to a "D" ring on the other
side.

FIGURE 9.14. The two straps connect in front with a safety-belt type of attachment.

child enters the water the vest could come off over his head. Vest manufacturers have therefore developed an alternative method of tying the straps so that it will fit the child, which requires the straps to go between the legs of the child. But this introduces the problem of what will happen when the vest is inflated after the straps are already pulled snugly between

FIGURE 9.15. Some vests have the straps already attached. When you put the vest over your head, you must put your arms through the loops.

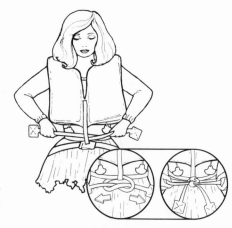

FIGURE 9.16. An unusual type of
vest which requires you to tie the straps
together.

the child's legs. Obviously, it could cause great discomfort, if not injury.
Some airlines suggest that one cell of the vest be inflated before the straps
are tightened (see Figure 9.17).

Inflating the Life Jacket

The question of when to inflate the vest is difficult because of the
variety of situations which can occur in a ditching. You would usually be
instructed to inflate the life vests when leaving the plane or after you are
outside. But there are two problems with this. If the plane breaks apart
the person could be thrown outside, and if he is unconscious or badly
injured he might not be able to inflate the vest. If the plane does not break
apart, the passenger may jump out an exit but then have difficulty finding
the inflation tabs. In ocean tests I found that when a person is in the water
the red inflation tabs are about ten inches below the surface, and not visible
on a bright day; even some experienced swimmers had difficulty locating
these tabs. A passenger who is not a good swimmer, and who doesn't hold
the tabs on entering the water, might not be able to find the tabs when
trying to inflate the vest.

On the other hand there are arguments for not inflating the vest inside
the plane. There is the idea (mistaken, I believe) that a fully inflated vest
would necessarily slow the escape of someone trying to get out a small

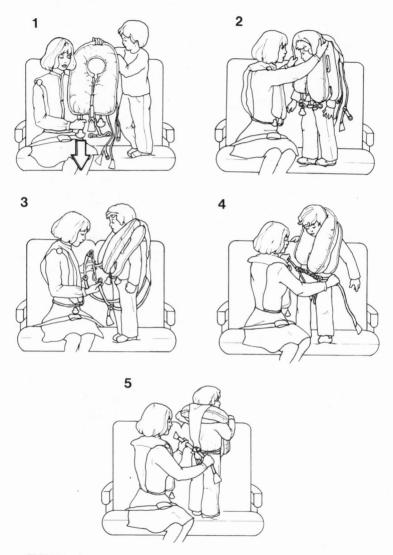

FIGURE 9.17. Some vests for children require the straps to go between the legs.

exit, such as the Type III exit. A study conducted by human factor researchers at Douglas Aircraft in the mid-1950s, when the DC-8 was being designed, showed that passengers exiting a Type III exit with life vests inflated were not significantly slower than those with uninflated vests on.[17] One potential criticism of this finding, however, was that the people in the test were experienced in getting out through the exit. Inexperienced passengers might be hampered if their vests were inflated. Moreover, the vests used in that test were not described and were probably smaller than the thirty-five pound buoyancy vests commonly found on current aircraft. But in 1980 I was with a flight attendant training instructor, with decades of experience, and weighing over 230 pounds, who was quite surprised to find that he could squeeze through a Type III exit wearing an inflated thirty-five-pound buoyancy life vest. And when the HS-748 ran off the end of the runway into the sea off the Shetland Islands, it was noted that "although a number of passengers reported that they had inflated their lifejackets before leaving the aircraft, a practice never to be recommended in normal ditching circumstances, on this occasion they were fortunate in having no apparent difficulty in escaping."[18] It was not stated in the report, however, whether passengers wearing the inflated life vests had used the small overwing exits or the large door exit.

On wide-body aircraft, where there are no Type III exits, it is even more unlikely that wearing an inflated life vest would slow your escape following a ditching.

Another argument against inflating the vest inside the plane I have encountered is that it could be accidentally deflated if the person brushed up against jagged metal during the escape. While this possibility may exist, it does not seem too convincing. After all, one could puncture the vest even if it were not inflated.

Possibly the most valid reason for not inflating it inside is that the cabin could fill with water so quickly that a passenger with an inflated vest would float to the ceiling and be unable to dive underwater to reach an exit. Although military fighter pilots have used automatic inflation devices (AID) successfully after bailing out of their planes over water,[19] potential entrapment inside the cabin has been the chief reason for not incorporating a mechanism that would sense water and automatically inflate the vest. In the case of nonswimmers, this is no issue. If they were inside a quickly filling cabin, it seems unlikely that many would be able to swim underwater to find their way through an exit; whether or not they had their vests inflated would matter little. However, for swimmers an inflated vest could be fatal in this situation.

It seems that the dilemma is this: if you don't inflate the vest prior to touchdown and the plane were to break apart, you could be thrown outside, unconscious or injured, and be unable to inflate it when you need it. But if you inflate it inside the plane, you could be trapped. Since you don't know if the plane will break up and throw you out, or remain intact but sink rapidly, you cannot make a rational decision beforehand on whether to inflate the vest before touchdown. My suggestion is that if you find yourself in a plane that is about to ditch, be ready to inflate the vest if it seems the plane is breaking up during impact. If not, inflate it as you leave the plane but before you enter the water. Luckily, a planned ditching is the only time you would have a vest on prior to touchdown. Since such ditchings are extremely rare, it is unlikely you will have to make this decision.

Most likely you will *not* know beforehand that you are about to end up in the water, so you will have to grab the life vest and take it with you. If the plane has remained relatively intact, and you are waiting in line to get out one of the exits, put the vest on and be ready to inflate it when you leave the plane. But if there is not enough time to put it on and secure the straps, take it with you and inflate it as you go out. Once outside, put the vest on, because even if you are a good swimmer you will probably need it if you are to survive.

WATER SURVIVAL WITHOUT A RAFT

Hypothermia

Your chances of surviving in the water without a raft are seven to ten times worse than if you were in a raft, according to Wayne Williams of the Institute for Survival Technology of Nova University near Fort Lauderdale, Florida.[20] The major reason for the low survival rate without a raft is cold water. A given volume of water absorbs twenty-five times more heat than the same volume of air. While an air temperature of 60°F may seem "brisk," 60°F water feels cold, and if you're in it long enough it can be fatal. Don deSteiguer, former chief of the Survival Research Unit of FAA's Civil Aeromedical Institute in Oklahoma, reports that a drop in body-core temperature starts within fifteen minutes after a person is in water between 65 and 70°F. The rate of temperature drop is greater the colder the water.[21] In 1963, a Greek ship off the African coast caught fire and 200 people went into the 64° water wearing life jackets. When the rescuers arrived three hours later, 118 were dead.[22] In colder water, survival time is less. Don deSteiguer predicts a survival time of thirty minutes or less in water that is 40°F or colder for people dressed as they would be on a commercial airplane. And he reports that the coastal waters along the northeast and northwest regions of the United States are almost always below 60°F. Only along the Florida and Gulf coasts are water temperatures not critical.

If you end up in cold water without a raft, your first impulse may be to swim to shore to get out of the cold. But this would be a deadly mistake unless you are very close to shore. Williams reports that in 1952 a DC-3 went into the Monongahela River near Pittsburgh and ten people died trying to swim the seventy-five feet to shore. It was winter and the water temperature was 35°F.[23] The U.S. Coast Guard reports that some good swimmers have been able to swim 0.8 miles in 50° water before being overcome by hypothermia (severe loss of body heat) while others have not been able to swim even 100 yards.[24]

The initial reaction to cold water is violent, uncontrollable shivering as the body attempts to generate heat through involuntary muscular contractions. In fact it may be ten or fifteen minutes before the temperature in the heart and brain starts to drop. But if the core temperature drops to 90°, shivering will subside and unconsciousness occur. Without a life jacket even the strongest swimmer would drown, thus the reason for carrying a life jacket and putting it on outside the plane. If the core temperature drops to about 85°F death usually occurs due to heart failure.

It may seem that swimming could increase your body temperature since vigorous exercise on land certainly produces excess body heat. But the heat generated from swimming is quickly lost in cold water. When floating stationary the water next to your skin will heat up slightly, but when you're swimming a constant flow of cold water washes over your body, accelerating heat loss 1.3–1.4 times faster than if you were not moving.[25]

You must reduce the rate of heat loss as much as possible. A method recommended by the U.S. Coast Guard, called the Heat Escape Lessening

Posture (HELP), involves holding your arms tightly against the sides of your chest and raising your thighs to reduce the water moving over your groin area[26] (see Figure 9.18). Reportedly, this simple practice can increase the predicted survival time by almost 50 percent.[27] Another recommended method is called the "Huddle," in which several people huddle together in the water so that their sides are pressed against those of their neighbors (see Figure 9.19). This not only has the effect of cutting down the water flow around each person, thereby conserving heat,[28] but since your group of people form a larger "target," it also increases the chance that rescue aircraft will spot you.[29]

The question of how long a person can survive in cold water depends on several factors in addition to the temperature of the water. The larger or fatter the person the slower the heat loss, hence the longer the survival time. Children would chill the fastest. A person treading water or swimming would cool faster than one remaining stationary with a life vest on (see Table 9.4). The HELP or Huddle positions, with vests on, conserve heat the longest.

If you should ever happen to rescue a hypothermia victim, there are a number of things to remember. Even after a person is removed from cold water he could still die as a result of "after drop." As the body cools, the arms and legs will cool faster than the trunk because they have more surface area per pound from which to lose heat. In the cold, the blood in the extremities becomes colder than the blood in the trunk and head. A person pulled from cold water should not have his arms and legs warmed first, for this would start the blood flowing from the extremities to the

FIGURE 9.18. Heat Escape Lessening Posture (HELP) that will reduce heat loss in the water.

FIGURE 9.19. The Huddle, another way of
staving off hypothermia by reducing heat loss.

heart. When this colder blood reaches the heart, it could cause a further
drop in core temperature (thus the term "after drop") and induce heart
failure. The Coast Guard recommends that a victim of severe hypothermia
have his trunk heated first as quickly as possible, such as by immersion
in water between 105 and 110°F. Also, contrary to folklore, the person
should not be given alcohol or rubbed with snow, as either of these procedures can increase heat loss. Furthermore, the person should not be
simply wrapped in a blanket without an auxiliary heat source, such as an
electric blanket or hot-water bottles, as this could also induce "after drop."[30]

TABLE 9.4
Predicted Survival Time for an Average Adult in 50°F Water in Various Situations

Situation	Predicted survival time (hours)
Treading water (no vest)	1.5
Swimming (vest on)	2.0
Remaining stationary (vest on)	2.7
Heat Escape Lessening Posture (vest on)	4.0
Huddle with others (vest on)	4.0

Source: *Hypothermia and Cold Water Survival*, a publication of the U.S. Coast Guard, AUX–202
(10–76), 1976.

Aircraft Flotation

A plane can float for a considerable period before sinking. In Chapter Two an accident was described in which a DC-8 on approach to Los Angeles International Airport struck the water several miles from the airport. The tail section broke off and sank, but the wings and forward section floated all night, sinking only after the passengers were rescued, while it was being towed to shore.

J. F. Goodwin has reported on a number of water landings and ditchings between 1953 and 1967.[31] On August 20, 1962, another DC-8, this one carrying 105 passengers and crew, made a water landing in Guanabara Bay near Rio De Janeiro. While everyone managed to get out, several drowned trying to swim to shore. The plane, however, floated for forty-five minutes. Based on calculations of the strength of the plane's skin surface, as well as its structural strength and buoyancy, Goodwin calculated that the DC-10, and probably other wide-body aircraft as well, has a ditching strength greater than the DC-8. In addition, the buoyancy of a wide-body plane is 50 percent greater than that of the DC-8; Goodwin figured that even with a hole in any one compartment in the cargo area, the plane should still float with all passenger door sills above the water level for a considerably longer period than is required for all of the passengers to escape.

While the DC-10 will most likely float level as it fills with water, not all planes will. This is important to know because you don't want to open an emergency exit if the door sill is underwater; this would flood the cabin and cause the plane to sink faster than it normally would.

Generally speaking, planes with engines on the wings will float level, while those with two or more engines in the rear of the plane will float tail-down. To my knowledge, all of the wide-body planes are calculated to float in a level position. DC-10s and L-1011s, both of which have an engine on each wing as well as one in the tail, should float level with their door sills above water. The A-300 and B-747, like the DC-8 and B-707, have only wing-mounted engines and are also expected to float level; thus initially after impact all exits should be above water level. On the other hand DC-9s and B-727s have all of their engines on the tail, and can therefore be expected to float in a tail-down position. Exits behind the wings in these planes should not be opened after a water landing because of the danger of flooding the cabin. Only the Type III exits, located at the overwing area, and the exits in the front of the plane should be used.

Of course there are always exceptions to any general rule. The B-737 has two engines, both mounted on the wings. One might think this plane would float level, but it may or may not. Some B-737s will float tail-down but others have been modified so that they will float in a level position. Another exception is the British-made HS-748, a propeller-driven plane with four engines, two on each wing. At least some models of this plane will float in the unusual nose-down position. On the other hand the Lear jet, a small business jet with two engines on the tail, will float level, not tail-down as one might expect. When one ditched in Lake Michigan it reportedly floated level. The safety information card on any plane should indicate which exits to use and which not to use following a water landing.

The planes described above all have "low wings," that is, the wings are level with the bottom of the fuselage, allowing a passenger to look out the window and see the top of the wing. In a ditching it is safer to be in a plane with low wings than in one with high wings. Townshend reports that ditching was one factor which led to the adoption of a low-wing rather than a high-wing version of the European "air bus," the A-300.[32] According to Townshend there are a number of reasons why low-winged planes are safer in a ditching. When flying very low to the ground, and probably also very low to the surface of the water, there is a cushioning effect (called "ground effect") which permits low-winged planes to fly until slower speeds are reached before touchdown as compared with high-winged planes. Another reason is that at touchdown all of the impact forces must be absorbed by the bottom of the fuselage of a high-winged plane, whereas on low-winged planes these forces are spread over most of the wings, substantially reducing the stresses on the fuselage.

Low-winged airplanes have several other advantages over high-winged planes in a ditching, according to Townshend. The wings, being watertight, provide buoyancy and will also keep the cabin in an upright position. High-winged planes, on the other hand, have several problems in this respect. If the impact forces do not damage the cabin then the cabin should remain buoyant, in which case the plane will heel over to one side or the other until a wing tip submerges enough so that its buoyancy offsets that of the cabin. But if the wing tip goes to the depth of the ten or fifteen feet necessary to achieve this buoyancy, the external water pressure may collapse the wing, allowing the plane to roll over onto its side or back. On the other hand if impact forces damage the cabin, water could quickly fill the cabin and the plane would sink to wing level where buoyancy of the wings should allow the plane to float. But then it would be questionable whether the passengers would have time to escape. Another advantage of low-winged planes is that the wings provide handy platforms from which to launch rafts, platforms which might not be available on a high-winged plane. It is fortunate that most planes which fly over water are of the low-winged variety.

Sharks

The chances of being attacked by a shark following a ditching or water landing are extremely small compared with the dangers of drowning or hypothermia. An authority on the topic, H. David Baldridge, described the factors surrounding the total record of shark attacks on man, which has involved 1,600 individuals.[33] The last year that comprehensive records were kept was 1968, when there were forty-one attacks of which only six were fatal. Baldridge's data showed a steady decline in shark attacks from a peak of fifty-five in 1958, as well as a decrease in the percentage that proved fatal, which peaked at 49 percent in 1940 but reached a low of 15 percent in 1968. The number of attacks on survivors of aircraft ditchings and bailouts is unknown, but is probably very few. In a 1978 document Dr. C. Scott Johnson reported that the last recorded attack on U.S. Navy personnel occurred in 1961 to one of three sailors who had floated in the mid-Atlantic for several hours. He survived with relatively minor injuries.[34] According to Johnson the Naval Safety Center, in Norfolk, Virginia, reported on 407 emergency ejections and bailouts over the open seas from 1966 through 1970. Of these, 362 survived and none of the recovered bodies received shark-caused injuries. But as Johnson noted, people still worry about shark attack. Actually, the solution for preventing a shark attack is the same as that for preventing immersion hypothermia—stay out of the water. Following a ditching or water landing, the best method is to stay on a plane that floats or get into a life raft.

LIFE RAFTS AND SLIDE RAFTS

Life rafts were originally the only rafts designed to be used following a water landing or ditching. But after inflatable escape slides were developed it became apparent that they too might function as rafts. It wasn't too long before these slides were so modified, and they came to be known

as slide/rafts. A life raft or slide/raft typically has the following characteristics, based on recommendations provided by the airline industry.[35] It
is composed of two identical air tubes, one superimposed on the other,
with a floor suspended between the tubes, and with a small inflatable section
on each side of the floor, and in the center for additional support. A circular
raft, therefore, looks like two doughnuts, one sitting on top of the other,
with a flexible fabric floor between them. An advantage of having a double-
ring type life raft is that either side may be the top so that after inflation
it wouldn't have to be turned over (see Figure 9.20).

Each life raft is equipped with a "boarding station," a small platform
on the side of the raft with a fabric stirrup hanging below the surface that
can be used as a foothold, and handles located on the edge of the raft
which can be used in pulling oneself aboard. In addition there is a life line
around the outside of the raft which people can hold when floating in the
water. Finally, there is a "heaving line," located near the boarding station,
which has a ring on the end several inches in diameter, and which can
float. This ring is thrown to people in the water so they can be pulled to
the raft.

Pulling the inflation handle fills both air tubes with carbon dioxide.
These tubes are separated, however, so if one is deflated the other will
not also lose air. In addition there are inflation valves for pumping up both
tubes accessible to passengers on either side of the floor; hence if a slow
leak develops, occupants can keep the raft inflated.

FIGURE 9.20. Life raft with inflatable section, for support, in center.

All rafts and slide/rafts have canopies to protect the passengers from exposure to the sun and cold wind, and to keep spray from entering the raft. Usually these canopies must be erected after the passengers are inside the raft, though on some slide/rafts these canopies are partially erected when the slide/raft is inflated (see Figure 9.21). Some rafts (presently found only on small corporate planes, not on large airliners) have canopies which automatically inflate when the rafts are inflated: this overcomes the common problem of passengers not erecting a canopy.[36] The problem arises because many do not know there is a canopy, do not know how to erect

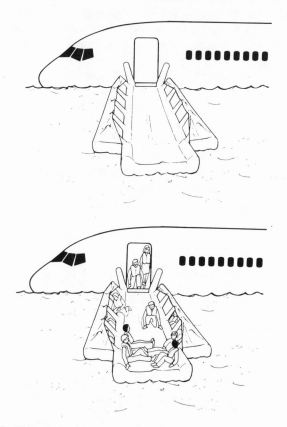

FIGURE 9.21. Slide raft after it is inflated (*top*) and while passengers are boarding (*bottom*). The partially erected canopy is seen on each side.

it, are unable to read the instructions (especially if it is dark), or have suffered injury or experienced feelings of depression and apathy following the accident. In any case, rafts with self-inflating canopies are not reversible as are those described above.

On long overwater flights you can expect to have either a number of life rafts stowed in containers around the plane, or there will be slide/rafts at most or all of the doors. With planes carrying many passengers, the capacity of the slide/rafts (forty to sixty passengers per slide/raft is not unusual) may not be great enough to accommodate everyone. In that case additional rafts, some of which can carry as many as forty-two passengers, must also be aboard to ensure that each passenger will have a place on a raft. Although most narrow-body planes on overwater flights will have only life rafts, and most wide-body planes will have only slide/rafts, there are exceptions. Some wide-body planes will have life rafts only, or a combination of slide/rafts and life rafts. The safety information card should indicate the types of rafts and their locations.

Slide/rafts automatically inflate when the door is opened. After the last person is aboard, the slide/raft is released from the plane by performing several steps. Typically, a flap located at the point where the slide/raft connects with the plane must be lifted and a handle underneath pulled. On some planes one handle located in the slide/raft must be pulled before the flap is lifted, and a second handle pulled to release the raft from the plane. (See Figures 9.22 and 9.23.) A knife, found on the side of the slide/raft near this line, can be used to cut the line. However, it was designed so that if it were not cut before the plane sank, the line would separate without damaging the raft.

As yet there have been no ditchings of planes with slide/rafts and no water landings where the slide/rafts were used. Nonetheless it seems that slide/rafts would be easier to deploy than life rafts. Life rafts are stored in containers, usually located in the ceiling or the overhead bins. On a few planes life rafts are stowed in closets near the exits. A life raft may weigh from 85 to 130 pounds, depending on its size, and must be carried from its container to an exit. The life raft is bulky so that two people are needed to carry it.

U.S. airlines have the life rafts stowed in containers near the exits through which they are to be launched, as required by federal regulations.[37] If passengers are to use the overwing window exits, it could be dangerous being on the wing in rough seas. Thus a life line, usually found inside the

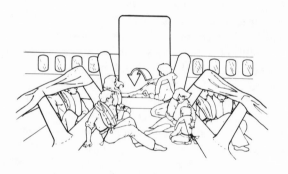

FIGURE 9.22. Opening a Type A door on some DC-10s results in a slide/raft's inflating. After passengers have boarded, lifting a flap near the doorway and pulling a handle will release the slide/raft from the plane.

FIGURE 9.23. To release the slide/raft on some B-747s, a handle must be pulled (*top*) before a flap is lifted (*middle*) and a second handle is pulled (*bottom*).

upper frame of the window after the emergency hatch is removed, is supposed to be taken by the first person out the exit and connected to a small ring on the wing. This ring is usually located in the center of the wing, about a third to half the distance from the window exit to the wing tip (see Figure 9.24). The life line, which is permanently connected to the

FIGURE 9.24. A life line should be connected to the wing before passengers get onto the wing to board the raft.

plane at the window frame, would be very helpful in high seas, but the rough waves might make it difficult to attach the line to the ring.

Before the life raft is pushed out through the exit, it must first be attached to the plane. In a relatively moderate wind an inflated but empty life raft could be blown away so quickly that even the best swimmer would have no chance of capturing it. Even if it were caught, there would be no way to get it back to the plane for use by other passengers. Thus the life raft must be attached to the inside of the plane before it is ever put out the exit.

A line, perhaps twenty feet or more long with a snap on its end, is used to attach the life raft inside the cabin by any of several means. Looping the line under a seat leg and snapping the line back onto itself is one way. Another is to snap the line to a safety belt. If the life raft is to be launched through one of the door exits, there is always a hand hold on the wall of the fuselage to one side of the door. Looping the line through this handle, then snapping the hook back onto the line, will keep the life raft from floating away. (See Figure 9.25.)

After hooking the life raft to the plane, it should be pushed out the exit. Doing this at overwing exits would of course result in the raft lying on the wing. From there it must be carried to the edge of the wing before inflation is attempted.

The line that connects the life raft to the plane is usually, but not always, the same line that must be pulled to inflate it. (Some life rafts are equipped with two lines, the inflation line and another line to attach the life raft to the plane.) In any case there is a red handle attached to the line that, when pulled, results in inflation of the life raft. This should only be done when the life raft is in the water since the accident could have created jagged metal edges on the wing which could deflate the raft. The raft should be at the forward edge of the wing rather than the rear edge. The pilot may have had the wing flaps, located on the rear of the wing, in the down position to slow his airspeed. The force of the water could have torn the flaps, producing dangerous jagged edges.

Another potential problem involves wind. If the pilot had time before touchdown to try to slow the plane, he most likely would have headed the plane into the wind. A life raft launched at the forward edge of the wing will then tend to be blown back over the wing, which could cause deflation if it came into contact with sharp metal. After passengers have boarded,

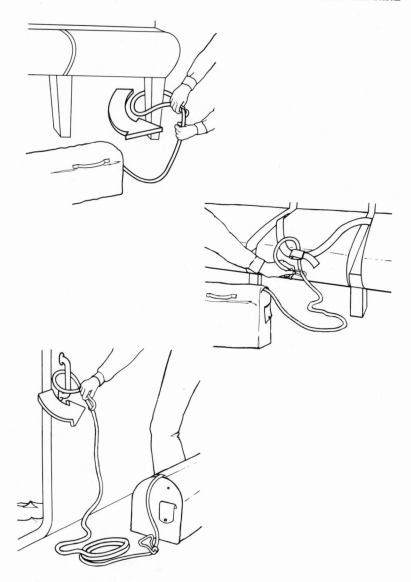

FIGURE 9.25. Life rafts can be connected to a seat leg (*top*), a safety belt (*middle*), or an assist handle located at each exit (*bottom*).

it is therefore important to try to get the raft to the tip of the wing before the wind blows it rearward.

Once passengers have boarded the life raft, it can be released by cutting the line with a knife attached to the raft. Or if the plane starts to sink, the line will separate without damaging the raft.

If one of the life rafts does deflate, all is not lost. There should still be enough room on the other rafts, assuming they all have been launched, for the remaining passengers.[38] The usable rafts should be tied together. The connecting line should be at least 25 feet long, otherwise wave action could turn one of the rafts over. If the rafts are connected they will be more easily spotted by rescue craft.

RESCUE

After everyone has gotten out of the plane, the next problem is to attract rescuers, and to survive until you are rescued. If your plane ends up in the water, it will probably be in the vicinity of an airport, not too far from shore, because most water landings occur during takeoff or landing. On a sunny day with calm seas there should be little problem in moving you from the rafts to rescue vehicles, whether they be boats or helicopters. Water landings, however, can just as easily occur when visibility is poor, which can cause problems for rescuers not only trying to find you, but once you are located, trying to pluck you from the ocean.

At 11:08 A.M. on the morning of October 26, 1978, an airborne U.S. Navy P-3c airplane carrying fifteen crewmen sent out a distress signal.[39] The plane was 465 miles from the island of Shemya in the Aleutian Islands south of the Alaska mainland. But it was another thirty minutes before the extreme nature of the emergency, which necessitated a ditching, was transmitted to the military station at Elmendorf, Alaska. By noon, search and rescue (SAR) planes were flying south toward the P-3. Prior to ditching, the crewmen on the stricken plane put on their specially designed exposure suits to provide some protection on the cold ocean's surface where the forty-mile-per-hour winds were blowing waves ten to twenty feet high and where the water and air temperature were between 40 and 44°F.

At 12:30 P.M. the plane, heading into the wind, touched down on the water in a direction parallel to the swells. It landed in a slightly nose-high position, resulting in a light skip, but the second impact, two or three seconds after the first, was more severe, pitching the nose down violently, the plane coming to rest a short distance away. Luckily, fourteen of the fifteen men survived the impact and got out of the plane in the two or three minutes it remained afloat. On impact the plane immediately began filling with water, and within thirty seconds the water in the cabin was three feet deep. Within sixty seconds the survivors were forced to swim through the exits. The emergency lighting, however, did not work, so that retrieving the survival gear in the dark cabin was difficult. Somehow two life rafts were launched, one with a canopy, the other without.

Neither raft had a heaving line—a line attached to the raft at one end with a ring on the other end, that could be thrown to someone in the water. This reportedly resulted in the death of the pilot. Apparently, when he got to the door of the sinking plane both rafts, which had been attached to the plane by a sixty-pound nylon cord, had already started to drift away. The force of the high seas had snapped the cords connecting the rafts to the plane. The pilot jumped into the water, but he couldn't swim fast enough to catch either raft; he was close enough, though, so that he could have grabbed a line if one had been available. Some of the men in one raft actually jumped into the frigid water and tried to swim it to him, but the enormous waves and wind made his rescue impossible.

Still, the other survivors were more fortunate considering the circumstances. The pilot had skillfully set the plane down on very rough seas without breaking it apart. They even had time to put on their exposure suits, and thirteen of the fifteen crewmembers actually got into rafts. But their ordeal was not over.

At 2:45 P.M. the rafts were sighted by a U.S. Navy SAR plane, another P-3. In the raft without the canopy sat nine men. A quarter- to half-mile away was the other raft, carrying the other four men. But the rafts became increasingly difficult to keep in sight, for by this time the clouds had lowered to 300 feet, accompanied by driving rain and snow squalls. The SAR crew had great difficulty in deciding where a survival kit should be dropped, because the wind appeared to go in one direction and the current in the opposite direction. Finally, at 5:30 P.M. a kit was dropped and successfully captured by the men in the raft with the canopy. The SAR plane kept visual contact with the rafts until a Coast Guard aircraft relieved it. The SAR plane then went in search of a ship that could rescue the men.

At 7:15 P.M. they sighted a Soviet fishing trawler, the *MYS Senyevina*. The Navy plane didn't have a radio frequency common with that of the ship, so, communicating with its landing lights, the plane directed the fishing boat toward the rafts. Soon afterward the Coast Guard plane and the Russian trawler made voice contact. The ship was then directed to the rafts, where at midnight, eleven and a half hours after the ditching, the men were lifted from the ocean. Ten survived, but three, all from the raft without the canopy, died even though they suffered no injuries in the accident.

There are a number of things you can do to affect your survival aboard a life raft. At least one raft aboard each commercial plane must have an emergency locator transmitter (ELT).[40] While some airlines may only have one raft with an ELT, many have voluntarily equipped all of their rafts with ELTs, realizing that if only one out of six or eight rafts had the ELT, then luck would have it that that raft might be the one that was accidentally deflated. Also, there is the problem that rafts drift apart; hence after several hours there may be considerable distance between them, and a rescue plane might have trouble spotting all the rafts if just one had an ELT.

When the ELT is submerged, a water-activated battery starts the device signaling its position on radio frequencies 121.5 and 243.0 MHz (see Figure 9.26). You cannot send voice signals with this transmitter, nor can you receive any kind of radio signals. It simply transmits signals that can be picked up by aircraft or satellites monitoring those frequencies.

Once the rescuer is in your general location, making yourself visible becomes your next significant effort. There is a requirement that aboard each raft there be one pyrotechnic device, which is usually a flare that gives off light and can be shot into the air.[41] But one flare is probably inadequate to gain the attention of rescuers, except under ideal circumstances. There have been a number of cases where people in lifeboats or rafts using aerial flares have been unable to attract the attention of ships within view. Maurice and Maralyn Bailey were able to get aboard a small life boat, with a rubber dinghy attached, after their yacht struck a whale and sank off the west coast of South America in 1973. They spent 118 days on the lifeboat, longer than any known survivor has ever spent in such a circumstance. They were finally rescued by a Korean fishing boat. During this four-month period they saw eight ships, some passing within a quarter mile of their raft. Eight days after the encounter with the whale

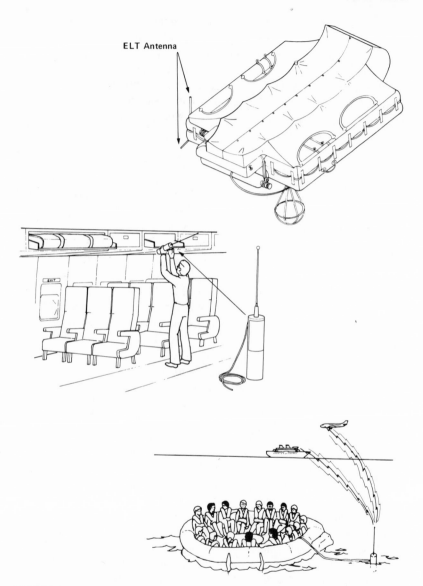

FIGURE 9.26. Some rafts and slide/rafts have ELT's attached to the raft (*top*). Some planes, however, have portable ELT's (*middle*), which must be carried along and attached to the inflated raft (*bottom*).

they spotted the first ship when it was about two miles away and approaching them. They estimated that it would pass within a mile from their boat. Maralyn collected their flares and laid them out, ready to use:

> As she drew level with us Maurice asked for the first flare—a smoke flare—and with mounting excitement I handed it to him. He tore off the tape and struck the top with the igniter—nothing happened. For long seconds we stared at the useless object and it was with a cry of exasperation that Maurice threw it into the sea. "It's a dud. A bloody dud!" I handed him a second flare and this time we both heaved a sigh of relief as it ignited. As the flare began to diminish I handed him a second red flare. There was no answering signal from the ship and she still maintained her course. A third flare was used—our hopes were fading rapidly. . . . I could see the boat going further and further away. We hadn't been seen. It was pointless using the other two flares. While Maurice sat dejectedly in the dinghy I began to wave my oilskin jacket although I knew it was no use. After a few minutes Maurice asked me to stop and save my energy and reluctantly I did so. By now the ship's funnel was only visible in the swells on the horizon and before many more minutes had passed the ocean was ours again.[42]

Apparently the first flare the Baileys attempted to use, which did not work, was a smoke flare. But the other flares, the "red" flares, were apparently light flares which are difficult to see in the daytime.

They spotted the second ship three weeks later, and this time it was dark. They had two remaining light flares, and as the ship, a tanker, drew near, Maurice ignited a red flare—but it too was a dud. He threw it into the sea and lit the second flare which illuminated the raft and a large area around them. They were confident that the lookouts aboard the ship would see them. As the flare faded Maurice began flashing S-O-S with the flashlight, but the ship continued on toward the horizon. Six more ships were to pass them before someone aboard a Korean fishing boat saw them desperately waving their jackets and returned to put an end to their ordeal. The crews, of course, were not searching for anyone. Thus it could be argued that they would not be as alert as a trained search and rescue team which, knowing the approximate position of a raft, would be much more likely to spot a flare.

Because the problem of the visibility of aerial flares, as well as other signaling devices, is of practical significance, I conducted some tests of the effectiveness of various signals that are found in the survival kits of some downed aircraft.[43] The tests were conducted in the desert near Twenty Nine Palms, California, but some of the results could easily apply to the ocean environment. Two trained rescuers, members of the San Diego

Mountain Rescue Team who had participated in numerous desert searches, were placed at observation points from which they could look for signals from the "victims." One rescuer was at ground level and the other on a hillside at about 250 feet above ground level to simulate a searcher aboard a low-flying airplane.

The "victims" selected were six men and five women with little previous experience in using signaling devices, but who were trained in using each signal prior to the test. Five groups of victims, two or three per group, were stationed at various distances ranging from one-half mile to five miles from the searchers. Tests were conducted in both day and night, using a number of different signals including smoke flares, hand-held and aerial light flares, mirrors, whistles, flashlights, and strobe lights, as well as various reflective materials. In the day tests, aerial and hand-held light flares (similar to a road flare but with a handle) simply were not effective. The aerial flares, tested at each location for both the day and night tests, were the type that shoot up to 300 or 400 feet, giving off a red light for seven to ten seconds. During the day tests these flares were seen less than 25 percent of the time, and then only at the closest distances of one mile or less. The most effective signal during the day was orange smoke, which was seen at the farthest distance during the day tests (four miles) and by the searchers on 81 percent of the trials. When the smoke canisters are ignited, however, they do not put out the maximum amount of smoke initially. Thus it took an average of fifty-three seconds for the searchers to see the smoke signals.

Even though the days were sunny, the signal mirrors were not very effective because some victims had trouble using them. The difficulty in trying to shine a mirror to enable someone to see it several miles away is that you can't tell where it's shining. Consequently you can't correct the position of the mirror to hit the target. Before the experiment all the victims were trained in a method of shining the beam between two fingers of the other, outstretched hand, and then using these fingers as a "sight" to point to the potential rescuers. Even so, some never became proficient in using the mirror. As Table 9.5 indicates, the mirrors were seen only during approximately half of the trials, but those that were seen were detected in about half of the time that it took rescuers to see the smoke.

At night, the hand-held light flares and the aerial flares were more effective than the other signals (see Table 9.6). A simple road flare, lit and dropped on the ground, was seen in 100 percent of the trials. For

TABLE 9.5
Signal Devices Ranked by Detection Distance and Percent of Trials Seen in Day Tests[a]

Device	Detection threshold (miles)	Percent of trials detected	Average mean detection time (sec.)
Hand-held smoke	4	81	53
Glass mirror	4	56	22
Hand-held light flare	2	22	47
Aerial flare	1	22	7
Road flare	0.5	5	20

[a] Detection threshold is that distance at which the device was detected 50% or more of the time. The road flare in the day tests was seen at 0.5 miles on half of the trials or more, but was seen only on 5% of the total trials.

obvious reasons a road flare is not practical aboard a raft, though a hand-held light flare, which might be practical, was seen on 90 percent of the trials; it was detected even more quickly than the road flare. The aerial flare, seen on 80 percent of the night trials, was detected very quickly—four seconds on the average compared to thirty-five seconds for the road flare. This is explained by the fact that searchers are trained to visually scan an area from left to right within ten seconds. Occasionally an aerial

TABLE 9.6
Signal Devices Ranked by Detection Distance and Percent of Trials Seen in Night Tests

Device	Detection threshold (miles)	Percent of trials detected	Average mean detection time (sec.)
Flare	5	100	35
Hand-held light flare	5	90	14
Aerial flare	5	80	4
Flashlight	3	60	9
Strobe light	2	40	49
Light stick	2	20	17
Whistle	0	—	—

flare would go off to the searcher's left while he was looking to the right; since the flare was only illuminated ten seconds or less, he would miss it. Flares with a longer life, such as the hand-held type, were seen more often, though they took longer to detect. At the end of the test a very large aerial flare was sent into the sky, which gave off 30,000 candlepower for a period of thirty seconds or longer. It seemed to light the whole valley, and was seen at the five-mile distance as soon as it was illuminated. It was undoubtedly the most effective signal used.

The least effective signal was the police whistle. Even though the night was quiet with no noticeable wind, the whistle could not be heard at a distance of one mile. In a follow-up test it was barely audible at half a mile.

If you are on the ocean with a limited number of the types of signals that extinguish after one use (aerial flares, smoke), you will need to match the type of signal with the prevailing conditions. In bright daylight don't use the aerial flare unless there is absolutely no better signal available. Smoke, a mirror, even reflective material would be better to use than to expend the aerial flare, which is designed for night use. If you have the choice between smoke and a mirror, realize that it will take a minute or more before the smoke will be dense enough to be seen. So in a situation where you do not detect a rescue plane until it is nearly overhead, or there is one far on the horizon which is not heading in your direction, then even the smoke should not be used. A mirror might be the best choice—after all, you can use it over and over, and with practice it can be an effective signal. In fact on a sunny day someone in the raft should constantly sweep the horizon with the mirror, for even though you may not see a rescue boat or plane, they could see the flash from your mirror. At night, anything that produces light should be ready to be used in case a potential rescuer appears suddenly.

While waiting for rescue there are some things to keep in mind. Hypothermia does not affect only those in the water—it can also affect those in the raft. Cold wind against wet clothes can lower body temperature to a dangerous level. The three sailors who died in the raft following the P-3 ditching were in a raft without a canopy. The rafts aboard commercial airplanes are supposed to have canopies, but Jack Grant, former head of cabin safety with Qantas Airways, reported there have been no known cases where survivors of airline accidents have ever erected the canopy.[44]

It is essential that someone in the raft take the initiative to make sure that the canopy is erected. Putting up the canopy might be impossible at night, but as soon as there is enough light, this must be done. The canopy will protect against the cold as well as the wind and sun, which can cause dehydration.

In cold weather, the next step after putting up the canopy is to reduce the amount of water in your clothes, as well as the excess water in the raft, using a bailing bucket which should be aboard the raft. Remove your wet clothes and squeeze them dry before putting them back on. Damp clothes are better at reducing heat loss than wet clothes.

There will be at least two openings, at opposite ends of the canopy, through which people should keep a lookout for rescuers. An appropriate signal device should be kept handy.

In warm weather a major survival problem is dehydration. According to some experts, we are bombarded with misinformation on how to survive in a situation where little drinking water is available. According to Dr. P. M. McGuigan, a U.S. Navy doctor, the idea of rationing a limited water supply is wrong.[45] He reports that many people have been found dead of dehydration with water remaining in their containers. His advice is consistent with that of Dr. Paul Nesbitt, former chief of the U.S. Air Force Arctic, Desert, Tropic Information Center at Maxwell Air Force Base, and his colleagues, Alonzo Pond, also of the Air Force, and William Allen of NASA, in their excellent publication *The Survival Book*. They reported that water must be conserved, but it is body water, not drinking water, that must be conserved—ration your sweat, not your water.[46] With minimal activity an average adult can survive for five days with no water or food. With just water, the same person can survive for many weeks. By minimizing activity, a person in a life raft can greatly reduce loss of water due to urine output and sweat. Humid air will also reduce the loss of water through the lungs. Stay under the canopy out of the sun and use sea water to cool the body to reduce water loss through perspiration. In this way you can get by with very little drinking water. But the cardinal rule still remains: don't drink sea water. Its high salt concentration will draw the water from your body and increase the rate of dehydration. Life rafts on commercial airplanes may contain a small amount of water in a survival kit stowed aboard the raft, but this is meant for infants, who require more water than adults to survive.

In summary, before any flight make sure you know what kind of flotation equipment is aboard your plane. Find out whether your seat cushion is for flotation—your safety information card should tell you if it is. If you are supposed to have a life jacket, check to make sure there is one near your seat; study the card, and watch the flight attendant, so that you know how to put it on and adjust it. Also, keep in mind the location of the rafts or slide/rafts, from what exits they will be launched, and if your safety card provides the information, how they are inflated. Know which exits might be underwater and should not be opened. Listen for and follow instructions from the crew members.

REFERENCES

1. Human Factors Group Chairman's Factual Report, Flight 980, May 2, 1970, Report no. DCA–70–A–7, National Transportation Safety Board, Washington, D.C., 1970; *Special Study, Passenger Survival in Turbojet Ditchings (A Critical Case Review), April 5, 1972*, Report no. AAS–72–2, National Transportation Safety Board, Washington, D.C., 1972.
2. *Federal Aviation Regulations,* part 121.340.
3. *Ibid.,* part 121.339.
4. Ernest B. McFadden, "Evaluation of Aircraft Seat Cushion Flotation Characteristics," in *Flotation and Survival Equipment Studies,* compiled by McFadden, Report no. FAA–AM–78–1, Office of Aviation Medicine, FAA, Washington, D.C., Jan. 1978.
5. Ernest B. McFadden, "Aircraft Flotation Seat Cushion Evaluation," in *Flotation and Survival Equipment Studies,* compiled by McFadden, Report no. FAA–AM–78–1, Office of Aviation Medicine, FAA, Washington, D.C., Jan. 1978.
6. Ernest B. McFadden and Hiley F. Harrison, "Use of Flotation Dummies in the Evaluation of Life Preserver Design," in *Flotation and Survival Equipment Studies,* compiled by McFadden, Report no. FAA–AM–78–1, Office of Aviation Medicine, FAA, Washington, D.C., Jan. 1978.
7. Coast Guard Study of Inflatable Life Preservers. Steven E. Weiss, *Inflatable Personal Flotation Device Study,* Report no. CG-M-5-81, U.S. Coast Guard, Washington, D.C., 1981.
8. *Code of Federal Regulations,* Title XXXIII, subpart 175.15.
9. Civil Aircraft Accident Report no. 1/81 (EW/C671), Department of Trade, Accidents Investigation Branch, Kingsgate House, London, 1981, pp. 15, 21.
10. *Aircraft Accident Report, Boeing 727-235, N4744NA, Escambia Bay, Pensacola, Fl., May 8, 1978,* National Transportation Safety Board, Washington, D.C.
11. "Luck Steers 'Lost' Hero to Rescue of Crash Survivors," *Los Angeles Times,* May 10, 1978.
12. *Aircraft Accident Report, Boeing 727-235, N4744NA, Escambia Bay, Pensacola, Fl., May 8, 1978.*
13. "Invalid Wife Safe, But Jet Passenger Forfeits Own Life," *Long Beach Independent-Press Telegram,* May 10, 1978.

14. "Luck Steers 'Lost' Hero to Rescue of Crash Survivors."
15. Daniel A. Johnson, "Effectiveness of Video Instructions on Life Jacket Donning," *Proceedings of the Human Factors Society Annual Convention,* Human Factors Society, Santa Monica, Calif., Oct. 1973.
16. Draft Technical Standard Order (TSO-C13d), Life Preservers, a request for comments requested to be returned to the Federal Aviation Administration, Washington, D.C., on or before Feb. 19, 1982.
17. J. A. Roebuck, "Effects of Opening Size Variables on Overwing Emergency Exit Time," Human Factors Group, Interiors Design Section, Douglas Aircraft Company, Santa Monica (now headquartered at Long Beach), Calif., paper presented at the Air Safety Seminar sponsored by Flight Safety Foundation, Inc., Palo Alto, Calif., Nov. 12, 1957.
18. Civil Aircraft Accident Report no. 1/81 (EW/C671), Department of Trade, Accidents Investigation Branch, Kingsgate House, London, 1981, pp. 15, 21.
19. S. J. Wojdan, Conax Corporation, Buffalo, N.Y. Personal communication, 1978.
20. Wayne Williams, "Water Survival," *Professional Pilot,* Oct. 1981.
21. Don deSteiguer, "Comments on Cold Water Immersion," in *New Trends in Air Transport Evacuation Systems,* SAFE Proceedings, SAFE Association, Canoga Park, Calif., 1979.
22. Williams, "Water Survival."
23. Ibid.
24. *Hypothermia and Cold Water Survival,* a publication of the U.S. Coast Guard, AUX-202 (10-76), 1976.
25. deSteiguer, "Comments on Cold Water Immersion."
26. *Hypothermia and Cold Water Survival.*
27. Jeanne M. Koreltz, "Hypothermia: Menace to Survival," *Cabin Crew Safety Bulletin,* Flight Safety Foundation, Arlington, Va., May-June 1982.
28. Ibid.
29. Williams, "Water Survival."
30. Koreltz, "Hypothermia."
31. J. F. Goodwin, "DC-10 Airplane: Design Ditchability Structural Aspects," paper presented to Pacific Air Safety Search and Rescue Symposium, San Francisco, Calif., Oct. 1968.
32. B. W. Townshend, "Ditching the Air Bus: A Matter of Self Preservation," *Technical Review* (Journal of the Society of Experimental Test Pilots), 1967, pp. 13-21.
33. H. David Baldridge, *Shark Attack* (Berkeley, Calif.: Berkeley Publishing Corp., 1975), as reported in C. Scott Johnson, "Surviving with Sharks," *SAFE Proceedings,* SAFE Association, Canoga Park, Calif., 1978.
34. C. Scott Johnson, "Surviving with Sharks," *SAFE Proceedings,* SAFE Association, Canoga Park, Calif., 1978.
35. *Specification—Airline Life Rafts,* Report no. NAS 800, National Aircraft Standards Committee, Aircraft Industries Association of America, Washington, D.C., 1958.
36. J. H. Grant, *Passenger Survival and Evacuation,* Qantas Airways, Ltd., Sydney, Australia, undated.
37. *Federal Aviation Regulations,* part 25.1411.
38. Ibid., part 121.339.
39. Unclassified Report, PACCO274 334/04 : 54Z, United States Navy, Washington, D.C., 1978.

40. *Federal Aviation Regulations,* part 121.339.
41. Ibid.
42. Maurice Bailey and Maralyn Bailey, *Staying Alive!* (New York: David McKay, 1974), pp. 55–56.
43. Daniel A. Johnson, *A Survival Kit Test Program: Experimental Evaluation of Signals in a Desert Situation,* Interaction Research Corporation, Olympia, Wash., Aug. 1977.
44. Grant, *Passenger Survival and Evacuation.*
45. Lt. P. M. McGuigan, M.D., Flight Surgeon, MC, USN, "Survival at Sea," AEWAR-RONPAC, at Ditching Seminar in Honolulu, March 4, 1969.
46. Paul H. Nesbitt, Alonzo W. Pond, and William H. Allen, *The Survival Book* (New York: Funk & Wagnalls, 1959): 204.

Chapter Ten

STRESS REACTIONS FOLLOWING ACCIDENTS

If you experience a severe airplane accident you may encounter a number of psychological and physiological reactions in the following weeks or months. Such reactions are certainly quite common after other types of disasters. Although there has not been any extensive research on the psychological reactions of passengers following aircraft accidents, anecdotal reports indicate that there are some similarities among their reactions.

Definitions may be useful. *Stress* is considered, in general, to be a response of the mind and body to any demand placed on it. It is an internal state caused by something in the environment which a person interprets to be in some way threatening. Being in an airplane accident, or losing a close friend or relative in one, can result in a severe state of stress. Nevertheless an environmental event need not be primarily negative in order to produce stress; winning a million-dollar lottery or receiving a promotion may seem to be very positive events, but either can cause stress if the person interprets them as events with which he will have to cope.

A *stressor* is whatever it is in the environment that causes stress. A stressor may have a physical basis, such as a poison, a high level of noise, a bout of cold weather, or an airplane accident. A stressor may also have a psychological basis, such as the possibility of not passing an important exam, losing one's spouse, or the prospect of flying after having just been in an accident. In general stressors are those factors in the environment which a person interprets as a threat, or as an obstacle to a goal.

If a person interprets an event as threatening, and more than he can easily cope with, then one or more *stress reactions* are likely to occur. These reactions can occur on the physiological, psychological, or behavioral levels.[1] Stress reactions can take numerous physiological forms such as nausea, skin rashes, and increased blood pressure, to name just a few. Increased emotionality or emotional numbing—which can occur when a person feels nothing following the loss of a close friend—are also two common stress reactions. Moreover, inability to concentrate, obsessive thinking about the accident, and forgetfulness are cognitive reactions to stress. A breakdown in social relationships can also occur as a result of severe stress.

Every person will react to the occurrence of an event regarded as threatening, trying to cope with it in one way or another. If the person is unable to cope, stress reactions may be evidenced by symptoms such as increased high blood pressure, tears, and anger; the exact method of expression may be based more on the person's prior learning than on any other single factor.

How you cope with the stress of having been in an accident, or having lost someone close to you in that accident, depends on many factors. Some people will overcome the stress reactions while others will find this difficult to do. The severity of the stress reactions may even increase for the latter group. But even those unable to cope, who exhibit more severe stress reactions as time progresses, should not be considered mentally ill, nor should they be treated as such. This is not to say, however, that their stress reactions should be considered unimportant, for if left untreated the condition could steadily worsen, even to the point of such self-destructive behaviors as alcoholism, drug abuse, and possibly suicide.

This chapter outlines some reseach on how people have coped with being in life-threatening situations, some of the stress reactions that occur following disasters, some of the factors which have an effect on the state of stress, and some methods of reducing or eliminating stress reactions.

THOUGHTS IN LIFE-THREATENING SITUATIONS

Those who have lost close friends or relatives in a plane accident may wonder what it was like for those on board during the last few moments. They grieve to think that the person died suffering tremendous fear and excruciating torment. This may be the case for some victims, but research with those who have survived life-threatening situations indicates that the last moments may not necessarily be as fearful or as horrendous as one might guess.

Two psychiatrists, Dr. Russell Noyes, Jr., and Dr. Roy Kletti, interviewed or administered questionnaires to 101 people who had been in life-threatening accidents. Most of these people (72 percent) experienced what has been termed "depersonalization."[2] Depersonalization occurs when one experiences a number of emotional feelings and perceptions, perhaps simultaneously, which are quite different from each other and which may even be contradictory. Many of the people interviewed by Drs. Noyes and Kletti reported that at the moment of the most extreme danger, their minds suddenly seemed to work on at least two different levels. In one case a twenty-three-year-old student was driving an old car at sixty miles per hour when the steering gave out. He later recalled that his mind seemed to speed up while time was drawn out—the accident actually took only a few seconds but it seemed to take five minutes. Some sensations seemed very acute, such as his grip on the steering wheel and the sound of grass brushing against the door; but other sensations were blurred—he doesn't remember seeing anything except for an instant when his attention was focused on the abutment ahead. At one level his mind was working rapidly, reviewing information he had learned in driver's education that might help him in the situation. On the other hand he remembers having a clear vision of himself being killed, of seeing the accident as if it were on a television screen which he was viewing from a point outside the car. At the same time the accident was occurring he felt calm, even detached. On one level he was trying to cope with the situation by reviewing what he had learned in the past which could affect his safety, even though it was apparently hopeless. On another level he became dissociated from himself (thus the term "depersonalization"), viewing the accident as if it were occurring to someone else.

Another young man was driving when his car skidded into the path of another on a wet curve. After the collision his car started to spin, and he remembers a relaxed kind of feeling, as if he were "stoned" on marijuana. He had no feeling of danger but felt rather that the situation was not really happening.

Another young man was on a motorcycle at night when he became aware of a stalled vehicle a short distance ahead. Knowing he couldn't avoid the crash, he at first felt terror, but then scenes from his life started flashing before his eyes in rapid succession. The scenes ranged from the time he was about two years old, dumping a bowl of cereal upside down on his head, to being spanked for a bad report card, to kissing a girl for the first time, and to other incidents. With each one he had the same emotion he felt when each scene was lived the first time, but also he felt detached, as if looking at the pictures in a family album. Most of the scenes aroused happy emotions.

Overall, 72 percent of the people in the study reported an altered awareness of the passage of time. Most of them referred to a slowing, as if time were strung out. But this apparent slowing of environmental events was in contrast to a speeding of mental processes, which was reported by 61 percent of the people. On the other hand 56 percent of the survivors reported a reduction or absence of emotion—they described their feelings as those of detached calm or peacefulness. One mountaineer claimed that during a fall he felt calm and detached, with no emotion. Thirty percent indicated they felt as though a wall existed between themselves and their feelings during the depersonalized state, though most reported a state of intense fear right before or right after the state of depersonalization.

Drs. Noyes and Kletti concluded that depersonalization, like fear, is a very common response to a life-threatening danger. It occurs instantly upon the realization of extreme danger, and disappears when the threat is past. They believe that depersonalization may be an adaptive process by which the realization of the danger of the situation intensifies alertness and ability to think, but at the same time part of the self becomes a detached observer, thereby reducing strong emotion which could disorganize the ability of the person to think and act.

If we can generalize these findings to what people experience just before and during airplane accidents, it would seem that many passengers and crewmembers might be aware of the danger of the situation but that some of them, especially the cockpit crewmembers, would be doing what they could to prevent the accident from occurring. Other crewmembers might be mentally reviewing what they would do as soon as the plane comes to a halt. One flight attendant I interviewed after an accident stated that as the plane swerved down the runway, all she could think of was how she would unbuckle her seatbelt, what she would yell to the passengers, and the steps she would take in opening the emergency exit. Some passengers may think of things they will do, such as moving from their seats to an exit, but others may not focus their minds on anything in general. If the report by Noyes and Kletti accurately describes what occurs in airplane accidents, then most of the plane's occupants will not experience the extreme fear one might think would occur.

PSYCHOLOGICAL AND PSYCHOSOMATIC STRESS REACTIONS

Every severe airplane accident results in injury. Efficient medical care can usually reduce or completely eliminate the adverse effects of some of the physical injuries. But even so, many survivors will still suffer from psychological stress. Even in nonsurvivable accidents there will still be living victims, people whose lives have been touched by the disaster, who find themselves unable to function normally afterward. The stress produced by an accident may be just as incapacitating as physical injuries. In some ways the stress reactions caused by an accident are analogous to the physical injuries caused by the same accident. Stress reactions may be as varied as the physical injuries suffered by passengers. Some people will not require treatment and will heal on their own; others will be incapacitated, and for some, their symptoms will even worsen unless quick, effective help is received. Some people may respond to the treatment quite readily and others not.

One discrepancy in the analogy between physical injury and psychological stress is that physical injury is usually apparent at the time of the accident, or soon after, whereas a stress reaction may not be noticed, even by the victim, perhaps for days, weeks, or even months. Because a stress reaction is not always immediately noticeable, and may not even be evident until sometime after the accident, people unfamiliar with stress may be suspicious, believing that such a reaction is not "real" but imagined, or even feigned, by the victim, as a means of receiving some benefit. While some who have been in disasters may deliberately try to defraud an insurance company by pretending to have severe stress reactions, it is quite obvious that others actually experience a high state of stress, and exhibit stress reactions that put the person at a considerable disadvantage.

Adverse reactions to the stress of being in a disaster are, of course, not limited to plane accidents. In October 1973 a small cargo ship capsized off the coast of Tasmania, Australia, and all ten crewmen managed to get aboard a raft. Five days after the accident one man died from exposure to the cold on the rough seas. Two more men died on the ninth day, soon after the raft reached shore. Three of the remaining seven men walked through dense brush on seriously swollen feet and were found on the thirteenth day. The other men were rescued by helicopter soon after. The survivors were interviewed within a few days of being found, and again between one and two years later, by two psychiatrists, Dr. Scott Henderson and Dr. Tudor Bostock.[3] During the initial examination it was learned that two of the survivors had previously been torpedoed on ships during World War II, and another had drunk excessively when on shore, but none had psychiatric disorders previous to the shipwreck. During the one to two years between the accident and the follow-up interview, some of the survivors had seen their family physicians. Only one had received psychological assistance during this period, although five of the seven men had developed severe stress reactions, the most common of which was depression. One man became depressive three months after the shipwreck; however, drugs prescribed by his family doctor helped him recover. Another had suffered insomnia since the shipwreck, but even though kept on drugs prescribed by a physician, he still was very anxious in bad weather at sea. A third man had severe anxiety which manifested itself in poor concentration, increased irritability, and insomnia. He also suffered nightmares relating to the time on the raft, and a loss of sex drive. Though under a physician's care, he still had to quit his job at sea and take one driving a truck, which resulted in a 50 percent reduction in his earnings. Another man, well for the first nine months following the accident, became depressed and suffered loss of sexual drive, increased insomnia, and tearfulness, as well as feelings of guilt and worthlessness. At the time of the second interview he was receiving psychiatric treatment for depression. A fifth man displayed extreme psychosomatic reactions, including a general impairment of health, frequent colds and bronchitis, as well as severe insomnia and nightmares. He had also become impotent. On the other hand two men seemed to have come out of the experience relatively intact. Apparently they had been able to cope with the stress of being in the accident and later of putting themselves back into the same situation— going back aboard ship. One seemed to have actually benefited from the experience, having more confidence in facing crises and feeling greater enjoyment in being married and a parent. This accident shows the variability in different people's reactions to the stress of a disaster. The severity of some of the stress reactions are not unique, as the following episode illustrates.

On March 7, 1957, a gasoline tanker collided with a freighter on the Delaware River, near Newcastle, Delaware. There was an explosion which killed nine crewmen instantly. Twenty-five of the twenty-seven survivors, none of whom was injured seriously, were examined twice by two psychiatrists, Drs. Robert Leopold and Harold Dillon. The first examination occurred within two weeks of the accident and the second examination took place 3.5–4.5 years later.[4] This case is of interest because there was no systematic psychotherapy available to the men during this 3.5- to 4.5-year period, and according to Drs. Leopold and Dillon, the element of litigation anxiety was considerably lessened because of the unique position of seamen with regard to compensation.[5] These circumstances provide us with some understanding of how people react to the stress of a disaster without the ameliorative effect of psychological assistance, and without the variable of symptoms being reported by victims for financial gain.

The first examination (which was of twenty-seven survivors, only twenty-five of whom were available for comparison in the second examination) showed that there were few physical injuries; the most common was concussion, present in six of the men. There were no broken bones; one man had several small first-degree burns. The most common physical complaint was of gastrointestinal disorders—nausea, vomiting, and diarrhea. This complaint, reported by one third of the men, is a common stress reaction following disasters. Since there appeared to be no external physical cause for this problem, the psychiatrists concluded that they were of a psychosomatic nature, resulting from the stress of having experienced the accident.

Some seamen experienced emotional and cognitive reactions to the accident. One man was very depressed, nearly to the point of suicide. Another exhibited a severe fear reaction, though what the man was fearful of was not made clear in the report. Similar but less extreme emotional disturbances were experienced by many of the men, though the exact numbers were not reported. Cognitive deficits, such as poor concentration and forgetfulness, were also present but less common. Only six of the men (22 percent) reported no stress reactions.

The increase in the severity of stress reactions that took place between the first exam in 1957 and the second in 1960 and 1961 was significant. Two-thirds of the men required some form of help for psychological complaints during that four-year period, and many of these men suffered from severe gastrointestinal disorders. The "psychological help," however, seemed to be primarily bed rest and sedation rather than psychotherapy. There were increases in the number of seamen complaining of emotional disturbances, including restlessness, depression, and "phobic reactions," or extreme fear reactions toward a specific object or place, such as a ship. In addition new stress reactions developed, including feelings of isolation and of being watched, and hostility toward and distrust of others. The number reporting sleep disturbances increased by 50 percent between the first and second exam, so that over half the seamen were suffering from this problem by 1960 and 1961. While six men had no stress reactions in the first exam, only one was symptom-free in the second exam, and even this man had a back disability which the doctors felt could have been partially due to the stress of the accident.

Two-thirds of the men returned to work within three months of the accident, and all but four eventually returned to work. But a third of those who did return were forced to give it up, mostly because of psychological reasons stemming from the accident—a couple quit because of physical problems not related to the accident. All the men who continued to work at sea were greatly disturbed emotionally, some so much that they could only work sporadically. All those who returned to sea did so because of necessity; the majority of the seamen were poorly educated—only about 15 percent had high school diplomas. As such, few if any could make comparable wages on shore. Some said they would never work on a tanker again, even though it was more lucrative. And even those who shipped on tankers preferred other ships, except for one man who said he was equally miserable on all ships.

The purpose of detailed descriptions of these two ship accidents is that they both report the stress reactions of people immediately after an accident as well as several years later. Information on how passengers react following aircraft accidents has not been gathered. However, a rather large and systematic study of how people respond during a variety of natural and man-made catastrophies was conducted by the National Opinion Research Center (NORC) in the early 1950s.[6] One purpose of the NORC study was to find out how people reacted during and immediately after a disaster. Hundreds of hours of taped interviews were conducted following such disasters as a tornado in Arkansas, the crash of an airplane into spectators at an air show in Colorado, a series of house explosions in New York, a mine explosion in Illinois, a series of plane crashes into a housing area in New Jersey, an earthquake in California, and other disasters. This study concluded that most of the participants suffered psychological and physiological stress reactions.

The NORC study found that about 16 percent of the participants experienced aggravation of preexisting ailments as a result of the disaster. Most common were increased heart and blood pressure disturbances, experienced by 6 percent of the people. Other parts of the body in which preexisting ailments were aggravated were the gastrointestinal and respiratory systems. The study also found that 19 percent of the people had acute psychosomatic reactions which were stress reactions occurring during, or within a few minutes after, the disaster. Most prevalent was nausea, reported by 8 percent of the survivors. A few people also reported having hot and cold flashes, fainting spells, and shaking and convulsive spasms.

In the weeks following the disaster, 68 percent of the people suffered some form of psychosomatic disorders. Most pervasive was insomnia (46 percent), followed by anorexia, or loss of appetite (29 percent), headaches (19 percent), respiratory disturbances (16 percent), and generalized weaknesses, rashes, and other disturbances, each of which was reported by less than 10 percent of the survivors.

A prolonged period of emotional disturbances was experienced by 62 percent of the people. The most frequently (49 percent) felt were increased nervousness, excitability, and hypersensitivity to unexpected noises or other stimuli. Less common were nightmares (18 percent), a feeling of being in a dazed condition (14 percent), and depression (9 percent). A few people felt anxious or more irritable, and had a low frustration tolerance.

In addition to the emotional and psychosomatic disturbances, prolonged cognitive disturbances were experienced by most (78 percent) of the survivors. Many experienced constant, almost obsessive, thinking about the disaster (45 percent), and some were unable to concentrate (37 percent), or were forgetful (21 percent); some (17 percent) had less capacity to work because of these symptoms.

A relatively common reaction following the disasters studied by the NORC interviewers was increased emphasis on religious beliefs and less materialism, reported by 28 percent of the people. A small percentage (1 percent) became more fatalistic.

STRESS REACTIONS FOLLOWING AIRPLANE
ACCIDENTS

It is difficult to document the incidence of stress reactions among passengers following airplane accidents. One reason for this problem is that passengers may live in different parts of the country, or even in different areas of the world, and they usually disperse soon after the accident. Also, some survivors resist answering questions for fear that their answers could adversely affect any legal claims they may have. If they have severe psychological reactions to the accident they will probably see private therapists in their own communities. For these reasons, apparently no statistical information on the types and incidence of stress reactions following plane accidents has been compiled. I have reason to believe, though, that reactions following these accidents are similar to those following other disasters. This opinion is based in part on interviews held with accident survivors who *can* be easily contacted following accidents— the crewmembers.

As a psychologist, I interviewed a flight attendant who had over ten years of experience when she was in a catastrophic accident. She survived with no greater injury than a broken bone and a sprained back. Nonetheless, many people did not survive, including a close friend of hers. When I interviewed her ten months after the accident she reported that her ability to concentrate was disturbed for several months and she felt she might not be able to perform in another emergency; she feared she might attempt to save herself rather than risk her life for others in a future accident. At the time of the interview she constantly thought about the accident as well as the possibility of another. She had not gone back to work. Even airplanes flying overhead frightened her. Her stress reactions stemming from the accident caused conflict in her marriage, which eventually ended in divorce. Even though she had seen a psychiatrist weekly since the accident she reported an increasing frequency of nightmares—at the time of the interview she was having three or four a week. Other symptoms included a reduced threshold for frustration and increased fatalism combined with a newly formed religious belief which she said helped give her a purpose for surviving the accident while others did not. At the time of the interview she felt considerable hostility to many of those associated with the accident.

Another flight attendant I interviewed had similar reactions. Within the first hour following the accident she suffered some acute psychosomatic symptoms, including faintness and tunnel vision (the inability to see anything peripheral to where her eyes were focused). These symptoms passed. She had a complete loss of appetite for four or five days after the accident, accompanied by severe free-floating anxiety which peaked in intensity two weeks after the crash, but which lasted for about a month. Free-floating anxiety is a fear which may attach itself to any object in the environment, even objects which are usually not fear-arousing. When she was being driven home several days after the crash she suddenly became terrified that the trees along the highway would fall on her car. A mild preexisting claustrophobia was aggravated by the accident; safety belts in the automobile suddenly seemed too confining, whereas this was not a problem before. After returning home she suffered three bad head colds in quick succession. She also had a generalized weakness for about three months. Minor tasks greatly fatigued her during this period. For about one month she was overly sensitive to external stimuli and would overreact to loud noises. She became irritable toward others, especially to her husband who had not wanted her to fly even before the accident. She was depressed during the first year after the accident. She never returned to flight duty because of her physical injuries.

I have interviewed several passengers following catastrophic accidents who have reported similar reactions. A common symptom of stress is fatigue and weakness which can last for several months. Two elderly passenger-survivors said that before the accident they were energetic, whereas afterward, if they even walked across the street to the store, they would have to sit and rest for several hours upon returning home. Interviewers in the NORC study also reported that some participants in disasters experienced fatigue.

Some people with severe stress reactions may respond with self-destructive behaviors, behaviors which can range from increased alcohol and drug intake to suicide. Since some crewmen in the ship accidents recounted earlier indicated higher alcohol consumption after the accident, it seems plausible that some survivors from plane accidents may also be prone to this and other types of self-destructive behavior. While some sedation may be prescribed as an acceptable method of handling the acute stress reactions immediately following an accident, in the long run better strategies must be worked out by each individual. Whereas some people are able to find methods of coping with their stress reactions on their own, others will need professional help.

SOURCES OF STRESS

Survivor Guilt

Flight attendants may respond quite differently to the accident than do passengers. For one thing, flight attendants have emergency duties which, if not performed, may cause considerable guilt. Such feelings of guilt can emerge even if it was not physically possible to perform these tasks. A flight attendant was knocked unconscious during the impact phase of an accident. She came to, perhaps three minutes later, still strapped in her seat. Apparently all of the passengers who could have escaped had already done so. The plane was canted to one side, burning. When she came to she was looking down at flames licking at her feet. Looking up toward the other side of the plane she saw the exit she was responsible for opening. She unfastened her safety belt and started to go to the front of the plane to see if anyone else was aboard. But there was a pile of rubble in the aisle. She crawled to the top of it and called, but it was very still and she saw smoke billowing toward her. Her only thought then was to escape. She crawled back down, saw an opening on the side of the plane opposite from the door, an opening which led directly down to the ground. It was large enough for her to crawl through, but it was surrounded by fire which burned her as she got out of the plane.

A day or two later, as she lay in the hospital, someone asked her why she hadn't opened the door. This question precipitated enormous guilt based on the implication (which may not have been intended) that if she had stayed aboard the plane a little longer, or opened the door, maybe someone else could have gotten out. She had been trained to believe that following an accident she would be able to, and was expected to, save lives. When the accident happened and she couldn't save lives, it resulted in extreme guilt.

Guilt suffered by survivors can be very irrational, but even so, it can cause considerable psychological pain. A young woman and her husband frequently invited her parents to spend the evening at their home, and they often accepted. On May 28, 1977, the parents declined and the young couple went to the Beverly Hills Supper Club, in Southgate, Kentucky—the night it burned down. The daughter and her husband, along with 162 other people, died in that fire, but they weren't the only victims. Months later her parents were still trying to overcome the guilt frequently suffered by the survivor.[7] They felt that if they had only accepted the daughter's invitation, she and her husband would still be alive. Though logically unsound, the parents reacted as if they had done something that caused the death of the young couple.

Another form of survivor guilt I have encountered following plane accidents involves a confusion of feelings—joy in surviving and sorrow that others did not. You would normally feel thankful if you lived through a harrowing experience, but if others died and you walked away unscathed, you might develop the belief, perhaps on a subconscious level, that your escape was somehow associated with, and therefore caused, their deaths. Survivor guilt can cause substantial stress, and if it is not dealt with, severe stress reactions may emerge.

Cause of the Accident

Some accidents appear to be more preventable than others. Victims of accidents which appear unnecessary because they were caused by neglect, and so could have easily been prevented, seem to suffer greater stress reactions than victims of those accidents which appear unpreventable. In one sense most airplane accidents seem preventable. When one occurs, all the possible factors are examined, including the way the plane was manufactured, how well it was maintained, the training and the physical condition of the pilots, how well they performed, how the air traffic control system functioned, and even how the airport was designed and maintained. Every possible cause of the accident is studied, and measures are recommended to ensure that identical conditions, which could lead to another accident, do not recur. An attempt is made to place the blame for the accident, if possible, on someone or some agency. In fact it is common for the NTSB to list a series of probable causes of an accident. In many cases blame is placed on human error. Pilot error is commonly named as the primary cause, though the reasons why pilots make the errors are not always explicable. Sometimes blame is placed on the FAA, the airplane manufacturer, or those responsible for maintaining the airport.

Accidents may appear unnecessary if they result from apparent negligence—a known defect in the plane which was not corrected, improper procedures by the pilot, inattention by air traffic controllers, and so on. Other accidents, however, are reported as being virtually unpreventable, such as when severe weather causes a properly operated airplane to crash.

If someone close to you was lost in a preventable accident the length of your grief reaction may well be longer than if that person's death were unpreventable.[8] Of course, the closer the person was to you, the more intense and long-lasting will be that grief. Those who grieve the longest are those who lost someone close to them in an accident which could have been avoided. Similarly, if you were in the accident you would be less able to cope with your injuries if someone else were to blame than if you were responsible for your injuries, or if your injuries were due to chance. Ronnie Bulman and Camille Wortman conducted in-depth interviews with twenty-nine people who had been seriously injured.[9] All of them had spinal-cord injuries suffered in accidents occurring in the year preceding the interview, and were either paraplegic (paralyzed in the lower half of the body) or quadriplegic (paralyzed from the neck down). One purpose of the study was to find out why some people were able to cope well with their injuries and others were not. One result of the study was that those who blamed another for their injury had the greatest difficulty in coping. Many in this category expressed resentment that the person who had caused the harm was not also victimized.

If we could generalize from this special group of victims to passengers on planes, then in those plane accidents where someone or some agency was held responsible, victims may be less able to cope with their injuries than if the accident had occurred by chance and appeared to be unpreventable.

Fear of Flying

If you have just survived an airplane accident, your chances of being in an accident on your next flight are no greater and no less than if you had not been in the accident. Yet I have talked to some accident survivors who simply would never fly again for fear of another accident. I have also talked to those who felt that they were immune from ever being in an another accident. One passenger who had just survived a very severe crash said that he had no fear of flying—it was obvious to him that he was not meant to die in a plane. Most people will not respond in either of these two extreme ways. Some will hesitate to fly on a certain type of airplane they believe to be unsafe. After a series of accidents, some people believed that the DC-10 was an unsafe plane and would not fly on one unless there was no other method of getting to their destinations. For example, after a DC-10 accident in Mexico City in which the pilot inadvertently landed on the wrong runway, a runway that was closed, some people were hesitant to fly on the DC-10, others were hesitant to fly into Mexico City airport, others considered not flying at all, at least for a period of time, and some had no problems whatever with getting aboard the next flight.

For those who must continue to fly but who have not resolved their internal conflict about flying, further flying may increase or decrease their stress reactions. One flight attendant who was in two catastrophic accidents in a six-week period, accidents in which fire destroyed the planes although no one was killed or seriously injured, continued to fly. She had very few reactions, except that for about three months afterward, whenever she boarded a plane she experienced a skin rash. Following that period she exhibited no symptoms of stress.

Flying for many people is stressful; in one study of phobias, researchers found that fear of flying was intense in 10 percent of the population, and mild in 20 percent.[10] Few of these people had been in plane accidents, so having been in an accident was not the cause of the fear. Fear of flying may be associated with a number of other fears including fear of confined places, height, falling, loss of control, and of being in an accident, to name just a few.

For survivors, simply being in a plane can become associated with being in another accident; thus the prospect of boarding a plane can increase anxiety, and stress reactions may occur.

Other Potential Causes of Stress

A number of other factors can increase the state of internal stress following airplane accidents. One is the severity and extensiveness of physical injury; those with more severe injuries will most likely suffer greater stress. In addition, injuries can strain the financial status of a person, and that of other family members, which can further exacerbate stress. For survivors who have lost someone close in an accident, additional stress will result during identification of the person and attempting to find and identify belongings. In other accidents considerable stress can be caused when the plane is lost and no body is ever found, or when, because of extreme impact forces, the victims can no longer be identified.

REDUCING STRESS REACTIONS

After a disaster some people will be able to cope with the stress and the subsequent stress reactions in the weeks and months that follow. However, in some cases the stress will be so great that professional help, in the form of psychotherapy, will be needed. Not all methods of psychotherapy are appropriate, however. Psychoanalysis, which was developed by Freud, and other types of in-depth therapy, such as the reflective technique developed by Carl Rogers, may not be effective in reducing the stress or eliminating the stress reactions. In fact Dr. Calvin Frederick of the National Institute of Mental Health says that classical psychotherapy procedures may not only be ineffective, but they are often inappropriate and even deleterious to reducing stress reactions. Such techniques can add to frustration and promote further mental stress.[11]

The most effective method of reducing the reactions to stress is a form of therapy called *crisis intervention*. It is a brief treatment, which is usually concluded within three months, though longer treatment is sometimes required. It is designed to provide relief from stress reactions and to help a person reestablish adaptive behavior so as to prevent the occurrence of more severe psychological problems.[12] Crisis intervention has been used following a number of disasters including earthquakes, floods, tornados, school bus/train accidents, and mid-air collisions.[13] A B-727 collided with a light two-passenger plane over San Diego on September 25, 1978, with the wreckage landing in the city. In addition to all 137 people on board the two planes, there were seven people on the ground who were killed from the tremendous impact. The scene which followed was of tremendous devastation and horror. There were between 80 and 150 officers from the San Diego Police Department involved in crowd control and body removal. It was obvious to Dr. Alan Davidson, along with other private clinical psychologists in the city, that there would be a need for crisis intervention for the police and other workers on the scene.

The city manager, told that about 100 psychologists were volunteering their services, passed this information on to the officers. It was made clear that any officer contacting a psychologist would receive free treatment at the therapist's office, and the officer's name would be kept confidential. The initial response was slow—within the first two weeks only a few police officers and rescue workers requested help, according to Dr. Davidson, who acted as liaison between the police department and the psychologists. But with time the response grew. When the program was terminated two months after the accident, thirty police officers had been seen by the psychologists. Most of them were senior men, including some lieutenants and sergeants along with some seasoned patrolmen and detectives.[14]

The stress reactions suffered by these police were similar to those experienced by passengers and crewmembers from other accidents. They included migraine headaches, stomachaches and other gastrointestinal disruptions, muscular aches in the back and neck, and a few cases of skin disorder. In addition many officers reported serious sleep disturbances, nightmares, loss of appetite and sex drive, and increased anxiety and hostility.

One method used in crisis intervention is to set up a situation wherein the person finds it acceptable to talk about his feelings relating to the disaster. Many times a person has no one to talk to who can understand, or wants to understand, what it was like during and after the disaster. Some police officers found it difficult to talk about their reactions to the scene in San Diego because of an image that others expect of them, which they have come to expect of themselves—that feeling pain and discomfort when exposed to an overwhelming stressful situation is a sign of weakness and emotional instability.[15] Furthermore, they may fear that if they were to speak of their feelings to their supervisors, the latter may hastily conclude that the officers were not really cut out for the job. This was an apparent concern with some of the police officers, who believed that any widespread knowledge of their participation in the crisis-intervention program would be embarrassing and possibly detrimental to their careers.[16]

Some flight attendants have told me that they have found it difficult to broach the subject of airplane accidents with their husbands or wives. Some spouses could not understand the sense of loss felt by a crewmember when another crewmember, whom neither knew personally, was killed in an accident. These spouses could not understand the identification that exists between people in a close-knit occupation such as that formed by pilots and flight attendants. When one flight attendant or pilot is killed, others are affected. Crewmembers undergo the same training, wear the same uniform, fly on the same planes, face the same problems within the organization, and have similar thoughts and fears. Any two crewmembers, without ever having met, will have much in common, and when one dies, the loss is felt by the others. Some spouses may not understand this, and indeed some crewmembers seem to be puzzled by the intensity of their own stress reactions when an accident takes the lives of people they didn't even know. But when they try to talk about this at home, some spouses may turn a deaf ear, effectively stopping them from expressing their thoughts and fears. When this happens, the internal conflicts aroused by the accident may not be resolved and stress reactions may increase.

Many passengers, as well as crewmembers, will have a need to discuss the accident, retelling their experiences over and over, and in great detail. This may be a way the person has of trying to solve some of the unresolved problems related to flying. Talking about the accident can also be a catharsis, allowing the person to express the emotions related to it. Discussion may also act to reduce fear of future accidents. If the possible reasons for the accident can be explained away as improbable and unlikely to occur again, or, because of steps taken as a result of the accident, that these causes will no longer precipitate future accidents, then fear can be reduced. Under any circumstances, however, talking about the disaster and expressing feelings associated with it are necessary in crisis intervention.

Dr. Davidson stressed the importance of confidentiality and individual therapy in crisis intervention with the police following the mid-air collision.[17] However, in working with crewmembers and passengers following accidents, I have found that these two factors are not important for some people, though they are important for others. Many flight attendants find it relatively easy to attend postaccident sessions to discuss their own reactions to the accident. Sessions with as many as 150 crewmembers have been held in which most of the flight attendants were able to talk about their fears and their stress reactions, and to cry openly about the loss of their friends. Many were reassured to learn that others were having similar experiences, and that these reactions were common not only after plane accidents but after many different types of disasters. These sessions also allowed the flight attendants to express the frustration and hostility they felt toward the plane manufacturers, or the federal government, or the airline itself, and to find out what was being done to prevent a similar accident in the future.

Although invited, pilots have seldom attended these meetings. One reason may be that they were not held in total confidentiality. In a sense, pilots are similar to police in that they must present an image of someone who will not display emotion under stress. If a pilot were to attend an open meeting such as those held with the flight attendants, and to admit to a feeling of fear, hostility, or loss, then this could jeopardize the pilot's career. Police and pilots learn to control their emotions under many conditions, including extremely stressful events, because of the necessity to make clear-headed, split-second decisions. If emotions are allowed to express themselves *on the job,* then the pilot, just as with the policeman, may end up making fatal mistakes. In fact depersonalization is a way the mind has of doing this very thing—dissociating the emotional reactions from that part of the mind involved in performing actions which could save the person's life. However, depersonalization occurs only under very rare circumstances and when extreme danger has already occurred. The pilot and others in high-risk occupations must learn to suppress emotion much of the time in order to prevent the dangerous situation from arising in the first place. But Dr. John Stratton, director of psychological services for the Los Angeles County Sheriff's Department, has reported on the dangers which can occur when emotion is repressed.[18] For some policemen, expressing emotion related to their job makes them uncomfortable. To overcome this discomfort, a wall may be built up between the person and his emotions, and some policemen reach a point where they cannot lower their emotional defenses regardless of the circumstances. At home they may come to appear more as a robot than a husband or father. But these people haven't rid themselves of their emotions, they have only hidden them. Over the years the stress can accumulate and cause problems of a psychological nature.

Consequently, some people in high-risk occupations may come to suppress emotions in all situations, and will not think highly of others who do express emotions, even when doing so is appropriate. Thus many pilots probably try to cope with these reactions alone, or with a small group of other pilots—perhaps on an informal basis—or to contact therapists privately. If they strive to cover up their emotions completely, however, they could develop a psychological wall that would prevent any emotions from affecting them.

GUIDELINES FOR PASSENGER-SURVIVORS

The following guidelines are meant for those who have been in an accident, or who have a close friend or relative who was involved in one. Following these guidelines should help in decreasing the intensity of the stress reactions. The guidelines also indicate when the reactions are of such severity that professional help is needed, help which should be sought sooner rather than later.

Discussion with Others

If you have been in an accident, it can be very beneficial to discuss your thoughts and feelings with another person. Select someone you can trust to hold your confidence, someone who has concern for you, who is a good listener and who won't try to interpret all of your feelings and thoughts. What you need is to express any painful thoughts and emotions related to the accident. Some people even find it helpful just to write out their reactions.

Activities to Reduce Stress

On the other hand expressing the thoughts and feelings may not suffice. The amount of stress may be so high that you will need to drain off some of the tension in the body that usually accompanies stress. Physical exercise can effectively reduce tensions and promote relaxation. Jogging, racquetball, and swimming are some of the best exercises for reducing stress, although calisthenics and weightlifting have also been successful in providing appropriate releases for hostility and aggression. Other forms of stress reduction, including systematic desensitization, deep-muscle relaxation, and hypnosis have also been used with success,[19] but these techniques require an experienced therapist.

Selecting a Therapist

While crisis intervention is a preferred treatment for overcoming the stress related to an accident, some people will have preexisting psychological problems exacerbated by the accident. In these cases the person may need to consult an experienced professional, such as a licensed clinical psychologist (Ph.D.), psychiatrist (M.D.), or licensed clinical social worker (M.S.W.). Should you experience stress reactions and feel you require professional help, select a therapist with the proper qualifications, but make sure the person you select has had training and experience in using crisis-intervention techniques following accidents. If you select a therapist from the telephone directory, ask specifically whether the person has had such training and experience, and if not, to recommend some other therapist in the community.

Stress reactions following airplane accidents can be quite severe and long-lasting, but with prompt treatment many of the adverse effects can be alleviated. Forcing yourself back into the same situation, before learning how to cope with the stress associated with it, is not the best course of action.

Precautions to Take

Operating Automobiles and Other Machinery. The grief felt by a person who has lost a close friend or relative is not only distressful, but it can even be dangerous. Strong waves of grief can wash over you, and you will have little or no control over your emotional reactions. As such, you should be careful if you are driving an automobile or operating machinery.

It is not unknown for a person to hallucinate and to believe the lost one is nearby, or is trying to communicate with him. Dr. Erich Lindemann, who treated a number of victims associated with the famous Coconut Grove fire in 1941, reported on a man who lost his daughter in the fire. For some time after the fire (how long is not reported) the man visualized his daughter in the telephone booth calling for him. He was much troubled by how loud she was calling his name, and at times became so preoccupied with the scene that he was oblivious to his surroundings.[20] Were this to occur in a situation requiring the man's attention, such as when operating heavy machinery, it would obviously be dangerous.

I interviewed one flight attendant who had lost a close friend in a plane accident several weeks earlier. After the accident the flight attendant was driving on the freeway when suddenly his dead friend "appeared" in the seat next to him. The shock was so great that he swerved off the road, nearly causing an accident.

Even the most common reaction to grief, crying, can be dangerous. Because your vision is affected it can adversely affect your operation of an automobile or other machinery. If you have been experiencing strong emotional states which result in crying, and you still must drive, be ready to pull over and park until the strong emotional reaction has passed. If your job requires you to operate machinery, take some time off to reduce the chance of your causing an accident.

Sickness. The stress of being in an accident, or losing someone who is close to you, can be great and can increase your chance of illness in the following months. While some common stress-related physical reactions are readily noticeable (respiratory infections), others (increased blood pressure, stomach ulcer development) may be symptom free. However, they may cause permanent physical damage unless detected and dealt with in time. You should schedule a medical check within a month or two after the accident and then periodically over the following year or two. Your physician will advise you how often you should be examined.

Social Relations. Having been in a major accident can adversely affect many of your social relationships. Physical injuries, of course, may preclude your returning to your occupation—you may have to learn a new occupation, or you may not even be able to work if you are permanently disabled. Even without physical injuries, however, social relationships may still be affected. Some of the people I have interviewed have reported that their close relationships deteriorated following an accident, while others reported that their relationships improved. Important relationships, such as marriage or career, should not be dissolved in the aftermath of a disaster.

Any dissatisfaction felt with the relationship might be more the result of the stress associated with the disaster than with some imperfection in the relationship. The relationship should not be dissolved because of this dissatisfaction which may be only temporary.

Helping Others

You may find yourself in the position of having to help another person who is unable to cope with the stress associated with a disaster. This person may be a close friend or relative, or someone you have met following the disaster. There may be few mental health experts available. The following guidelines have been drawn from a National Institute of Mental Health publication,[21] and indicate how to determine whether a person should be referred to a mental health professional.

The most important role you should take if approached by someone who has just undergone a tragedy is to be a good listener, which involves the following:

1. Having genuine respect and regard for the other;
2. Being nonjudgmental and accepting of the other person even if he has different attitudes and feelings;
3. Establishing trust by stating clearly only what you can do, not what you would like to do or what he would want you to do that is not possible; and
4. Understanding that many times what is actually said may be a cover for vastly different feelings.

Keep in mind that a person attempting to cope with the stress produced by a disaster should not be considered weak or "crazy." Some may reject help for fear that others will think of them in these terms. Therefore it is essential not to use words which imply mental illness. Instead, consider the person as having problems in adjusting to stress and not as someone who is neurotic or psychotic.

Below are several criteria which can help you decide whether professional help should be sought. Under the following four categories, "Alertness," "Actions," "Speech," and "Emotion," there are "mild" and "severe" symptoms. People with mild symptoms will probably not require referral to professionals while those with severe symptoms should definitely be referred.

Alertness

Mild. If a person is slightly confused or dazed, or shows some slight difficulty in thinking clearly, or concentrating on a subject, this is not to be taken too seriously. Likewise, if the person seems to concentrate more on small problems and neglects more pressing ones, or denies that any problems really exist, or blames all his problems on others, these temporary symptoms need not be taken too seriously.

Severe. Consider referral if the person is unable to give his own name or the current date, doesn't know where he is, cannot recall events of the past twenty-four hours, and complains of memory gaps.

Actions

Mild. Don't be too concerned if the person is restless, mildly agitated and excited, has sleep difficulty, wrings his hands, or appears still and rigid.

Severe. Be concerned if the person is very depressed and shows agitation or apathy, or is unable to care for himself—doesn't eat, drink, bathe, or change clothes. Consider referral if the person repeats ritualistic acts or uses alcohol or other drugs excessively.

Speech

Mild. A less serious form of stress reaction is unusually rapid or halting speech, or the person may talk constantly, as if under pressure.

Severe. Hallucinations—hearing voices, seeing visions, or having strange bodily sensations—indicate the need for professional help. In addition, if the person is excessively preoccupied with one idea or thought, has the delusion that someone is out to get him, or is unable to make simple decisions or to carry out everyday functions, then referral is indicated.

Emotions

Mild. Sympathetic listening on your part can help if the person is crying or weeping with continuous retelling of the disaster, has blunted emotions with little reaction to what is presently going on around him, has inappropriately high spirits, or is easily irritated and angered over trifles.

Severe. Refer a person if he is completely withdrawn and cannot be emotionally aroused or on the other hand is excessively emotional and unpredictable in his emotional reactions.

SUMMARY

The experience of being in an airplane accident, or of losing someone close in such an accident, can be very stressful. Most people will be able to cope with the thoughts and emotions that result. Some, though, will be affected to the point that they will be unable to function well at work or at home, and will need a compassionate friend, someone willing to listen to them and to help when possible. For a few, time and a compassionate friend will not be enough, and professional help will be needed if they are to overcome the stress reactions that will, if left untreated, continue to plague them.

REFERENCES

1. Raymond W. Novaco, "The Cognitive Regulation of Anger and Stress," in Philip C. Kendall and Steven D. Hollon (Eds.), *Cognitive-Behavioral Interventions* (New York: Academic Press, 1979), p. 244.
2. Russell Noyes, Jr., and Roy Kletti, "Depersonalization in Response to Life-Threatening Danger," *Comprehensive Psychiatry* 18 (July-Aug. 1977).
3. Scott Henderson and Tudor Bostock, "Coping Behaviour after Shipwreck," *British Journal of Psychiatry* 131 (1977): 15–20.
4. Robert L. Leopold, M.D., and Harold Dillon, M.D. "Psycho-Anatomy of a Disaster: A Long Term Study of Post-Traumatic Neuroses in Survivors of a Marine Explosion," paper presented at the 118th Annual Meeting of the American Psychiatric Association, Toronto, Canada, May 7–11, 1962.
5. Ibid.
6. D. B. Dill, "Human Reactions in Disaster Situations," Report no. DA 18–108–CML–2275, National Opinion Research Center, University of Chicago, June 1954.

7. Reginald Stuart, "Clinic Is Allaying 'Survivors' Guilt' over Deaths in Supper Club Fire," *New York Times,* Sept. 18, 1977.
8. Ronald W. Perry and Michael K. Lindell, "The Psychological Consequences of Natural Disaster: A Review of Research on American Communities," *Mass Emergencies* 3 (1978): 105–15.
9. Ronnie Janoff Bulman and Camille B. Wortman, "Attributions of Blame and Coping in the 'Real World': Severe Accident Victims React to Their Lot," *Journal of Personality and Social Psychology* 35, no. 5 (1977): 351–63.
10. S. Agras, D. Sylvester, and D. Oliveau, "The Epidemiology of Common Fears and Phobias," *Comprehensive Psychiatry* 10 (1969): 151–56.
11. Calvin J. Frederick, "Current Thinking about Crisis or Psychological Intervention in United States Disasters," *Mass Emergencies* 2 (1977): 43–50.
12. James N. Butcher, "The Role of Crisis Intervention in an Airport Disaster Plan," paper presented to the 51st Annual Meeting of the Aerospace Medical Association, May 14, 1980.
13. Ibid.
14. Alan Davidson, "Air Disaster: Coping with Stress: A Program That Worked," *Police Stress,* Spring 1979.
15. Ibid.
16. Ibid.
17. Ibid.
18. John G. Stratton, "Coping with Stress," Training Key no. 257, Bureau of Operations and Research, International Association of Chiefs of Police, Gaithersburg, Md., 1978.
19. Davidson, "Air Disaster"; Stratton, "Coping with Stress."
20. Erich Lindemann, "Symptomatology and Management of Acute Grief," *American Journal of Psychiatry* 101 (1944): 142.
21. *Human Problems in Disasters: A Pamphlet for Government Emergency Disaster Services Personnel,* DHEW Publication no. (ADM) 78–539, Department of Health, Education and Welfare, Washington, D.C., 1978.

EPILOGUE

Improvements in airline safety continue to be made, perhaps more so than in any other mode of transportation. Because of these improvements, travel on commercial aircraft is undoubtedly safer than on any other mode of transportation. One area in which significant improvements can be expected is fuels. Fuels will be used that are less likely to burn when spilled during an accident. Another area of significance involves the making of seat cushions and other plastic materials in the cabin. They will be made fire-resistant or fireproof, and in such a way that no increase in toxic fumes will occur. Yet another possible improvement in the near future will pertain to the manufacture of seats. The structure by which they are attached to the floor will enable the seats to tolerate greater forces without tearing away from the floor or otherwise failing. These stronger seats, however, will have to be designed so that the greater impact forces will not be transmitted in such a way as to increase the likelihood of injury to passengers. Moreover, expect better and earlier warnings of turbulence and wind shear which will aid pilots in avoiding dangerous situations. Furthermore, you may look forward to life jackets that will be simpler to put on, and inflatable escape slides that will be less likely to deflate from the heat of a nearby fire.

Even if these changes are forthcoming, you will still need to have a basic knowledge of how to survive an airplane accident. You must be mentally prepared to use an oxygen mask in a decompression, and to do so quickly. If the mask drops from its compartment, don't just sit there looking at it. And don't do as one subject did in an experiment I was conducting: When the compartment in the seatback in front of him opened up, presenting the oxygen masks, he quickly closed the compartment again. Thinking the compartment door had broken, he was trying to fix it! Remember, too, that on most planes you will have to pull your mask to start the oxygen flow; do this before helping anyone else.

Inflight turbulence will continue to be the cause of numerous injuries, though most will be of a relatively minor nature. Even so, they can be painful and even incapacitating. Don't wait until the plane is on its final approach and the safety belt sign is lighted to visit the restroom. This is probably one of the least safe places to be on a plane at a low altitude or at the time of landing.

If you have a choice of seating locations, select one that is near an exit, and if possible, near the middle or rear of the plane. Before takeoff or landing, wear a jacket, preferably one of leather or wool rather than one made of a material that could melt. Also, don't wear high-heeled shoes since they could deflate an escape slide or life raft; you may be requested to remove them before leaving the plane.

If it becomes apparent that a landing accident is imminent, be ready to get into an appropriate brace position, one that depends not only on whether your seat is facing forward or aft, but one that is correct for the distance between your seat and the one in front of you, and is also suitable for your height and agility. Being in a good brace position is one of the most important factors determining your survivability in an accident.

If there is an inflight fire, the flight attendants may have time to distribute wet towels to breathe through (to filter out some of the smoke particles) before landing. This, however, may not be possible, or smoke could spread throughout the cabin after an accident during landing or takeoff. In any case the smoke will probably stratify, accumulating near the ceiling. Since some toxic fumes may also be heavy and form a layer near the floor, you may have to bend over to find a level where the fumes are least concentrated. When the plane has stopped moving, you must get to an exit as quickly as possible.

Knowing the locations of the exits aboard your plane, how to operate them, and when *not* to open them, is of crucial importance. Though you may not be seated close to an exit, if you know where the nearest one is, and how to get there even if you can't see, there is a chance that you could be out of your seat and to the exit before anyone else. This being the case, then consider it your responsibility to know what to do, and what *not* to do, to open that exit. First, check to make sure that there is no fire or smoke immediately outside. If there is an escape slide, be ready to inflate it. If there are stairs, be ready to lower them. You can't be sure that a flight attendant will be there to do these jobs for you.

If any portion of your flight occurs over water, know before takeoff which kind of flotation equipment—life preserver or seat flotation cushion—is aboard the plane for *your* individual use. If there is supposed to be a life preserver under your seat, feel the pouch to ensure that it is not empty. Read the safety information card which describes how to use it, and watch the flight attendant demonstration closely. The card should also tell you if your seat cushion can be used for flotation. Consider whether or not the plane is likely to float level before deciding on which exit you would use in a water landing. If there are life rafts or slide/rafts, read the safety information card and note where they are located and from which exits they will be launched.

The safety equipment on commercial airliners is designed to be easily used, for the most part, by the passenger who has made the effort to learn a little about it. Many of the chapters in this book discuss how to use the safety equipment, and describe some of the problems you might encounter with it. This was done in the belief that if you know what problems to expect, you will be more likely to avoid them—or if they do occur, you will be more able to cope with them. Although you will probably never be in one, I hope you have gained some confidence in your ability to survive an airplane accident.

APPENDIX

Some Accidents in Which Passengers Had to Open Emergency Exits:
1970–1980[a]

Date	Aircraft	Location: Summary
May 2, 1970	DC-9	Caribbean: Ditching. No fire. 63 occupants, 40 survivors. A passenger opened one exit through which 31 survivors escaped. Crewmembers opened three other exits through which 9 survivors escaped.
July 19, 1971	B-737	Philadelphia: Aborted takeoff. No fire. 61 occupants, 61 survivors. Passengers opened two overwing window exits. Crew opened three door exits. (No information on how many used each exit.)
Dec. 20, 1972	DC-9	Chicago: Takeoff collision, fire. 45 occupants, 35 survivors. One passenger opened and escaped through an overwing window exit. One flight attendant opened the left overwing window exit, through which 4 passengers escaped. One flight attendant opened the forward boarding door, through which 27 passengers escaped.
June 20, 1973	DC-8	Bangor, Maine: Aborted takeoff, fire. 261 occupants, 261 survivors. Passengers opened three overwing window exits and one door exit. Flight attendants opened five door exits. Passengers assisted crew in opening one other door exit. (No information on how many passengers used each exit.)

Date	Aircraft	Location: Summary
Jan. 6, 1974	B-707	Los Angeles: Landing accident, fire. 65 occupants, 65 survivors. Passengers opened four overwing window exits, through which 11 escaped. Flight attendants opened four door exits through which 54 escaped.
Jan. 30, 1974	B-707	Pago Pago: Landing accident, fire. 101 occupants, 5 survivors. Passenger opened an overwing window exit through which 9 escaped (4 died later). Flight attendants did not (could not?) open any exits.
Aug. 7, 1975	B-727	Denver: Takeoff accident, no fire. 131 occupants, 131 survivors. Passengers initiated evacuation. Passengers opened four door exits and four overwing window exits. Three of the four flight attendants were temporarily incapacitated.
April 5, 1976	B-727	Ketchikan, Alaska: Landing accident, fire. 47 occupants, 46 survivors. Passengers opened two overwing exits. Passenger opened main cabin door, and helped incapacitated flight attendant out.
April 26, 1976	B-727	St. Thomas: Landing accident, fire. 88 occupants, 46 survivors. Passengers opened two overwing window exits through which all surviving passengers left. Two flight attendants went out through breaks in fuselage.
June 23, 1976	DC-9	Philadelphia: Landing accident, no fire. 106 occupants, 106 survivors. Passengers opened all seven exits. Forward flight attendant was injured, and rear flight attendant was unable to force rear door open; passengers opened it.
May 8, 1978	B-727	Near Pensacola, Florida: Water landing, no fire. 55 occupants, 55 survivors. Crew opened three exits used by about 19. Passengers opened three overwing exits and one cabin door, used by about 36 people.
July 31, 1979	HS-748	Shetland Islands: Ran off runway into sea, no fire. 47 occupants, 30 survivors. 18 out by doors opened by crew; 12 through overwing hatches opened by passengers.
Sept. 3, 1980	B-727	Costa Rica: Skidded off runway, fire. 67 occupants, 47 survivors. 59 left through three exits opened by crew; 8 left by overwing exits opened by passengers.

Date	Aircraft	Location: Summary
Nov. 21, 1980	B-727	Yap, Western Caroline Islands: landed short of runway, fire. 73 occupants, 73 survivors. Crew opened one exit in cockpit through which 2 escaped, passengers opened four (?) exits through which 71 escaped.

Exits opened by	Number (%) of occupants escaping through exits
Passengers	506 (72%)
Crewmembers	194 (28%)

[a] These data are not meant to be a complete summary of all accidents in which exits were opened by crew or passengers during the 1970–1980 period. Accident reports do not always provide information on which exits were opened, who opened them, and how many escaped through each.

INDEX